PRINCIPLES OF

FORM AND DESIGN

PRINCIPLES OF

FORM AND DESIGN

WUCIUS WONG

JOHN WILEY & SONS, INC.
New York   Chichester   Weinheim   Brisbane   Singapore   Toronto

Library of Congress Cataloging-in-Publication Data:

Wong, Wucius.
    Principles of form and design / Wucius Wong.
        p.   cm.
    Includes index.
    ISBN 0-471-28552-8
    1. Computer-aided design.   I. Title.
TA345.W66   1993
745.4—dc20   93-13883

Printed in the United States of America

20   19 18 17 16 15 14

PREFACE

It was exactly two decades ago when my first book on design, *Principles of Two-Dimensional Design*, was published. Subsequently, I wrote three more books: *Principles of Three-Dimensional Design* published in 1977, *Principles of Color Design* published in 1987, and *Principles of Two-Dimensional Form* published in 1988. Each of these books was meant to be self-sufficient, but there is a common terminology and approach that links the separate texts. This prompted the publisher and I to look into the feasibility of a combined volume, including a general introduction, glossary, and index with appropriate cross references that would integrate these books. Because there is a limit to the physical size and weight of a book that can be conveniently handled by the reader and produced by the publisher, the present combined volume does not include the book *Principles of Color Design*. Its subject matter, dealing with color theories, makes it the best candidate to remain apart from the other books.

As modest attempts at presenting a workable system of visual grammar, *Principles of Two-Dimensional Design*, constituting Part 1, lays down the basics with concentration on flat, abstract forms; *Principles of Two-Dimensional Form*, constituting Part 2, elaborates on the creation of forms with an emphasis on the representational aspects to extend one's visual vocabulary; and *Principles of Three-Dimensional Design*, constituting Part 3, examines the use of linear and planar materials for constructing free-standing objects in reality. In one single book the interrelationships among all three may become much clearer, since each tackles essentially the same design principles, but on different levels.

The texts, diagrams, and illustrations of these earlier books are included here more or less in their original form, only in a larger page format. All the key terms in the three books are explained in the newly written glossary which, with preceding notes, also serves as a handy reference to my particular version of visual grammar. The index, listing only the more important topics and frequently occurring terms, provides immediate access to various relevant parts of the texts.

The new general introduction concentrates on computer methods and techniques to help readers who wish to avail themselves of the new technology. Whereas all the two-dimensional illustrations featured in the earlier books were the result of many hours of sketching and finishing work by my former students, now the same work can be done on a computer in only a fraction of the time. The development of computer hardware and software in recent years has already begun to effect a fundamental change in our ways of creating, teaching, and learning design. Becoming computer literate now seems a must for designers.

In the preparation of this combined volume, my son, Benjamin, contributed many of the diagrams and illustrations and designed the cover and various sectional pages. My wife, Pansy, helped with the general coordination of the materials and word-processing work. I am grateful for the generous support of the Aldus Corporation, which provided the graphics software programs *Aldus SuperPaint* and *Aldus FreeHand*, with which all the new diagrams and illustrations were created, and also the *Aldus Pagemaker* program, which was used for the page layouts.

W.W.

Englewood Cliffs, N.J.

CONTENTS

8

GENERAL INTRODUCTION

GENERAL INTRODUCTION

GENERAL INTRODUCTION

Marks or shapes can happen spontaneously as we explore with tools, media, or substances for pictorial, textural, or sculptural effects and, in the process, decide on what is beautiful or exciting without consciously knowing how and why. We may pour in feelings and emotions during the process, resulting in a kind of artistic expression that reflects our personality in the form of our tastes and inclinations. This is the intuitive approach to visual creation.

Alternatively, we can create having prior recognition of particular problems that must be dealt with. When we define the goals and the limits, analyze the situations, consider all available options, choose the elements for synthesis, and try to come up with the most appropriate solutions, this is the intellectual approach. It requires systematic thinking with a high degree of objectivity, although personal response to and judgment of beauty, harmony, and excitement must be present in all visual decisions.

Obviously, in an attempt to sort out and articulate the principles, I have stressed the intellectual approach. Principles concern specific relationships and structures of elements, shapes, and forms. Some bias toward regularity may seem to prevail, for regularity of relationships and structures invariably has a mathematical basis and can be more precisely described. Regularity frequently becomes a point of departure, however, from which one can look into possibilities of partial or total transformation, modification, and deviation.

To visualize any design of regularity using traditional tools and methods is often a laborious task. After sketching out the ideas, we use rulers and probably also compasses to construct shapes and structures, draw the outlines with a pen, and fill the open areas with a brush. This can take considerable time and effort, and the result may not always be satisfactory. If changes are necessary, the process might have to be repeated again and again. Much of the work is mechanical and painstaking and it presents considerable frustrations for a beginner in design, who has to struggle with all the meticulous finishing techniques.

The advent of the computer has not only revolutionized our ways of information processing, but also provided new methods for design creation. As the computer is primarily a "number-crunching" machine, it is particularly suitable for producing configurations of strict mathematical order. With the rapid development of many graphics software programs and related peripherals in recent years, the computer is now capable of accomplishing with great efficiency most of the design work that is normally done with pencil, pen, and brush. Thus, it opens new horizons.

Operating a computer today is relatively simple and requires only a short period of training. The computer, engineered with highly sophisticated technology, can be simply a new and powerful tool to the designer, who does not really have to know how electronic signals work inside the circuitry to yield the on-screen image. What is fascinating is that, in simple computer operations, a designer can produce with great exactitude many visual effects relating to principles of form and design and that transformations and changes are unbelievably easy to make. When done manually, without the computer, these same efforts would, of course, take many more renewed attempts and hours to perform.

We can well anticipate that the computer will soon become an indispensable tool in any designer's office or in design teaching studios of colleges and institutions. Our concern here is what basic equipment and software

will suit a designer's particular requirements and how we can work with the computer to pursue or implement the design principles later elaborated in the main text.

Basic Computer Setup

Computers come in different sizes and with varying capabilities and price tags. Generally, what a designer needs is a personal computer of desktop size. Many personal computers belong to the IBM-compatible category and are simply referred to as PCs. They come in numerous brands and models. The other major category is the Macintosh, which is made by only one manufacturer, and probably at a higher cost. What distinguishes the Macintosh is that it is the first computer to introduce *graphical user interface*. This enables the designer to work directly with pictorial elements with built-in commands instead of merely typing verbal commands, and to get printed results similar to what is displayed on screen. Because of this, Macintoshes have the support of many more graphics software programs than the PCs. The gap between the Macintoshes and the PCs are narrowing, however, as some Macintosh software programs are becoming available in PC versions.

At this moment, the Macintosh still represents the choice of the design profession, and therefore it is this system on which my discussion of computer techniques will concentrate. For working efficiently with most currently available software programs, a computer for graphics purposes should have a *random-access memory* (RAM) of no less than 4 *megabytes* and an internal or external *hard drive* with a memory exceeding 50 megabytes. Other essential equipment includes a black-and-white *PostScript* laser printer, for a crisp output of the results on paper, and a scanner, which can be acquired at a later date, to deal with photographic and existing printed images.

All computers are equipped with a *central processing unit*, a *monitor,* a *keyboard*, and a *mouse*. The central processing unit is the main component. It has an opening at the front to accept *floppy disks*, so that software programs recorded on such disks can be installed into the hard drive inside the unit or into a separate external drive. The monitor usually sits on top of the central processing unit, and its screen displays information and shapes in monochrome or in full color. The keyboard is similar to that of a typewriter, but it also includes keys that perform functions other than those of a typewriter. The mouse is a palm-size input device for moving a *pointer* on screen and has a button that can be depressed. When the pointer is in a desired location, the button of the stationery mouse can be "clicked" or it can be firmly held down while the mouse is "dragged." Clicking and dragging are the two basic mouse operations.

A computer is practically useless without proper software. Software programs exist for many purposes, most commonly for word-processing or for producing spreadsheets, databases, or graphics. Word-processing programs are used for writing letters, articles, and books. Spreadsheet programs are used for accounting and financial work. Database programs are for storing and sorting information to produce reports, tables, and lists in a desirable order. Graphics programs are for creating pictorial images as artistic expression, as visual communication, as all-over surface patterns, and for page layouts in desktop publishing work.

Graphics Programs

Obviously, graphics programs are our main concern. In these, the screen takes the place of a piece of blank paper, with the mouse pointer assuming the role of a finger to move, point, and select, or that of a pen, pencil, or brush to create marks and shapes. On screen as a program is launched, a *tool-box* appears, containing a range of *tools*. As we click with the mouse on one of the tools in the tool-box, the pointer becomes a *cursor* in a particular shape representing the selected tool and performs the function designated for the tool. On top of the screen is a *menu bar* from which we can access a number of *pull-down menus* by dragging the pointer. A menu is an on-screen display listing all available *commands* for editing and viewing as well as for special graphic effects beyond what is possible with the tools (Fig. 1). Each command may have *submenus* and may provide a *dialog box* for entering data or for selecting options.

The screen is composed of a matrix of dots that are initially white in color. Some dots will appear in black, or sometimes in a chosen color, as you drag a tool cursor to make marks or shapes. Each dot stands for

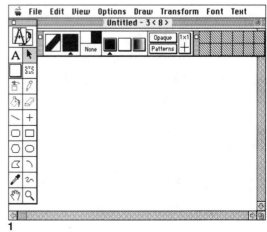

1

a picture element or *pixel*. There are normally 72 pixels to an inch, which is the standard screen resolution. Printing on a PostScript laser printer gives a much higher resolution to the shapes created. Resolution is measured in terms of number of dots per inch, or *dpi*. A laser printer can provide crisp outputs from 300 dpi to over two thousand. PostScript, a page description programming language developed by Adobe Systems to work with laser printers, helps to eliminate all ragged edges that might be visible on the screen.

Moving the mouse pointer on screen locates a tool, clicking activates a command or selects an element, and dragging creates a line or shape. Mouse operation is also used in combination with depression of the *shift*, *option* and/or *command* keys on the keyboard. Although the keyboard is basically for typing with different fonts and sizes, it can be used for issuing short-cut commands and for entering numerical data to determine measurements and angles of the lines and shapes. It also contains a set of arrow keys for moving the mouse-pointer or selected elements up, down, left, or right.

There are roughly six types of graphics programs: paint, draw, page layout, image processing, font manipulation, and three-dimensional modeling. A paint program enables us to "paint" intuitively on screen and produce *bit-mapped images* as strokes and shapes (Fig. 2). Bit-mapped images composed of pixels do not work with the PostScript language and tend to show some raggedness along any curved or diagonal edges. They are composed of densely packed independent square dots, representing the affected pixels, and can be magnified to facilitate editing with a *pencil* tool that adds new dots or removes existing ones (Fig. 3). Other tools particular to any paint program are the *brush* tool of different sizes and shapes for making lines or strokes of different widths and effects (Fig. 4) and a choice of patterns in the strokes (Fig. 5), a *spray* tool to sprinkle dots (Fig. 6), a *fill* tool to add color and pattern to an enclosed area or an unenclosed background (Fig. 7), an *eraser* tool to regain the original white color of the screen so that corrections can be made (Fig. 8). Each time as a line, stroke, or shape is formed on the screen, the new element fuses with all earlier ones it overlaps and becomes inseparable from them.

2

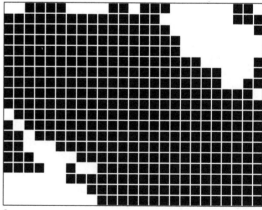

3

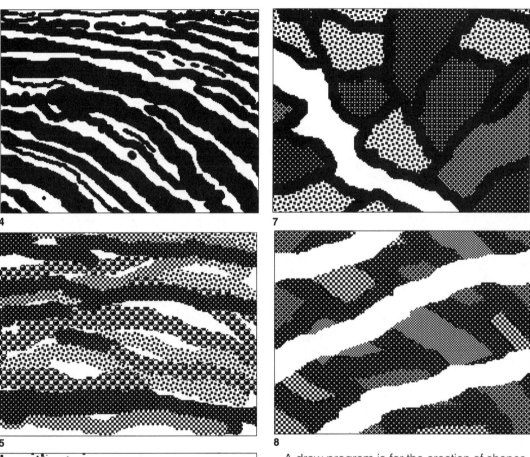

4

7

5

8

6

A draw program is for the creation of shapes as *object-oriented images* that are not bit-mapped but are stored in the computer's memory as mathematical formulas defining the positions of anchoring *points* and *paths*. Although the screen display may appear very much the same as the bit-mapped images in a paint program, a selected *object* is indicated with open or solid black dots along its outlines or at its four corners (Fig. 9). It can be enlarged unrestrictedly and printed without the jaggedness that is associated with bit-mapped images (Fig. 10). Each shape or even each

18

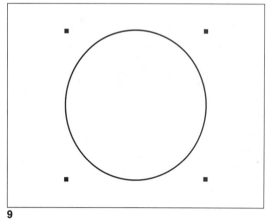

9

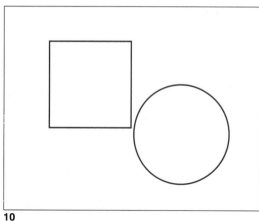

10

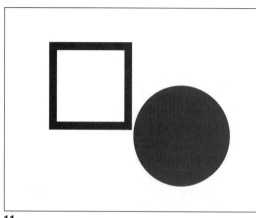

11

component of a shape remains independent and can be separately selected at any time for alteration, transformation, or deletion. This allows the designer great flexibility in making subsequent changes. The tool-box features a special set of *point* tools for the construction of paths. Elements first appear on screen as thin black lines that can be changed into any weight, color, tone, or pattern (Fig. 11). Positioning is aided with rulers, guides, grids, and various commands.

A page layout program imports text and graphics from a variety of files, effects placement, sizing, scaling, and cropping of different page elements, and organizes pages in a sequential order. Text and illustrations flow from one page to the next and can be reshuffled, if desired. A master page can be used to determine the general layout and recurring elements for a whole section of pages. The program has word-processing capabilities for changing font styles and sizes and for editing the text. Its graphics capabilities are limited to the adding of simple geometric elements, background color and shades, borders, and frames.

An image processing program allows scanning of images from photographs, sketches, or existing printed materials. It provides tools and commands for modification or transformation of the original images in the form of adjusting contrasts, tones, and colors; adding textures and patterns; retouching details; and introducing other special effects, as desired. Most of the tools and commands, however, can also be used on the blank screen for creation of bit-mapped images as in a paint program.

A font manipulation program is for altering and customizing existing fonts and may also be used to create new fonts. Some of these programs have special transformation tools or commands for planar, spherical, or cylindrical distortions of typographical elements and imported graphic images.

A three-dimensional modeling program combines plane and elevation views to establish forms of illusory volume and depth. The forms can be swiveled to show how they are seen from different angles, with a change of light source. Some programs may include animation capabilities.

Choosing a Program

Every type of program just described is desirable, and ultimately it would be necessary to get all of them to meet different requirements. Most people tend to choose a paint program for their first attempt to create electronic pictures. A paint program is by far the easiest to use and can also provide considerable fun. Simple paint programs produce only black-and-white images. The more sophisticated ones, however, enable you to tackle all colors of the spectrum — or a full range of grays if you work only with black-and-white outputs — and can simulate effects of actual painting and sketching on canvas or rough paper with dry or wet media.

A paint program, however, is not designed for precision work. A paint composition contains shapes and brush strokes intermingled with one another in an almost irreversible process, although some programs may allow you to *undo* several times beyond the latest operation. Shapes and brush strokes are simply marks formed of loose pixels that are either affected or unaffected by the movement of a selected tool. Edges of the marks are not clear-cut boundaries. To work with most of the concepts and principles in this book, in which geometric elements, smooth

curves, sharp edges, and structures of strict regularity are often required, a paint program is inadequate.

For a modest start, all that may be needed is a good draw program. You can choose from several high-end draw programs on the market with similar features but distinctly different capabilities. My current choice is the *Aldus FreeHand* from Aldus Corporation, available in both Macintosh and PC versions, that facilitates working directly with shapes in their visual attributes, allows numerous levels of undoing, arranges elements in multiple layers, and provides visible grids for accurate positioning, among other features. It is on this program that most of my explanations of computer techniques will be largely based.

There is the *Aldus SuperPaint*, also from Aldus Corporation, that the reader could consider as an alternative choice. Aldus SuperPaint combines paint and draw programs on interchangeable layers so that one can first create an image on the paint layer and immediately transfer it to the draw layer, or vice versa. The combination has definite advantages, particularly if you think you may want to do some painting work on screen. Many special effects are included on the paint layer for experimental work. Nevertheless, the drawing capabilities of Aldus SuperPaint are certainly not as extensive as those of the Aldus FreeHand.

Starting to Draw

With an appropriate draw program properly installed in the hard disk drive, the program can be launched. On screen, the menu bar and the tool-box appear. Opening a new file causes a vertically oriented rectangular frame to appear in the center of the screen.

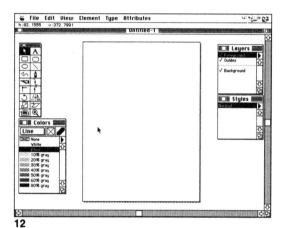

12

This is the *fit-in-window* view, showing the entire page reduced (Fig. 12). A command from the *view* menu on the menu bar changes this to a 100% view or a view of desirable magnification/reduction. Activating a *preview* command from this view menu enables you to work not just in key-line mode but directly with lines and shapes showing all intended attributes. The view menu also allows the display of rulers with appropriate markings, palette boxes for attribution of colors, line weights and control of layers, and an information bar containing measurements and angles of the elements, and vertical/horizontal positions of the pointer. Furthermore, there are guides in dotted or colored lines that can be dragged from the rulers, and a grid in a matrix of equidistant dots established with the *document setup* command in the *file* menu.

More than half of the tools in the tool-box are for originating shapes. The point tools include a *corner* tool, a *curve* tool, a *connector* tool, and a *pen* tool. The corner tool plots points to make straight paths and sharp bends (Fig. 13). The curve tool plots points to make winding curved lines (Fig. 14). The connector

tool plots points between straight and curved paths to ensure a smooth linear flow without noticeable bumps (Fig. 15). Plotting a point is accomplished by clicking with a tool cursor. The pen tool combines the function of the corner tool and the curve tool. It plots points to make straight lines with clicking and makes curved lines as you drag the mouse (Fig. 16).

Other tools include a *rectangle* tool for drawing squares and rectangles (Fig. 17), a *rounded-rectangle* tool for drawing rounded-corner squares and rectangles (Fig. 18),

13

an *ellipse* tool for drawing circles and ellipses (Fig. 19), a line tool for drawing straight lines (Fig. 20), and a *freehand* tool for drawing irregular curves (Fig. 21). All these tools effect shapes when the mouse is dragged.

In addition, there is the *type* tool for originating characters on the keyboard, which can be transformed into the desirable size and font style for use as shapes in a design. Pictorial fonts such as the Zapf Dingbats, consisting of symbols and naturalistic shapes, are also a handy choice for the designer

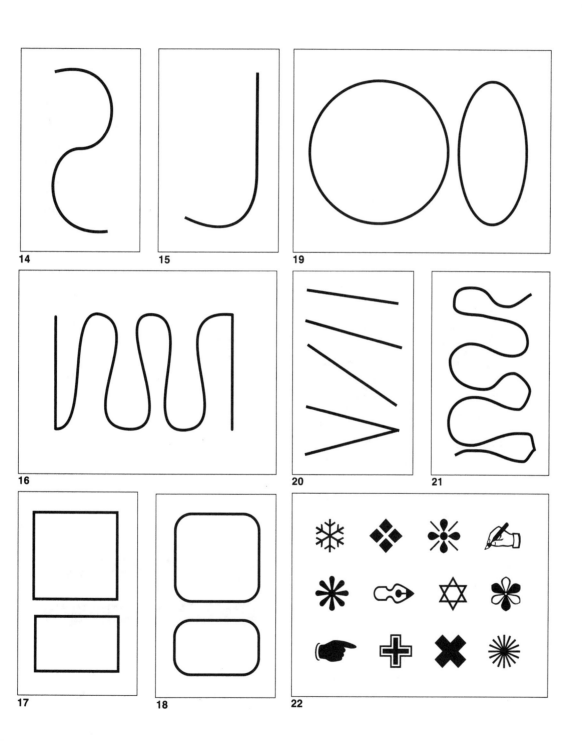

14

15

19

16

20

21

17

18

22

Creating a Shape

Points mark the beginning and end of a path and can occur along any part of the path. An open path is one that has disconnected end points. Connecting end points establishes a closed path. The rectangle or ellipse tool produces a closed path right away.

Any shape is constructed of points and paths. Points define key positions of a path. The path must take on attributes to be visible. This is accomplished with the *fill and line* command in the *attributes* menu, which provides a dialog box for separately

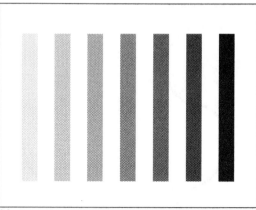

24

23

Caps and *joins* can also be specified for any open path. Caps, which may be square or round, are added to the endings of lines (Fig. 25). Joins occur where two lines meet at an angle, and they can be in a miter, round, or beveled shape (Fig. 26). Moreover, the line can be continuous or dashed (Fig. 27) and can be patterned (Fig. 28).

A closed path allows the covering of a plane with a flat fill, a *graduated* fill, a *radial* fill, or a patterned fill that could be in a gray tone or color (Fig. 29). As the closed path is filled, line attributes should be chosen in

entering fill and line data. An open path takes the shape of a line with attributes that include weight, color, and pattern. The weight of a line can be so thin as to be barely visible and as thick as two inches (Fig. 23). The color of a line can be in any gray ranging from 10% to 80% black (Fig. 24), plus solid black, white, and none, if you do not work in full color. White and none may appear the same on screen, but white refers to an opaque element that can hide anything beneath it; whereas none is transparent and invisible.

25

26

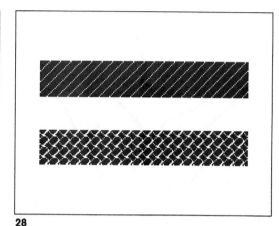

28

27

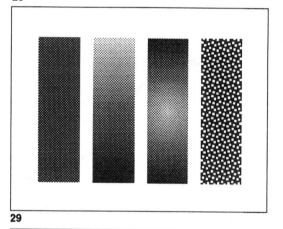

29

order to obtain an outlined shape (Fig. 30). If you do not want an outline, you can just enter *none* for the line attributes in the dialog box.

Paths can be edited before or after the attributes. Any point on a path can be specially selected and moved with the *arrow* tool pointer and can be dragged to any desirable new location to effect change in the path. There are three types of points, the *corner* point, the *curve* point, and the *connector* point, normally resulting from the use of those respective tools. One type of point can be substituted for another, using the *points*

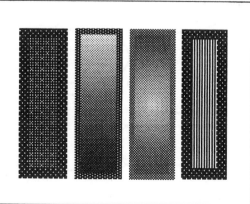

30

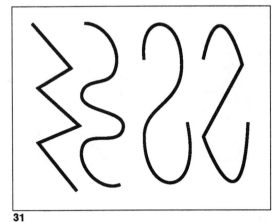

31

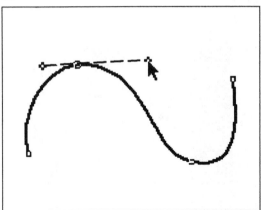

32

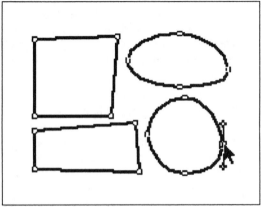

33   34

command in the element menu. In this way, an angular path can become smooth, or a smooth path can become angular (Fig. 31). There are two nonprinting *control handles* associated with every curve point. They are displayed on screen when the curve point is selected. Dragging each handle with the arrow pointer adjusts the convexity or concavity of a curved path (Fig. 32). A point can be added to the path with any appropriate point tool to facilitate manipulation or removed with the points command. Point removal can change a shape significantly.

Holding down the shift key on the keyboard as you drag with the rectangle tool produces a perfect square, and the ellipse tool a perfect circle. Rectangles, squares, ellipses, and circles all come with four handles, and without un-grouping you can drag any handle to resize and reshape the path without irregular distortion (Fig. 33). With activation of the *ungroup* command in the element menu, the handles change into points and each point can be dragged freely to change the shape (Fig. 34).

The tool-box also contains tools for effecting changes in existing shapes. The *rotating* tool is for making directional changes (Fig.

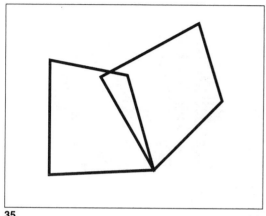

35

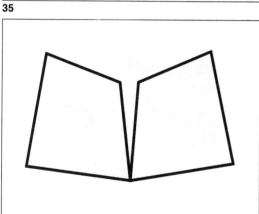

36

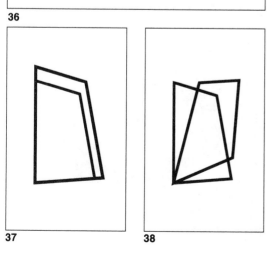

37   38

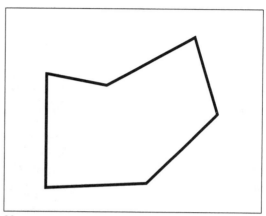

39

35). The *reflecting* tool is for flipping the shape to obtain its mirrored image (Fig. 36). The *scaling* tool is for resizing and reproportioning (Fig. 37). The *skewing* tool is for slanting a shape upward, downward, or sideways (Fig. 38). The *magnifying* tool is for blowing up any portion of the shape to help with critical modifications. The *tracing* tool is to perform automatic tracing of the outlines of any shape (Fig. 39). The *knife* tool is for cutting and splitting a path.

Achieving a Composite Shape
A composite shape consists of two or more shapes in a process involving *addition*, *subtraction*, *multiplication*, or even *division*. Addition is the overlapping of two or more shapes that can remain separately discernible with conspicuous line attributes or different fills (Fig. 40) or fuse together with the same fill but no line attributes (Fig. 41). Subtraction is the effect of placing an opaque white shape, which functions as a negative shape, in front of a filled shape (Fig. 42). Multiplication is creating the same shape more than once, by using the *copy* and *paste* commands, the *clone* command, or the *duplicate* command,

all in the edit menu (Fig. 43). Each copy of the shape can be moved with the arrow pointer or any of the arrow keys on the keyboard to attain the desirable configuration. You can have as many copies as desirable, and each copy can be separately moved, rotated, and reflected.

Division requires a more complicated procedure. This is possible with an ungrouped closed path, such as a rectangle or ellipse, on which you can engage the knife tool to insert breaking points. Afterwards, each segment or pair of segments is moved away from the path with the arrow pointer. Then the *join*

44

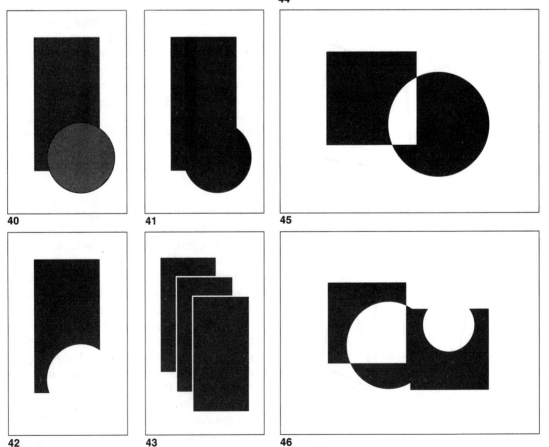

40

41

45

42

43

46

command in the same menu is used to join points of separate segments with straight lines. The process must be repeated to obtain a number of divisions. Individual shapes resulting from division can be shifted and rotated to establish a new configuration (Fig. 44).

Overlapping shapes can interpenetrate one another, with the overlapped area or areas showing the white of the screen. This is achieved by activating the join command as the shapes are selected and ungrouped (Fig. 45).

All the above methods can be combined to achieve a composite shape (Fig. 46).

Establishing Repetition

As just discussed, a shape in *repetition* can be used to create a composite shape. Any shape can become a *unit form* for repetition in a composition (Fig. 47). A group of connected or disconnected shapes can also be used as superunit forms for repetition (Fig. 48). If a shape or a group of shapes is copied by the computer, it stores the entire configuration in a *clipboard* file and can repeatedly paste the configuration at locations indicated by the arrow pointer on screen to attain an informal composition.

Activating the clone command places a copy of the shape directly on top of the original. The copy remains unnoticeable until it is moved with the arrow pointer or the arrow keys. If necessary, the dialog box associated with the move command can be accessed in order to enter numerical descriptions for a precise vertical/horizontal move. After the copy is moved once, activating the duplicate command will cause subsequent copies to appear with identical moves. All such moves can form a row or column, which can again be cloned, moved, and duplicated to spread the repetition vertically, horizontally,

47

48

49

28

50

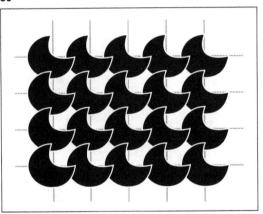

51

52

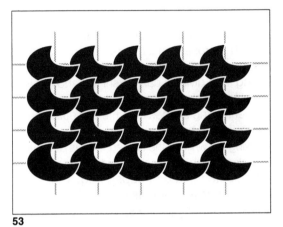

53

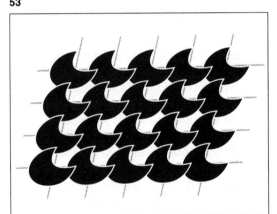

54

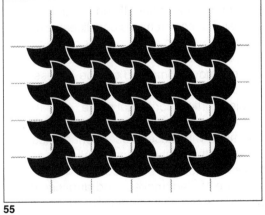

55

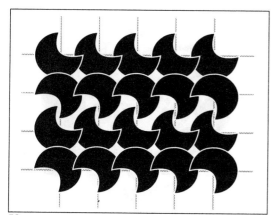

56

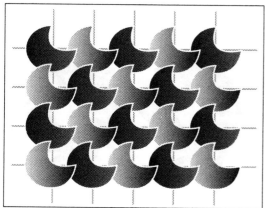

57

or diagonally. In this way a formal composition can be achieved with repetitive positioning of shapes that have identical attributes (Fig. 49).

Accurate positioning can be aided by having horizontal and vertical rulers on display from which nonprinting guides can be dragged to form a linear grid. Both the *rulers* and *guides* command are in the view menu. There is a *document setup* command in the *file* menu for erecting a *visual grid* with a matrix of equidistant dots and a separate *snap-to grid* command to effect snapping action. There is also an *alignment* command

in the element menu for aligning and evenly distributing selected unit forms.

A formal composition with unit forms or superunit forms evenly distributed vertically and/or horizontally implies the existence of an underlying *repetition structure*. A repetition structure can be designed with the line tool, the corner tool, or the rectangle tool. A repetition structure consists of *structural lines* that divide the picture area into *structural subdivisions* of the same shape and size. After the structure is formed, the next steps are selecting all the elements, locking them with the *lock* command in the element menu, and clicking the word *background* on the *layers* palette, obtainable from the *windows* command in the view menu. When this last step is done, the entire structure moves to the background layer, becoming a nonprinting template as the lines appear dotted or grayed. Clicking the word *foreground* in the palette causes a return to the working layer. Unit forms can occupy the center or the same corner of each structural subdivision in the template, or the junctions of the structural lines, and they can touch (Fig. 50), overlap (Fig. 51), or stay separate from one another (Fig. 52).

As you approach a certain stage in the composition, you can transform the entirety with the scaling tool (Fig. 53) or the skewing tool (Fig. 54), reflect (Fig. 55) or rotate (Fig. 56) it with respective tools, give a finished composition a new set of attributes (Fig. 57), select a few shapes for necessary changes (Fig. 58), or repeat or reflect the composition after resizing or other changes to attain further complexity (Fig. 59). Finally, you can crop and frame the composition with a *clipping path* by using the *cut* and *paste inside* commands in the edit menu (Fig. 60).

58

61

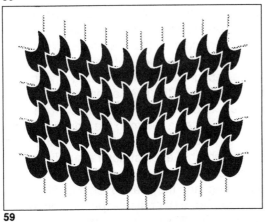

59

62

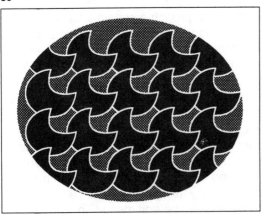

60

63

Establishing Radiation

Any element or shape inside a repetition structure may be individually rotated with the rotating tool. Systematic rotation of the unit forms properly arranged can give a composition the effect of *radiation* (Fig. 61). First, the information bar may be displayed to show the desirable degrees of rotation, and then, for precision control, the data shown can be entered in a dialog box provided by the rotating tool.

Before rotating a series of shapes in regular intervals, the shape must be cloned. Upon rotating, the unrotated original and the rotated copy are brought next to each other. Then the duplicate command is used to obtain all necessary further rotated copies to complete the series (Fig. 62). The crucial thing here is the placement of the center of rotation, which can affect the composition significantly (Fig. 63).

Elements can be rotated to create a radiating composite shape to be used as a superunit form or to establish a formal composition showing an underlying *radiation structure*. A radiation structure template can be designed by rotating lines regularly in a full revolution, with their convergence or intersection marking

65

the center, and superimposing on these a series of concentric circles (Fig. 64). With the completed radiation structure locked and transferred to the background layer, arrangement of unit forms can revolve around the same center with the same angle of rotation as the structural lines (Fig. 65).

If you do not use a structure template, you can directly clone and rotate a shape with subsequent duplications. The result is sometimes unpredictable and the rotation may have to be redone over and over to achieve desirable effects.

Establishing Gradation

The element menu provides a *blend command* that produces *gradation* almost instantaneously. To effect a blend, you must first select two shapes defining the beginning and the end of the blend. Each shape must be first ungrouped so that one of the points on its path can be selected to constrain the blend. A dialog box appears as the command is activated and in this can be entered the number of steps, which can range from one to hundreds. Not only shapes can be blended, but also line weights and colors. After blending, the series

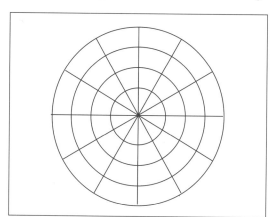

64

66

69

67

70
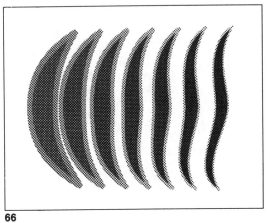
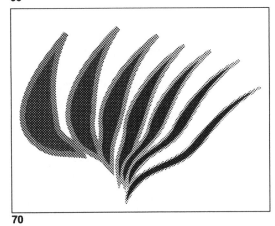

68

71

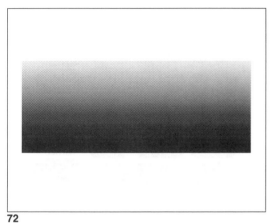

72

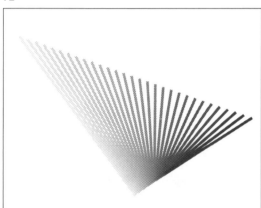

73

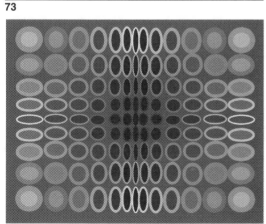

74

of shapes appear as a group, but you can hold down the option key as you use the arrow pointer to subselect a shape at the beginning or end of the blend and make necessary changes (Figs. 66–68). Any change will affect the entire series of blended shapes. The entire series can be further transformed (Fig. 69) and can also be ungrouped in order to effect change in individual shapes within the series (Fig. 70).

Blending places intermediate shapes equidistantly, providing a range of unit forms in gradation that can subsequently be repeated or reblended to achieve a composition with an underlying repetition structure (Fig. 71). Blending two parallel lines of the same weight but different grays in many steps can result in a very smooth tonal gradation of a plane (Fig. 72). Blending two linear shapes of different directions can establish the effect of radiation (Fig. 73). The blend command does not, however, provide for instantly erecting a *gradation structure*. This must be independently constructed with guides or lines made with an appropriate tool. With a gradation structure as a background template, you can then use the blend command to create a series of unit forms in tonal, shape, or other kinds of gradation for manual positioning (Fig. 74).

Establishing Similarity

In a composition containing repeated shapes in a formal structure, random variations of size, direction, and general attributes can be created to achieve the effect of similarity (Fig. 75–77), or individual shapes can be freely manipulated to attain shape changes (Fig. 78). You can also use the blend command to produce a series of gradually changing shapes for rearrangement in a nonsequential order to accomplish the effect of similarity (Fig. 79).

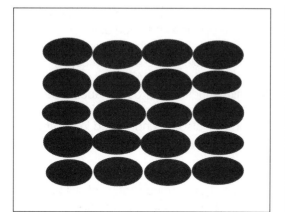

75

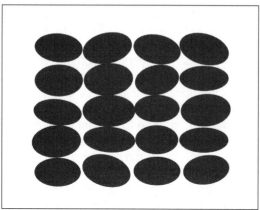

76

77

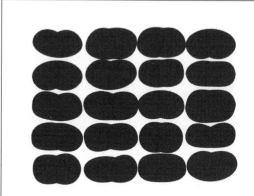

78

79

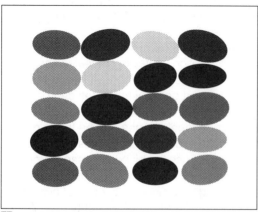

80

The existence of an underlying *similarity structure* can be implied if the arrangement of shapes in a repetition structure is deliberately inconsistent inside particular structural subdivisions (Fig. 80). A similarity structure can be constructed with the line tool or any point tool, but it is not worth the trouble unless the structure is active or visible.

Active and Visible Structures

Structural lines divide the picture area into subdivisions. In an *inactive structure*, shapes and their surrounding space flow uninterruptedly between subdivisions. In an *active structure*, each subdivision is an independent *spatial cell* with the background assuming the status of a shape with desirable attributes. Shapes and cells can alternate as positive and negative elements (Fig. 81), or they can have different attributes (Fig. 82). If the background has a fill of opaque white, shapes in adjacent cells intruding into it can be blocked at its borders (Fig. 83). Converting the background shape of the cell into an attributable shape can be done by tracing its bordering outlines with an appropriate tool to form a closed

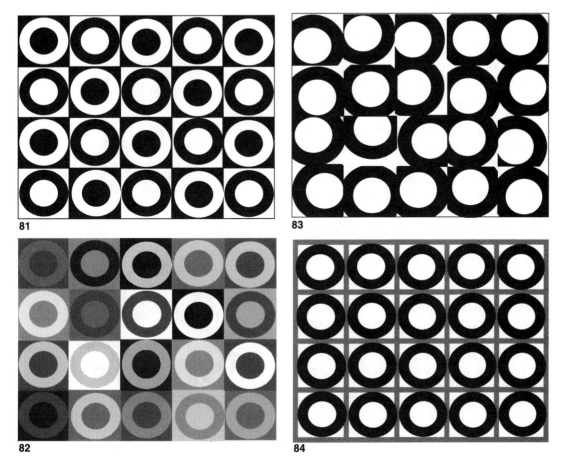

81

83

82

84

path and sending it behind the unit form with the *send backward* or *send to back* command in the element menu. This background shape and the associated unit form can be seen as a composite shape.

Giving line attributes to the background shape, which may or may not have a fill, produces a *visible structure*. Structural lines thus become lattice-like elements working with the unit forms (Fig. 84).

Representational Forms

Shapes obtained with the type tool, using a pictorial font, can be representational forms. After their conversion to paths, they can have line and fill attributes, and can be transformed and repeated to establish a composition (Fig. 85). A shape can also be traced with the tracing tool, but automatic tracing of complex shapes may not always produce satisfactory results.

Connecting a scanner to the computer, you can import a photographic or printed image that can be manipulated and repeated (Fig. 86) or used as a template on which you can trace with the tracing tool or redraw with the freehand or pen tools. After being traced or redrawn, the shape can be given any desirable line and fill attributes and can be used with or without transformation as a unit form in a composition (Fig. 87).

Three-Dimensional Images

A drawing program is not specifically intended for creation of three-dimensional images. Blending of simple shapes that overlap in a row, however, can establish an illusion of a three-dimensional form composed of serial planes (Fig. 88). Also, a simple linear framework that gives a three-dimensional illusion can be created with the pen tool or any other

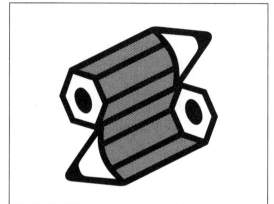

85

86

87

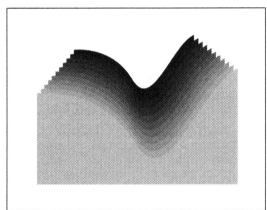

88

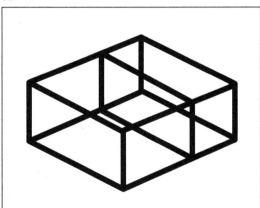

89

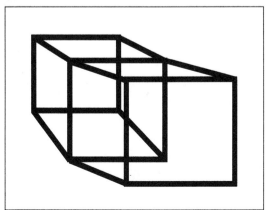

90

appropriate tool (Figs. 89, 90). In most cases, a three-dimensional form that looks good in one particular two-dimensional view can be very ordinary or even disappointing in real life and may be impossible for construction with physical materials when elements must be solidly joined or supported. Exercises in three-dimensional design should be accomplished with actual models. Computer-aided design is only for the advanced user who relies on the computer mainly for expediting production of planes and elevations and for perspective presentations.

Getting on with the Main Text
Full explanations of some of the design terms and concepts are in the main text. Descriptions of computer techniques here may not be complete, and can never be totally adequate. Thus, the reader will need to refer to special manuals for the computer and its peripherals, as well as to the user manual and guide books for any chosen software program. Software programs get updated frequently, with improved conveniences and added features, and hardware can become easily antiquated when newer models with increased power appear on the market. This general introduction is intended only to help the reader see the essential link between the language of visual form and computer language. Then the challenge becomes getting on with the effort to tackle all the concepts, principles, and exercises in form and design with growing computer literacy, increasing aesthetic sensitivity and technical competence.

TWO-DIMENSIONAL DESIGN

TWO-DIMENSIONAL DESIGN

CHAPTER 1: INTRODUCTION

What Is Design?

Many people would think of design as some kind of effort in beautifying the outward appearance of things. Certainly mere beautification is one aspect of design, but design is much more than this.

Look around us. Design is not just ornamentation. The well-designed chair not only has a pleasing outward appearance, but stands firmly on the ground and provides adequate comfort for whoever sits on it. Furthermore, it should be safe and quite durable, able to be produced at a comparatively economic cost, packed and shipped conveniently, and, of course, it should have a specific function, whether for working, resting, dining, or other human activities.

Design is a process of purposeful visual creation. Unlike painting and sculpture, which are the realization of artists' personal visions and dreams, design fills practical needs. A piece of graphic design has to be placed before the eyes of the public and to convey a predetermined message. An industrial product has to meet consumers' requirements.

A good design, in short, is the best possible visual expression of the essence of "something," whether this be a message or a product. To do this faithfully and effectively, the designer should look for the best possible way this "something" can be shaped, made, distributed, used, and related to the environment. His creation should not only be just aesthetic but also functional, while reflecting or guiding the taste of the time.

The Visual Language

Design is practical. The designer is a practical person. But before he is ready to tackle practical problems, he has to master a visual language.

This visual language is the basis of design creation. Setting aside the functional aspect of design, there are principles, rules, or concepts in respect of visual organization that may concern a designer. A designer can work without conscious knowledge of any of these principles, rules, or concepts, because his personal taste and sensitivity to visual relationships are much more important, but a thorough understanding of them would definitely enhance his capability in visual organization.

In the first year's curriculum of every art school or university art department, regardless of the fields of specialization the students are to follow later, there is always a course variously called Basic Design, Fundamental Design, Two-Dimensional Design, etc., which deals with the grammar of this visual language.

Interpreting the Visual Language

There are numerous ways of interpreting the visual language. Unlike the spoken or written language of which the grammatical laws are more or less established, the visual language has no obvious laws. Each design theorist may have a completely different set of discoveries.

My own interpretations, as unfolded in this book, may appear to be much on the rigid side and oversimplified. Readers will soon find that my theorization has a lot to do with systematic thinking and very little to do with emotion and intuition. This is because I prefer to tackle the principles in precise and concrete terms with maximum objectivity and minimum ambiguity.

We must not forget that the designer is a

problem-solving person. The problems he is to face are always given. This means that he cannot alter any of the problems but must find appropriate solutions. Certainly an inspired solution can be attained intuitively, but in most cases the designer has to rely on his enquiring mind, which probes into all the possible visual situations within the requirements of individual problems.

Elements of Design

My theorization begins with a list of elements of design. This list is necessary because the elements will form the basis of all our future discussions.

The elements are, in fact, very much related to each other and cannot be easily separated in our general visual experience. Tackled individually, they may appear rather abstract, but together they determine the ultimate appearance and contents of a design.

Four groups of elements are distinguished:
(a) conceptual elements
(b) visual elements
(c) relational elements
(d) practical elements

Conceptual Elements

Conceptual elements are not visible. They do not actually exist but seem to be present. For instance, we feel that there is a point at the angle of a shape, there is a line marking the contour of an object, there are planes enveloping volume, and volume occupying space. These points, lines, planes, and volumes are not really there; if they are really there, they are no longer conceptual.

— (a) **Point** — A point indicates position. It has no length or breadth. It does not occupy any area of space. It is the beginning and end of a line, and is where two lines meet or

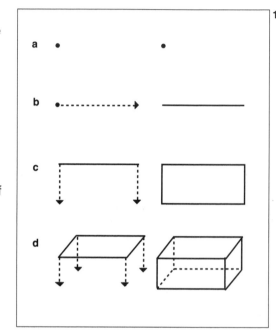

intersect. (Fig. 1a)

— (b) **Line** — As a point moves, its path becomes a line. A line has length but no breadth. It has position and direction. It is bound by points. It forms the border of a plane. (Fig. 1b)

— (c) **Plane** — The path of a line in motion (in a direction other than its intrinsic direction) becomes a plane. A plane has length and breadth, but no thickness. It has position and direction. It is bound by lines. It defines the external limits of a volume. (Fig. 1c)

— (d) **Volume** — The path of a plane in motion (in a direction other than its intrinsic direction) becomes a volume. It has position in space and is bound by planes. In two-dimensional design, volume is illusory. (Fig. 1d)

Visual Elements

When we draw an object on paper, we

employ a line that is visible to represent a line that is conceptual. The visible line not only has length but also breadth. Its color and texture are determined by the materials we use and the way we use them.

Thus, when conceptual elements become visible, they have shape, size, color, and texture. Visual elements form the most prominent part of a design because they are what we can actually see.

(a) **Shape** — Anything that can be seen has a shape which provides the main identification in our perception. (Fig. 2a)

(b) **Size** — All shapes have size. Size is relative if we describe it in terms of bigness and smallness, but it is also physically measurable. (Fig. 2b)

(c) **Color** — A shape is distinguished from its surroundings because of color. Color here is used in its broad sense, comprising not only all the hues of the spectrum but also the neutrals (black, white, and all the intermediate grays), and also all their tonal and chromatic variations. (Fig. 2c)

(d) **Texture** — Texture refers to the surface characteristics of a shape. This may be plain or decorated, smooth or rough, and may appeal to the sense of touch as much as to sight. (Fig. 2d)

Relational Elements

This group of elements governs the placement and interrelationship of the shapes in a design. Some are to be perceived, such as direction and position; some are to be felt, such as space and gravity.

(a) **Direction** — Direction of a shape depends on how it is related to the observer, to the frame that contains it, or to other shapes nearby. (Fig. 3a)

(b) **Position** — The position of a shape is

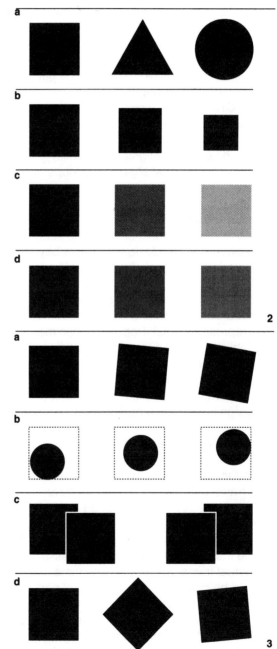

43

judged by its relationship to the frame or the structure (see Chapter 4) of the design. (Fig. 3b)

(c) **Space** — Shapes of any size, however small, occupy space. Thus, space can be occupied or left blank. It can also be flat or illusory to suggest depth. (Fig. 3c)

(d) **Gravity** — The sense of gravity is not visual but psychological. As we are pulled by the gravity of the earth, we tend to attribute heaviness or lightness, stability or instability to individual shapes or groups of shapes. (Fig. 3d)

Practical Elements

The practical elements underlie the content and extension of a design. They are beyond the scope of this book, but I would like to mention them here:

(a) **Representation** — When a shape is derived from nature or the man-made world, it is representational. Representation may be realistic, stylized, or near-abstract.

(b) **Meaning** — Meaning is present when the design conveys a message.

(c) **Function** — Function is present when a design is to serve a purpose.

The Frame of Reference

All the above elements normally exist within a boundary which we call a "frame of reference." The frame of reference marks the outer limits of a design and defines an area within which the created elements and left-over blank space, if any, all work together.

The frame of reference is not necessarily an actual frame. If it is, then the frame should be considered as an integral part of the design. The visual elements of the visible frame should not be overlooked. If there is no actual frame, the edges of a poster, the page of a magazine, the various surfaces

of a package all become frames of reference for the respective designs.

The frame of reference of a design can be of any shape, though it is usually rectangular. The die-cut shape of a printed sheet is the frame of reference of the design that is contained in it.

The Picture Plane

Within the frame of reference lies the picture plane. The picture plane is actually the plane surface of the paper (or any other material) upon which the design is created.

Shapes are directly painted or printed on this picture plane, but they may appear to be above, below, or unparallel to it because of spatial illusions, which will be fully discussed in Chapter 12.

Form and Structure

All the visual elements constitute what we generally call "form," which is the primary concern in our present enquiry into the visual language. Form in this sense is not just a shape that is seen, but a shape of definite size, color, and texture.

The way form is created, constructed, or organized along with other forms is often governed by a certain discipline which we call "structure." Structure which involves the relational elements is also essential in our studies.

Both form and structure will be thoroughly discussed in the chapters to follow.

CHAPTER 2: FORM

Form and the Conceptual Elements

As already pointed out, the conceptual elements are not visible. Thus point, line, or plane, when visible, becomes form. A point on paper, however small, must have shape, size, color, and texture if it is meant to be seen. So must a line or a plane. Volume remains illusory in two-dimensional design.

Visible points, lines, or planes are forms in the true sense, although forms as points or lines are still simply called points or lines in common practice.

Form as Point

A form is recognized as a point because it is small.

Smallness, of course, is relative. A form may appear fairly large when it is confined in a tiny frame of reference, but the same form may appear rather small when it is put inside a much greater frame of reference. (Fig. 4)

The most common shape of a point is that of a circle which is simple, compact, non-angular, and non-directional. However, a point may be square, triangular, oval, or even of a somewhat irregular shape. (Fig. 5)

Thus the main characteristics of a point are:

(a) its size should be comparatively small, and

(b) its shape should be rather simple.

Form as Line

A form is recognized as a line because of two reasons: (a) its breadth is extremely narrow, and (b) its length is quite prominent.

A line generally conveys the feeling of thinness. Thinness, like smallness, is relative. The extreme ratio between length and breadth of a shape makes it a line, but there is no absolute criterion for this.

Three separate aspects should be considered in a line:

The overall shape — This refers to its general appearance, which is described as straight, curved, bent, irregular, or hand-drawn. (Fig. 6a)

The body — As a line has breadth, its body is contained within two edges. The shapes of these two edges and the relationship between them determine the shape of the body. Usually the two edges are smooth and parallel, but sometimes they may cause the body of the line to appear tapering, knotty, wavy, or irregular. (Fig. 6b)

The extremities — These may be negligible when the line is very thin. But if the line is quite broad, the shapes of its extremities may become prominent. They may be square, round, pointed, or any simple shape. (Fig. 6c)

Points arranged in a row may evoke the feeling of a line. But in this case the line is conceptual and not visual, for what we see is still a series of points. (Fig. 6d)

Form as Plane

On a two-dimensional surface, all flat forms that are not commonly recognized as points or lines are forms as plane.

A planar form is bound by conceptual lines which constitute the edges of the form. The characteristics of these conceptual lines and their interrelationships determine the shape of the planar form.

Planar forms have a variety of shapes, which may be classified as follows:

(a) **Geometric** — constructed mathematically. (Fig. 7a)

4

5

a

b

c

d

6

a

b

c   d

e   f

7

46

(b) **Organic** — bounded by free curves, suggesting fluidity and growth. (Fig. 7b)

(c) **Rectilinear** — bound by straight lines which are not related to one another mathematically. (Fig. 7c)

(d) **Irregular** — bound by straight and curved lines which are not related to one another mathematically. (Fig. 7d)

(e) **Hand-drawn** — calligraphic or created with the unaided hand. (Fig. 7e)

(f) **Accidental** — determined by the effect of special processes or materials, or obtained accidentally. (Fig. 7f)

Planar forms may be suggested by means of outlining. In this case the thickness of the lines used should be considered. Points arranged in a row can also outline a planar form.

Points or lines densely and regularly grouped together can also suggest planar forms. They become the texture of the plane.

Form as Volume

Form as volume is completely illusory and demands a special spatial situation. A full discussion of this will be found in Chapter 12.

Positive and Negative Forms

Form is generally seen as occupying space, but it can also be seen as blank space surrounded by occupied space.

When it is perceived as occupying space, we call it "positive" form. When it is perceived as blank space surrounded by occupied space, we call it "negative" form. (Fig. 8)

In black-and-white design, we tend to regard black as occupied and white as unoccupied. Thus, a black form is recognized as positive and a white form as negative. But such attributions are not always true. Especially when forms interpenetrate or intersect one another (see the section on the inter-

relationships of forms later in this chapter), what is positive and what is negative are no longer easily distinguishable.

Form, whether positive or negative, is commonly referred to as the "figure," which is on a "ground." Here "ground" denotes the area surrounding the form or the "figure." In ambiguous cases, the figure-ground relationship may be reversible. This will be discussed in Chapter 12.

Form and Color Distribution

Without changing any of the elements in a design, the distribution of colors within a definite color scheme can have a large range of variations. Let us have a very simple example. Suppose we have a form which exists within a frame, and we can only use black and white. Four different ways of color distribution can be obtained:

(a) white form on white ground (Fig. 9a)

(b) white form on black ground (Fig. 9b)

(c) black form on white ground (Fig. 9c)

(d) black form on black ground (Fig. 9d)

In (a), the design is all white, and the form disappears. In (b), we have a negative form. In (c), we have a positive form. In (d), the design is all black, and the form disappears in the same way as in (a). Of course, we can have the form outlined in black in (a), and outlined in white in (d). (Fig. 10)

If the design increases in complexity, the different possibilities for color distribution will also be increased. To illustrate once again, we have two circles crossing over each other within a frame. In the previous example, we have only two defined areas where we can distribute our colors. Now we have four areas. Still using black and white, we can present sixteen distinct variations instead of only four. (Fig. 11)

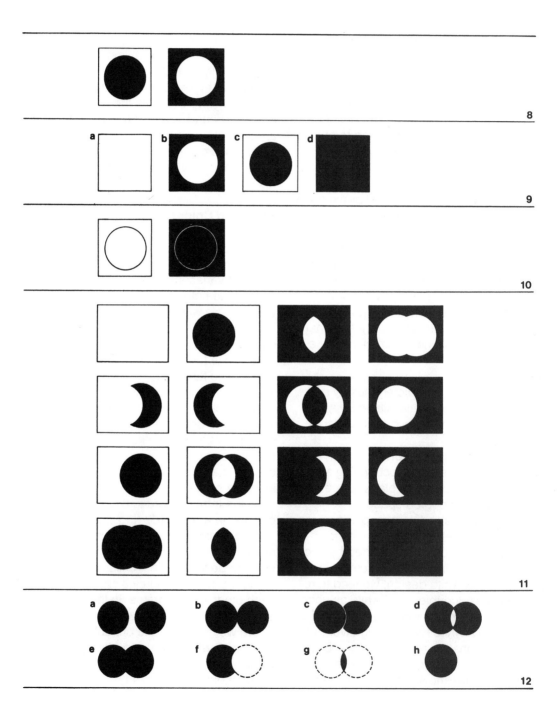

8

9

48

10

11

12

The Interrelationships of Forms

Forms can encounter one another in numerous ways. We have just demonstrated that when one form crosses over another, the results are not as simple as we may have thought.

We now again take two circles and see how they can be brought together. We choose two circles of the same size to avoid unnecessary complication. Eight different ways of interrelationship can be distinguished:

(a) **Detachment** — The two forms remain separate from each other although they may be very close together. (Fig. 12a)

(b) **Touching** — If we move the two forms closer, they begin to touch. The continuous space which keeps the two forms apart in (a) is thus broken. (Fig. 12b)

(c) **Overlapping** — If we move the two forms still closer, one crosses over the other and appears to remain above, covering a portion of the form that appears to be underneath. (Fig. 12c)

(d) **Interpenetration** — Same as (c), but both forms appear transparent. There is no obvious above-and-below relationship between them, and the contours of both forms remain entirely visible. (Fig. 12d)

(e) **Union** — Same as (c), but the two forms are joined together and become a new, bigger form. Both forms lose one part of their contours when they are in union. (Fig. 12e)

(f) **Subtraction** — When an invisible form crosses over a visible form, the result is subtraction. The portion of the visible form that is covered up by the invisible form becomes invisible also. Subtraction may be regarded as the overlapping of a negative form on a positive form. (Fig. 12f)

(g) **Intersection** — Same as (d), but only the portion where the two forms cross over each other is visible. A new, smaller form emerges as a result of intersection. It may not remind us of the original forms from which it is created. (Fig. 12g)

(h) **Coinciding** — If we move the two forms still closer, they coincide. The two circles become one. (Fig. 12h)

The various kinds of interrelationships should always be explored when forms are organized in a design.

Spatial Effects in Form Interrelationships

Detachment, touching, overlapping, interpenetration, union, subtraction, intersection, or coinciding of forms — each kind of interrelationship produces different spatial effects.

In detachment, both forms may appear equidistant from the eye, or one closer, one farther away.

In touching, the spatial situation of the two forms is also flexible as in detachment. Color plays an important role in determining the spatial situation.

In overlapping, it is obvious that one form is in front of or above the other.

In interpenetration, the spatial situation is a bit vague, but it is possible to bring one form above the other by manipulating the colors.

In union, usually the forms appear equidistant from the eye because they become one new form.

In subtraction, as well as in interpenetration, we are confronted with one new form. No spatial variation is possible.

In coinciding, we have only one form if the two forms are identical in shape, size, and direction. If one is smaller in size or different in shape and/or direction from the other, there will not be any real coinciding, and overlapping, interpenetration, union, subtraction, or intersection would occur, with the possible spatial effects just mentioned.

50

a

b

c

d

e

13

a

b

c

d

e

14

CHAPTER 3: REPETITION

Unit Forms

When a design is composed of a number of forms, those that are of identical or similar shapes are "unit forms" which appear more than once in the design.

The presence of unit forms helps to unify the design. Unit forms can be easily discovered in most designs if we search for them. A design may contain more than just one set of unit forms.

Unit forms should be simple. Overly complicated unit forms often tend to stand out too much as individual forms, and the effect of unity may be destroyed.

Repetition of Unit Forms

If we use the same form more than once in a design, we use it in repetition.

Repetition is the simplest method in designing. Columns and windows in architecture, the legs of a piece of furniture, the pattern on fabrics, tiles on the floor are obvious examples of repetition.

Repetition of unit forms usually conveys an immediate sense of harmony. Each repetitive unit form is like the beat of some kind of rhythm. When the unit forms are used in larger size and smaller numbers, the design may appear simple and bold; when they are infinitely small and in countless numbers, the design may appear to be a piece of uniform texture, composed of tiny elements.

Types of Repetition

In precise thinking, repetition should be considered in respect of each of the visual and relational elements:

(a) **Repetition of shape** — Shape is always the most important element. Repetitive shapes can have different sizes, colors, etc. (Fig. 13a)

(b) **Repetition of size** — Repetition of size is possible only when the shapes are also repetitive or very similar. (Fig. 13b)

(c) **Repetition of color** — This means that all the forms are of the same color but their shapes and sizes may vary. (Fig. 13c)

(d) **Repetition of texture** — All forms can be of the same texture but they may be of different shapes, sizes, or colors. In printing, all solidly printed forms with the same type of ink on the same surface are regarded as having the same texture. (Fig. 13d)

(e) **Repetition of direction** — This is possible only when the forms show a definite sense of direction without the slightest ambiguity. (Fig. 13e)

(f) **Repetition of position** — This has to do with how forms are arranged in connection with the structure which will be discussed in the next chapter.

(g) **Repetition of space** — All forms can occupy space in the same manner. In other words, they may be all positive, or all negative, or related to the picture plane in the same way.

(h) **Repetition of gravity** — Gravity is too abstract an element to be used repetitively. It is difficult to say that forms are of equal heaviness or lightness, stability or instability, unless all other elements are in strict repetition.

Variations in Repetition

Repetition of all the elements may seem monotonous. Repetition of one element alone may not provoke the sense of order and

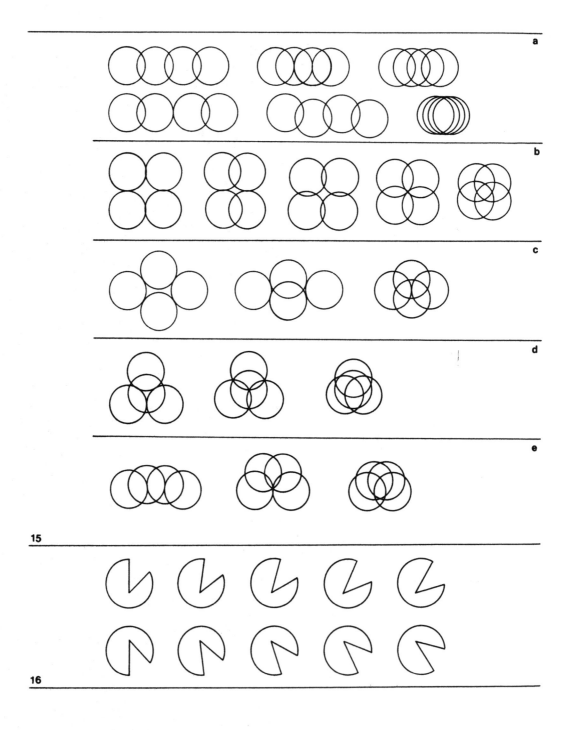

harmony which we normally associate with the repetition discipline. If most of the visual elements are in repetition, possibilities in directional and spatial variations should be explored.

Directional variations — With the exception of the plain circle, all forms can vary in direction to some extent. Even circles can be grouped to give a sense of direction. Several kinds of directional arrangements can be distinguished:

(a) repeated directions (Fig. 14a)
(b) indefinite directions (Fig. 14b)
(c) alternate directions (Fig. 14c)
(d) gradational directions (Fig. 14d)
(e) similar directions (Fig. 14e)

Repeated and the more regularly arranged directions can be mingled with some irregular directions.

Spatial variations — These can be obtained by having the forms encounter one another in a multiple of interrelationships as described in the previous chapter. Imaginative use of overlapping, interpenetration, union, or positive and negative combinations can lead to surprising results.

Subunit forms and Superunit forms

A unit form can be composed of smaller elements that are used in repetition. Such smaller elements are called "subunit forms."

If the unit forms, in the process of being organized in a design, are grouped together to become a bigger form which is then used in repetition, we call these new, bigger forms "superunit forms." Superunit forms can be used along with regular unit forms in a design if necessary.

Just as we can have more than one single type of unit form, we can have a variety of superunit forms if so desired.

The Encounter of Four Circles

To illustrate the formation of superunit forms, we will now see how four circles of the same size can be grouped together. The possibilities are definitely unlimited, but we can examine some of the common ways of arrangement as follows:

(a) **Linear arrangement** — The circles are lined up as guided by a conceptual line which passes through the centers of all the circles. The conceptual line may be straight, curved, or bent. The distance between the circles may be regulated as desired. Note, in an extreme case, that each of the circles crosses over all the other three simultaneously, producing as many as thirteen distinct divisions. (Fig. 15a)

(b) **Square or rectangular arrangement** — In this case the four circles occupy four points which, when joined together, can form a square or a rectangle. As in (a), an extreme case also shows thirteen divisions when all the circles deeply interpenetrate one another. (Fig. 15b)

(c) **Rhombic arrangement** — Here the four circles occupy four points which, when joined together, can form a rhombus. Regulating the distance between the circles, various types of superunit forms can emerge. (Fig. 15c)

(d) **Triangular arrangement** — Here the four circles are arranged so that three occupy the three points of a triangle, with the fourth in the center. This also produces interesting superunit forms. (Fig. 15d)

(e) **Circular arrangement** — Four circles in circular arrangement turn out the same result as in square arrangement, but circular arrangement can be very unique with more circles. Four circles can be arranged to suggest the arc of a circle, but this may be similar to a linear arrangement. (Fig. 15e)

Repetition and Reflection

Reflection is a special case of repetition. By reflection we mean that a form is mirrored, resulting in a new form which looks very much like the original form, except that one is left-handed, and the other is right-handed, and the two can never exactly coincide.

Reflection is only possible when the form is not symmetrical, because a symmetrical form turns out to be the same form in reflection.

Rotation of a form in any direction can never produce its reflected form. The reflected form has a completely different set of rotations. (Fig. 16)

All symmetrical forms can be divided into two parts: one component form and its reflection. The union of these two parts produces the symmetrical form.

Notes on the Exercises

Figures 17a, b, c, d, e, and f all represent the results of one simple problem: repetition of unit forms (circles) of the same shape and size. There is no restriction on the number of circles used.

Figures 18a, b, c, d, e, f, g, and h all represent the results of a more complex problem: students were asked to use two to four unit forms (circles) of the same shape and size to construct a superunit form, which is then repeated four times to make a design. Two levels of thinking are involved here. First, unit forms are not directly used to create the design but are grouped together to form superunit forms. Second, the superunit forms are used for the final design. The number of circles to be used in this problem should be no less than eight and no more than sixteen.

The results of the first problem appear to be more pleasing because there are fewer

17

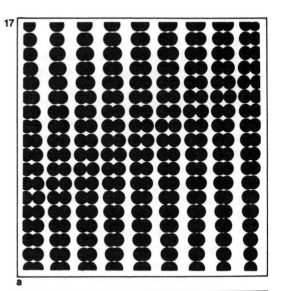

a

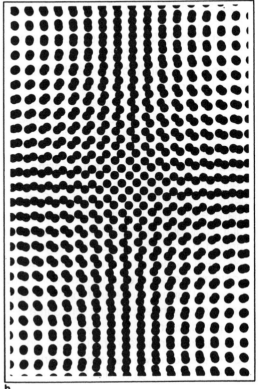

b

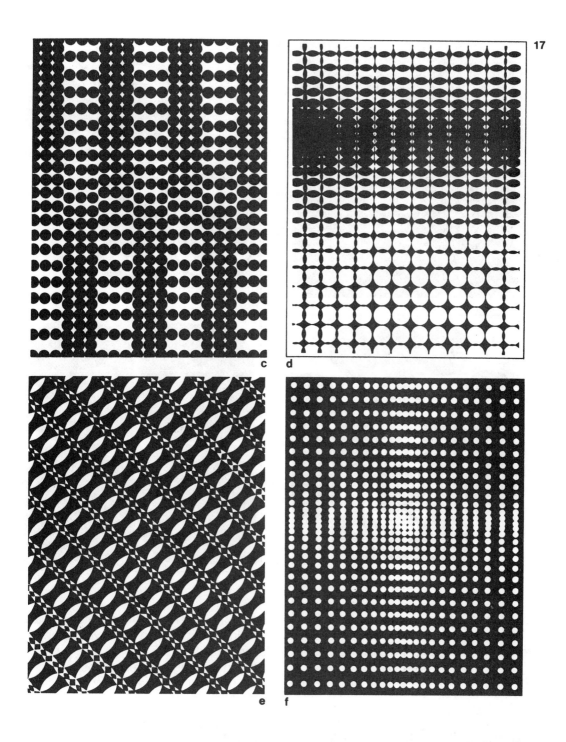

c

d

17

55

e

f

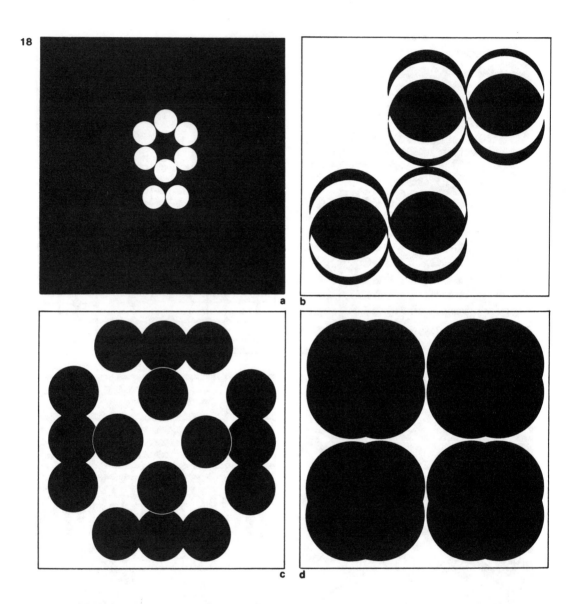

18 a b c d

restrictions; furthermore, the students were not totally unfamiliar with some of the structures to be covered later in this book when they attempted the exercise.

The second problem is more difficult. The results, however, all demonstrate special efforts in the exploration of the various interrelationships of forms.

It is interesting to compare the results of each problem and see how much one can

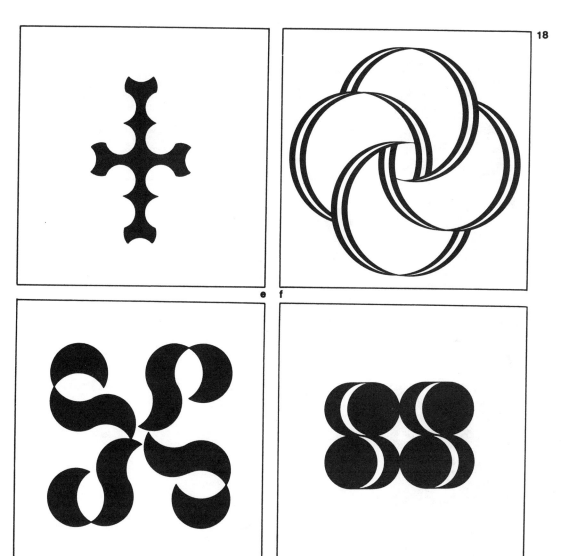

e   f

18

g h

do with the repetition of a circle in just black and white. I should like to point out here that all the exercises illustrated in this book have been done in black and white without any intermediate gray tones. This may impose much limitation but may help the beginner to gain a thorough understanding of black and white relationships which are so essential in all design jobs requiring the technology of printing.

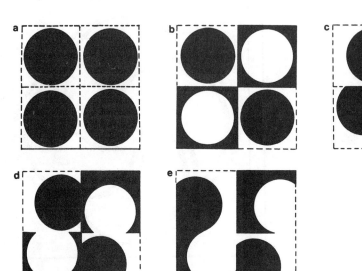

19

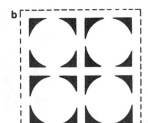

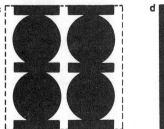

20

CHAPTER 4: STRUCTURE

Most designs have a structure. Structure is to govern the positioning of forms in a design. Why is one group of unit forms displayed in a row and equidistant from one another? Why does another group of unit forms suggest a circular pattern? Structure is the underlying discipline for such arrangements.

Structure generally imposes order and pre-determines internal relationships of forms in a design. We may have created a design without consciously thinking of structure, but structure is always present when there is organization.

Structure can be formal, semi-formal, or informal. It can be active or inactive. It can also be visible or invisible.

Formal Structure

A formal structure consists of structural lines which are constructed in a rigid, mathematical manner. The structural lines are to guide the entire formation of the design. Space is divided into a number of subdivisions equally or rhythmically, and forms are organized with a strong sense of regularity.

The various types of formal structure are repetition, gradation, and radiation. Repetition structures will be discussed later in this chapter. The other two types of formal structure will be dealt with in Chapters 6 and 7.

Semi-formal Structure

A semi-formal structure is usually quite regular, but slight irregularity exists. It may or may not consist of structural lines to determine the arrangement of unit forms. Semi-formal structures will be discussed in Chapters 5, 8, and 10.

Informal Structure

An informal structure does not normally have structural lines. Organization is generally free and indefinite. We will come to this type of structure when we discuss contrast in Chapter 9. It will also be touched upon in Chapter 10.

Inactive Structure

All types of structure can be active or inactive.

An inactive structure consists of structural lines which are purely conceptual. Such structural lines are constructed in a design to guide the placement of forms or unit forms, but they never interfere with their shapes nor divide the space up into distinct areas where color variations can be introduced. (Fig. 19a)

Active Structure

An active structure consists of structural lines which are also conceptual. However, the active structural lines can divide the space up into individual subdivisions which interact with unit forms they contain in various ways:

(a) The structural subdivisions provide complete spatial independence for the unit forms. Each unit form exists in isolation, as if it had its own small frame of reference. It can have a ground of different color from that of its neighboring unit forms. Alternate, systematic, or random play of positive and negative forms can be introduced effectively. (Fig. 19b)

(b) Within the structural subdivision, each unit form can move to assume various off-center positions. It can even slide partially beyond the area defined by the structural

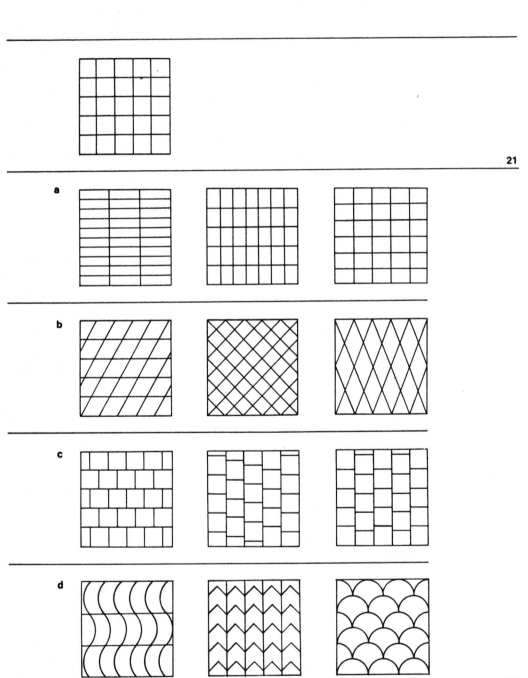

21

22

subdivision. When this happens, the portion of the unit form that is outside the confines as clearly marked by the active structural lines may be cut off. Thus, the shape of the unit form is affected. (Fig. 19c)

(c) When the unit form intrudes into the dominion of an adjacent structural subdivision, this situation can be regarded as the encounter of two forms (the unit form and its adjacent structural subdivision), and interpenetration, union, subtraction, or intersection can take place as desired. (Fig. 19d)

(d) Space isolated by a unit form in a structural subdivision can be united with any unit form or structural subdivision nearby. (Fig. 19e)

Invisible Structure
In most cases, structures are invisible, whether formal, semi-formal, informal, active, or inactive. In invisible structures, structural lines are conceptual, even though they may slice a piece off from a unit form. Such lines are active but not visible lines of measurable thickness.

Visible Structure
Sometimes a designer may prefer a visible structure. This means that the structural lines exist as actual and visible lines of desired thickness. Such lines should be treated as a special kind of unit form because they possess all the visible elements and can interact with the unit forms and the space contained by each of the structural subdivisions. (Fig. 20a)

Visible structural lines can be positive or negative. When negative, they are united with negative space or negative unit forms, and they can cross over positive space or positive unit forms. Negative structural lines

are considered as visible because they have a definite thickness which can be seen and measured. (Fig. 20b)

Positive and negative visible structural lines can be used in combination in a design. For example, all horizontal structural lines can be positive, and all vertical structural lines negative. (Fig. 20c)

Visible and invisible structural lines can also be used together. This means we can have only the verticals or the horizontals visible. Or visible and invisible structural lines can be used alternately or systematically, so that the visible structural lines mark off divisions, each of which actually contains more than one regular structural subdivision. (Fig. 20d)

Repetition Structure
When unit forms are positioned regularly, with an equal amount of space surrounding each of them, they may be said to be in a "repetition structure."

A repetition structure is formal, and can be active or inactive, visible or invisible. In this type of structure, the entire area of the design (or a desired portion of it) is divided into structural subdivisions of exactly the same shape and size, without odd spatial gaps left between them.

The repetition structure is the simplest of all structures. It is particularly useful in the construction of all-over patterns.

The Basic Grid
The basic grid is the most frequently used in repetition structures. It consists of equally spaced vertical and horizontal lines crossing over each other, resulting in a number of square subdivisions of the same size. (Fig. 21)

The basic grid provides each unit form the same amount of space above, below, left, and

62

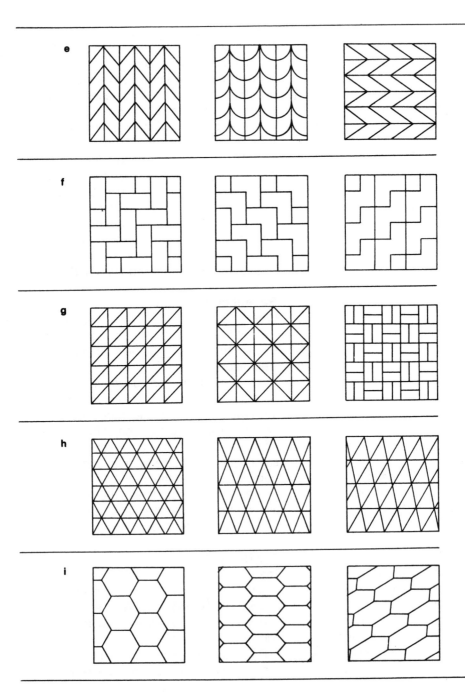

right. Except for the direction generated by the unit forms themselves, the vertical and horizontal directions are well-balanced, with no obvious dominance of one direction over the other.

Variations of the Basic Grid

There are many other types of repetition structures, usually derived from the basic grid. Such variations of the basic grid are suggested as follows:

(a) **Change of proportion** — The square subdivisions of the basic grid can be changed into rectangular ones. The balance of the vertical and the horizontal directions is thus transformed, and one direction gains greater emphasis. (Fig. 22a)

(b) **Change of direction** — All the vertical or horizontal lines, or both, can be tilted to any angle. Such diversion from the original vertical-horizontal stability can provoke a sense of movement. (Fig. 22b)

(c) **Sliding** — Each row of structural subdivisions can slide in either direction regularly or irregularly. In this case, one subdivision may not be directly above or next to another subdivision in an adjacent row. (Fig. 22c)

(d) **Curving and/or bending** — The entire set of vertical or horizontal lines, or both, can be curved and/or bent regularly, resulting in structural subdivisions still of the same shape and size. (Fig. 22d)

(e) **Reflecting** — A row of structural subdivisions as in (b) or (d) (provided that the two outer edges of the row are still straight and parallel to each other) can be reflected and repeated alternately or regularly. (Fig. 22e)

(f) **Combining** — Structural subdivisions in a repetition structure can be combined to form bigger or perhaps more complex shapes. The new, bigger subdivisions

should, of course, be of the same shape and size, and fit together perfectly without gaps in the design. (Fig. 22f)

(g) **Further dividing** — Structural subdivisions in a repetition structure can be further divided into small or perhaps more complex shapes. The new, smaller subdivisions should, again, be of the same shape and size. (Fig. 22g)

(h) **The triangular grid** — Tilting of the direction of structural lines and further dividing the subdivisions thus formed, we can obtain a triangular grid. Three well-balanced directions are usually distinguished in this triangular grid, although one or two of the directions may appear to be more prominent. (Fig. 22h)

(i) **The hexagonal grid** — Combining six adjacent spatial units of a triangular grid produces a hexagonal grid. It can be elongated, compressed, or distorted. (Fig. 22i)

It is necessary to note that inactive (and invisible) structures should be rather simple, because the shape of the subdivisions remains unseen. Active (both visible or invisible) structures can be more complex. Since the shape of the subdivisions is to affect the design, care should be taken in relating them to the unit forms.

Multiple Repetition Structures

When the structure consists of more than one kind of structural subdivisions which repeat both in shape and size, it is no longer a repetition structure but a "multiple repetition structure."

A multiple repetition structure is still a formal structure. The various kinds (usually two, but there can be more) of structural subdivisions are woven together in a regular pattern. Examples of this type of structure are

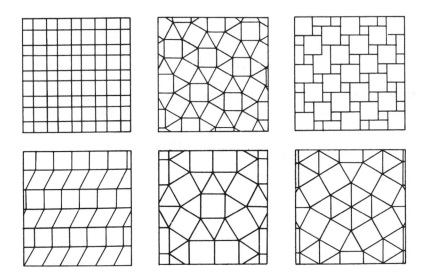

23

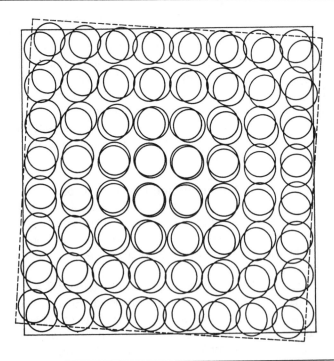

24

mathematical semi-regular plane tessellations and structures consisting of repetitive shapes with regular gaps. (Fig. 23)

Unit Forms and Structural Subdivisions

In an inactive (and invisible) structure, unit forms are either positioned in the center of structural subdivisions, or at intersections of structural lines. They can fit exactly, be smaller or bigger than the subdivisions. If bigger, all adjacent unit forms will touch, overlap, interpenetrate, unite, subtract, or intersect one another. Sometimes they can be so big that one can cross over several others simultaneously.

In an active (visible or invisible) structure, each unit form is confined to its own spatial subdivision, but it is not necessarily placed right in the center of the subdivision. It can just fit, be smaller or bigger than the subdivision, but it is seldom so big that it extends too much beyond the area of the subdivision. Variations of position and direction can occur.

Superunit forms are related to the structural subdivisions in the same way, except that we may contain them in superstructural subdivisions which consist of several regular subdivisions joined together.

Repetition of Position

This has been mentioned in the preceding chapter. Repetition of position means that the unit forms are all positioned inside each subdivision in exactly the same way.

In an inactive (and invisible) structure, there is always a repetition of position, because if the positioning of unit forms inside each subdivision varies, the regularity of the repetition structure may be easily destroyed.

In an active (visible or invisible) structure, repetition of position is not always necessary.

25

a

b

c

65

The active or visible structural lines provide sufficient discipline of repetition so that the freedom of positioning the unit forms, plus directional variations, may be fully explored.

Superimposition of Repetition Structures
One repetition structure, along with the unit forms it carries, can be superimposed upon another repetition structure. The two structures and their unit forms can be the same or different from each other. Interaction of the two structures may produce unexpected results. (Fig. 24)

Notes on the Exercises
Figures 25a, b, c, d, e, and f exemplify the use of repetitive unit forms in an inactive (and invisible) repetition structure. The unit form here is a smaller circle enclosed by a bigger circle. The relationship of the smaller circle and the bigger circle has to remain consistent within each design.

The use of active (and invisible) repetition structures is demonstrated in figures 26a, b, c, d, e, and f. The unit form here is similar to the one used in our problem for inactive repetition structure, except that the ring-like shape is broken, suggesting a form very much like the letter C.

Comparing the results of the two problems, we should easily notice that straight lines are present in the designs with active structures but absent in those with inactive structures. The straight, active structural lines not only affect the shape of unit forms and space surrounding them, but also change the nature of the design.

25

d

e

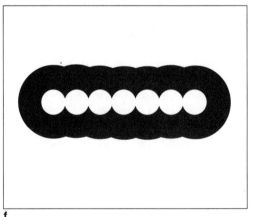

f

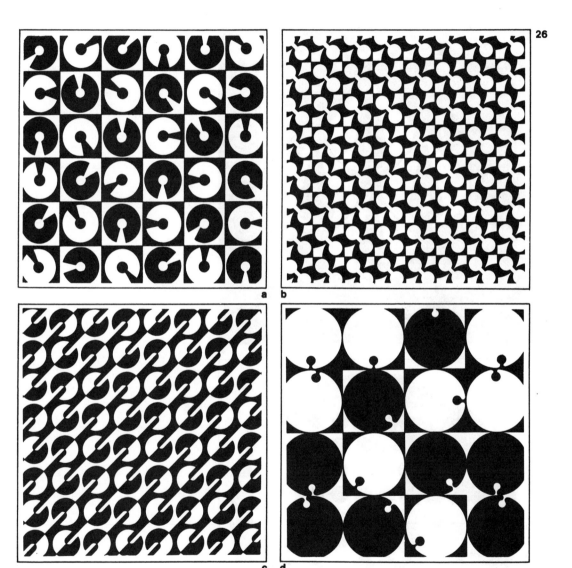

26

26

e

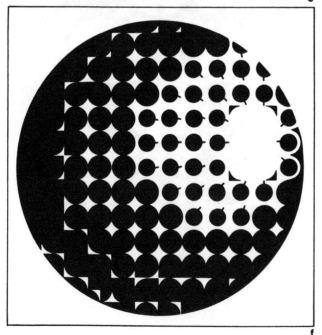

f

CHAPTER 5: SIMILARITY

Forms can resemble each other yet not be identical. If they are not identical, they are not in repetition. They are in similarity.

Aspects of similarity can be easily found in nature. The leaves of a tree, the trees in a forest, the grains of sand on a beach, the waves of the ocean are vivid examples.

Similarity does not have the strict regularity of repetition, but it still maintains the feeling of regularity to a considerable extent.

Similarity of Unit Forms

Similarity of unit forms in a design usually refers to, primarily, the similarity of shapes of unit forms. Inside a repetition structure, the sizes of unit forms have to be similar as well.

As in the case of repetition, similarity should be considered separately in respect of each of the visual and relational elements. Shape is always the main element in establishing a relationship of similarity, because forms can hardly be regarded as similar if they are similar in size, color, and texture, but different in shape.

Of course, the range of similarity of shape can be quite flexible. Shape A may look very different from shape B, but in contrast with shape C, shapes A and B can possess some relationship of similarity. Just how wide or how narrow the range of similarity should be is determined by the designer. When the range is narrow, the similar unit forms may appear to be almost repetitive. When the range is wide, the similar unit forms are seen more as individual forms, only vaguely related to one another.

Similarity of Shape

Similarity of shape does not simply mean that the forms appear more or less the same in our eyes. Sometimes similarity can be recognized when the forms all belong to a common classification. They are related to one another not so much visually as perhaps psychologically.

Similarity of shape can be created by one of the following ways:

(a) **Association** — Forms are associated with one another because they can be grouped together according to their type, their family, their meaning, or their function. The range of similarity is particularly flexible here. For instance, alphabets of one single typeface and weight definitely look alike, but we can expand the range to include all alphabets, regardless of typeface or weight. The range can still be widened as to include all forms of human writing. (Fig. 27)

(b) **Imperfection** — We can start with a shape which is regarded as our ideal shape. This ideal shape does not appear in our design, but instead we have all its imperfect variations. This can be achieved in numerous ways. The ideal shape can be disfigured, transformed, mutilated, cut up or broken up, as seen appropriate. (Fig. 28)

(c) **Spatial distortion** — A round disc, if turned in space, will appear elliptical. All forms can be rotated in the same manner, and can even be bent or twisted, resulting in a great variety of spatial distortions. (Fig. 29)

(d) **Union or subtraction** — A form can be composed of two smaller forms that are united, or obtained by subtracting a smaller form from a bigger form. The multiple ways

AcdBACD

27

28

29

30

31

in which the two component forms are related produce a chain of unit forms in similarity. If we allow the shapes and sizes of the component forms to vary, the range of unit forms in similarity becomes even more extensive. (Fig. 30)

(e) **Tension or compression** — A form can be stretched (by an internal force which pushes the contour outwards) or squeezed (by an external force which presses the contour inwards), resulting in a range of unit forms in similarity. This can be easily visualized if we think of the forms as something elastic, subject to tension or compression. (Fig. 31)

Similarity and Gradation
When a group of unit forms in similarity is used, it is essential that they should not be arranged in the design in such a way as to show a discernible systematic gradational change. As soon as the regularity of a gradational change is apparent, the effect of similarity will vanish.

Gradation is a different kind of discipline, which will be discussed in our next chapter.

Compare figures 32a and b. While both use the same kind of unit forms, 32a shows the effect of similarity, whereas 32b shows the effect of gradation. The results are quite distinct. In similarity, the unit forms are seen in slight agitation but they stick to one another to form a unity. In gradation, the unit forms are organized to suggest progression and movement in a highly controlled manner.

The Similarity Structure
It is not easy to define a similarity structure, but we can say it is semi-formal, and does not have the rigidity of a repetition structure nor even the regularity of a multiple repetition structure.

Two basic types of similarity structure are suggested here:

Similar structural subdivisions — Structural subdivisions are not repetitive, but similar to one another. Quadrilaterals, triangles, or hexagons, all with unequal sides, can be linked together to form all-space-filling patterns. This type of structure can be active or inactive, visible or invisible. (Fig. 33)

Visual distribution — This means that the unit forms are positioned within the frame of reference of the design, visually, without the guidance of structural lines. Visual distribution in this case should allow each unit form to occupy a similar amount of space as judged by the eye. Visual distribution is related to our concept of concentration, which will be discussed in Chapter 9. (Figs. 65f and g)

Notes on the Exercises
Figures 34a, b, c, d, e, and f all exemplify the use of similar unit forms in a repetition structure which is active but invisible. The unit forms are based on the letter "C," just like those used for the problem on active repetition structure in Chapter 4.

If we think systematically, the unit form can be formulated as $A - (B + C)$. Here A stands for the bigger circle, which is constant both in shape and size; B stands for the smaller circle, which may either be constant or variable in shape, size, and position within the bigger circle A; and C stands for the link between B and the space surrounding A, which may also be either constant or variable in shape, size, and position. Thus, a good range of unit forms in similarity can be created in this way.

By comparing the results of this problem and the active structure problem in Chapter 4, we can easily find that the discipline of similarity is more dynamic in nature than the discipline of repetition.

a

b

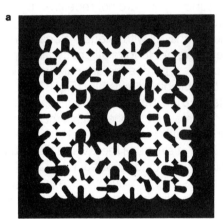
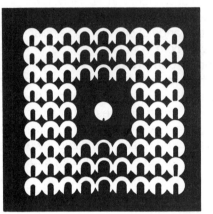

32

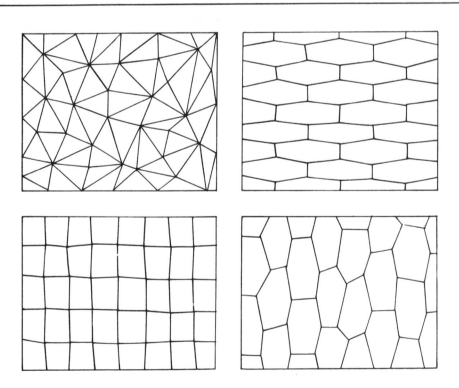

33

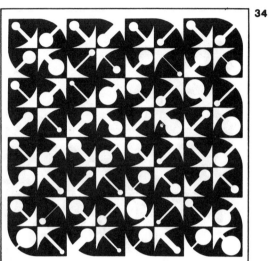

34

a

b

c

d

34

e

f

CHAPTER 6: GRADATION

We have already compared the different effects of similarity and gradation in the last chapter (figs. 32a and b). Obviously gradation is a much stricter kind of discipline. It demands not just gradual change, but gradual change in an orderly way. It generates optical illusion and creates a sense of progression, which normally leads to a climax or series of climaxes.

Gradation is a daily visual experience. Things that are close to us appear large and those that are far from us appear small. If we look at a tall building with a façade of regular window patterns from a very low angle, the change in size of the windows suggests a law of gradation.

Gradation of Unit Forms

Within a repetition structure, unit forms can be used in gradation. Most visual and relational elements can be used singly or combined in gradation to achieve various effects. This means that the unit forms can have gradation of shape, size, color, texture, direction, position, space, and gravity. However, three of these elements will be dropped from our present discussion. One of these is color, which is beyond the scope of this book. The next is texture, which will be thoroughly dealt with in Chapter 11. The third is gravity, which depends on the effects produced by other elements. Eliminating these, the rest fall into three main groups: planar gradation, spatial gradation, and shape gradation.

Planar Gradation

Planar gradation does not affect the shape or the size of unit forms. The relationship between the unit forms and the picture plane always remains constant. Two kinds of planar gradation can be distinguished:

Planar rotation — This indicates the gradual change of direction of the unit forms. A shape can be rotated without diversion from the picture plane. (Fig. 35a)

Planar progression — This indicates the gradual change of position of the unit forms within the structural subdivisions of a design. The unit forms can ascend or descend, or shift from one corner of the subdivisions to another, in a sequence of regular, gradual movements. (Fig. 35b)

Spatial Gradation

Spatial gradation affects the shape or the size of unit forms. The relationship between the unit forms and the picture plane is never constant. Two kinds of spatial gradation can be distinguished:

Spatial rotation — With gradual diversion from the picture plane, a unit form can be rotated so that we see more and more of its edge, and less and less of its front. A flat shape can become narrower and narrower until it is almost a thin line. Spatial rotation changes the shape of a unit form. (Fig. 35c)

Spatial progression — This is the same as the change of size. Increase or decrease of the size of unit forms suggests the forward or backward progression of unit forms in space. The unit forms are always parallel to the picture plane, but they may appear far behind the picture plane when it is small, or even in front of the picture plane when it is large. (Fig. 35d)

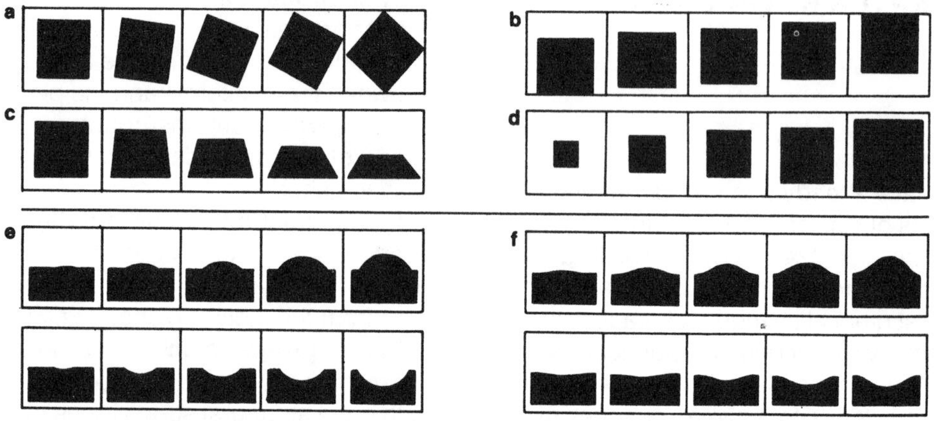

35

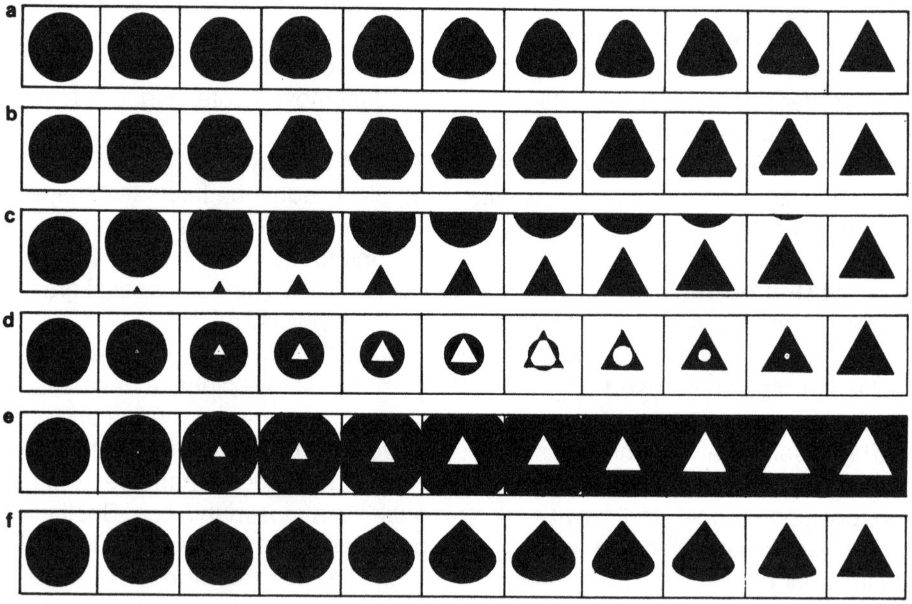

36

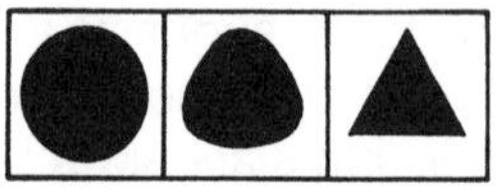

37

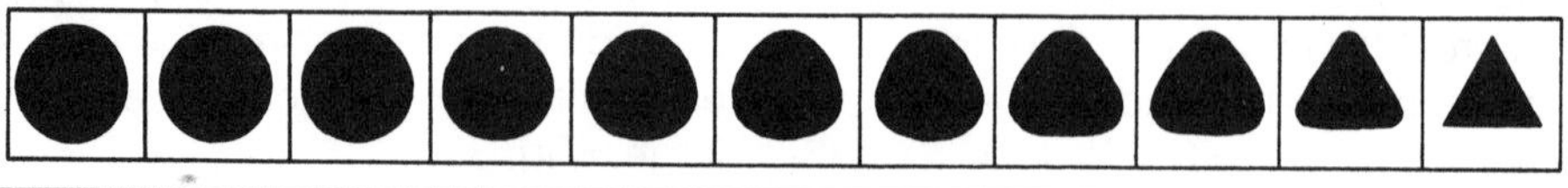

38

Shape Gradation

This refers to the sequence of gradations which are the results of actual change of shape. Two common kinds of shape gradation are suggested:

Union or subtraction — This indicates the gradual change of positions of subunit forms which make up the unit forms proper by union or subtraction. The shape and size of each of the subunit forms may also undergo gradual transformations at the same time. (Fig. 35e)

Tension or compression — This indicates the gradual change of shape of unit forms by internal or external forces. The shape appears as if it is elastic, easily affected by any slight push or pull. (Fig. 35f)

The Path of Gradation

Any form can be gradually changed to become any other form. How the change takes place is determined by the path of gradation chosen.

There are multiple paths of gradation. The designer can choose a path of planar, spatial, or shape gradation, or a combination of all these. The path can be straightforward or roundabout.

For instance, if we wish to change a circle into a triangle by shape gradation, the circle can be stretched and squeezed to become more and more triangular (Fig. 36a), or it can be subtracted from three sides until it becomes a triangle (Fig. 36b). By planar gradation, the circle can be shifted upwards followed by a triangle which will occupy the entire structural subdivision when the circle has completely moved out (Fig. 36c). By spatial gradation, the circle can gradually diminish while the triangle can emerge simultaneously, first as a dot and then as a

small triangle which gradually expands (Fig. 36d). Or the circle can gradually expand beyond the confines of the structural subdivision when the triangle also emerges (Fig. 36e). We can also consider the circle as the bottom of a cone which rotates to give the triangular front elevation (Fig. 36f).

All the paths of gradation just described are straightforward. If a roundabout path is desired, the circle can first be changed to a square (or any other shape) before it approaches the shape of the triangle in the sequence.

The Speed of Gradation

The number of steps required for a form to change from one situation to another determines the speed of gradation. When the steps are few, the speed becomes rapid, and when the steps are many, the speed becomes slow.

The speed of gradation depends on the effects a designer wishes to achieve. A rapid gradation causes visual jerks, whereas a slow gradation evolves smoothly and sometimes almost imperceptibly. Optical illusion is usually the result of slow gradation.

It is necessary to point out that rapid gradation should be used with great caution. If a form changes too rapidly, there may not be a feeling of gradation at all, and the result may be a group of only vaguely related forms (Fig. 37). Indeed we cannot change a circle effectively into a triangle in less than five steps, for normally this would require ten steps or more.

Extremely slow gradation may approach the effect of repetition, but careful arrangement of the pattern can produce very subtle results.

The speed of gradation can be changed in the middle of a sequence, or gradually quickened or slowed down for special effects. (Fig. 38)

39

1	2	3	4	5
1	2	3	4	5
1	2	3	4	5
1	2	3	4	5
1	2	3	4	5

1	1	1	1	1
2	2	2	2	2
3	3	3	3	3
4	4	4	4	4
5	5	5	5	5

1	2	3	4	5
2	3	4	5	6
3	4	5	6	7
4	5	6	7	8
5	6	7	8	9

40

3	3	3	3	3
3	2	2	2	3
3	2	1	2	3
3	2	2	2	3
3	3	3	3	3

5	4	3	4	5
4	3	2	3	4
3	2	1	2	3
4	3	2	3	4
5	4	3	4	5

3	2	1	2	3
2	2	1	2	2
1	1	1	1	1
2	2	1	2	2
3	2	1	2	3

41

6	5	6	5	6
5	4	5	4	5
4	3	4	3	4
3	2	3	2	3
2	1	2	1	2

2	3	4	5	6
1	2	3	4	5
2	3	4	5	6
3	4	5	6	7
2	3	4	5	6

3	4	5	4	3
3	3	4	4	3
3	2	3	4	3
3	2	2	3	3
3	2	1	2	3

42

1	1	1	1	1	4	4	4	4	4
2	2	2	2	2	5	5	5	5	5
3	3	3	3	3	6	6	6	6	6
4	4	4	4	4	7	7	7	7	7
5	5	5	5	5	6	6	6	6	6
6	6	6	6	6	5	5	5	5	5
7	7	7	7	7	4	4	4	4	4
6	6	6	6	6	3	3	3	3	3
5	5	5	5	5	2	2	2	2	2
4	4	4	4	4	1	1	1	1	1

1	1	1	1	1	5	4	3	2	1
2	2	2	2	2	5	4	3	2	1
3	3	3	3	3	5	4	3	2	1
4	4	4	4	4	5	4	3	2	1
5	5	5	5	5	5	4	3	2	1
1	2	3	4	5	5	5	5	5	5
1	2	3	4	5	4	4	4	4	4
1	2	3	4	5	3	3	3	3	3
1	2	3	4	5	2	2	2	2	2
1	2	3	4	5	1	1	1	1	1

9	8	7	6	5	1	2	3	4	5
8	7	6	5	4	2	3	4	5	6
7	6	5	4	3	3	4	5	6	7
6	5	4	3	2	4	5	6	7	8
5	4	3	2	1	5	6	7	8	9
1	2	3	4	5	9	8	7	6	5
2	3	4	5	6	8	7	6	5	4
3	4	5	6	7	7	6	5	4	3
4	5	6	7	8	6	5	4	3	2
5	6	7	8	9	5	4	3	2	1

43

a

1	2	3	4	5
5	4	3	2	1
1	2	3	4	5
5	4	3	2	1
1	2	3	4	5

b

1	2	3	4	5
6	5	4	3	2
1	2	3	4	5
6	5	4	3	2
1	2	3	4	5

c

1	2	3	4	5	A
9	8	7	6	5	B
1	2	3	4	5	A
9	8	7	6	5	B
1	2	3	4	5	A

Without alteration to the speed of gradation, a roundabout path of gradation normally takes more steps than a straightforward path.

Patterns of Gradation

In a gradation design, two factors are of importance in pattern construction: the range of gradation, and the direction of movement.

The range of gradation is marked by a starting situation and a terminating situation. In some cases, where the path of gradation is not straightforward but roundabout, intermediate situations should be taken into account. The number of steps between the starting and the terminating situations determines both the speed and the breadth of the range of gradation.

The direction of movement refers to the orientations of the starting and the terminating situations and their interrelationship. The unit forms of the starting situation can all be lined up in a row and proceed lengthwise, breadthwise, or both, with regular steps towards the terminating situation. Diagonal or other ways of progression are also possible. Some typical movement patterns in gradation are:

Parallel movement — This is the simplest. Unit forms are transformed gradually in parallel steps. In parallel movement, the climax is usually a straight line. (In figure 39, please note that the numerals signify the varying degrees of gradation and that the solid lines divide the area into zones, with each zone containing unit forms of the same step.)

Concentric movement — This means that the unit forms are transformed in concentric layers. If the starting situation is at a corner of the design, then the pattern is only partially concentric. In concentric movement, the climax may be a point, a square, or a cross. (Fig. 40)

Zigzag movement — This means that the unit forms of the same step are arranged in a zigzag manner and are transformed at equal speed. (Fig. 41)

In our diagrams, only twenty-five structural subdivisions (five rows of five subdivisions each) are shown. Of course, a normal gradation pattern is much bigger, and the number of steps can be extended infinitely. Also, small standardized gradation patterns may be repeated and arranged to form a bigger pattern of gradation. For example, sections of parallel movement can be joined to form a gradation design in the ways suggested in figure 42.

It is essential to note that gradation can proceed from the starting situation to the terminating situation and then back to the starting situation with the reversal of the steps, as in the example 1-2-3-4-5-4-3-2-1. The sequence can be repeated and repeated if necessary, with smooth transitions. If regular breaks of the gradation pattern are desirable, the gradation can proceed from the starting to the terminating situation and immediately start all over again, as in 1-2-3-4-5-1-2-3-4-5.

The Gradation Structure

A gradation structure is similar to a repetition structure except that the structural subdivisions do not remain repetitive but change in size, shape, or both, in a gradual, systematic sequence.

Most repetition structures can be converted into gradation structures. Let us examine such possibilities in the same way as we discussed the variations of the basic grid in Chapter 4:

(a) **Change of size and/or proportion** — The structural subdivisions of a basic grid can increase or decrease in size (with or without change of proportion) gradually from one to the next. The vertical or horizontal

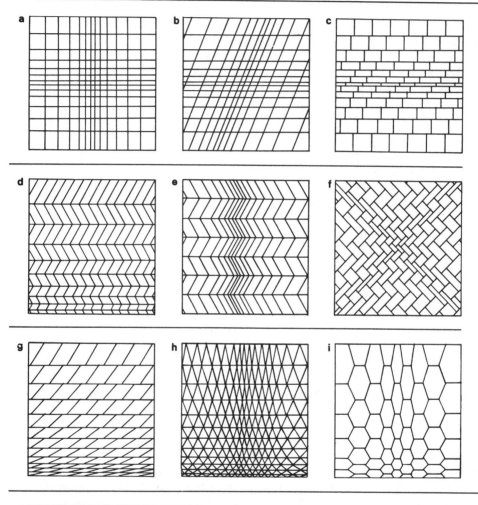

44

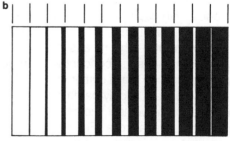

45

structural lines or both of the basic grid can be spaced with gradually increasing or decreasing widths. Gradation can proceed from narrow to wide, and then wide to narrow again, or can be arranged in any rhythmical sequence. (Fig. 44a)

(b) **Change of direction** — The entire set of vertical or horizontal structural lines, or both, in (a) can be tilted in any desired direction. (Fig. 44b)

(c) **Sliding** — The entire row of vertical or horizontal structural subdivisions in (a) or (b) can be made to slide regularly so that one subdivision is not directly next to or above another. (Fig. 44c)

(d) **Curving, bending** — The entire set of vertical or horizontal structural lines, or both, in (a), (b), or (c) can be curved or bent gradually or regularly. (Fig. 44d)

(e) **Reflecting** — A row of non-right-angled structural subdivisions as in (b) or (d) can be reflected and repeated alternately or regularly. (Fig. 44e)

(f) **Combining** — Structural subdivisions in (a) or (b) can be combined to form bigger or more complex shapes with the effect of gradation. (Fig. 44f)

(g) **Further dividing** — Structural subdivisions in all gradation structures can be subdivided into smaller or more complex shapes. (Fig. 44g)

(h) **The triangular grid** — The triangular grid of a repetition structure can be transformed into a gradation structure by gradually varying the size and shape of the triangles. (Fig. 44h)

(i) **The hexagonal grid** — The hexagonal grid of a repetition structure can be transformed into a gradation structure by gradually varying the size and shape of the hexagons. (Fig. 44i)

Alternate Gradation

Alternate gradation provides unusual complexity in a gradation design. It means that gradually changing unit forms or structural subdivisions from opposite directions are interwoven together. The simplest way to achieve alternate gradation is to divide the structure (either the vertical or the horizontal rows) into odd and even rows, and have all the odd rows observe a discipline different from the even rows.

To illustrate this, we have figure 43, in which A stands for the odd rows and B stands for the even rows. To have alternate gradation of unit forms, we can arrange in A rows unit forms to be transformed from left to right, and in B rows the exact opposite (figure 43a and also figure 17c, which is a finished design). However, it is not necessary that the steps of gradation in A and B rows should be the same. Variations of these are suggested in figures 43b and c. Manipulating the range, speed, and direction of gradation, we can have almost unlimited kinds of variation. Unit forms, if they are not used gradationally in both A and B rows, can be used gradationally in one set of the rows, and repetitively (in straight or alternate repetition) in the other set of rows.

If the unit forms are in gradation of size, the space left over by diminishing unit forms can be used for the accommodation of a set of unit forms in reverse gradation. Here the original unit forms can occupy the central portion of the structural subdivisions, whereas a new set of unit forms can occupy intersections of the structural lines. (Fig. 45a)

In a gradation structure, alternate gradation can be obtained if the A rows gradually diminish while the B rows gradually expand simultaneously in the same direction. This is illustrated in figure 45b with black bands standing for the A rows and white bands for the B rows. The illustration may look rather complicated, but the method of construction can be very simple. The combined width of every pair of A and B rows should always remain constant (or in very slow gradation). Thus we can first divide the entire width of the design area into combined rows of A+B, and then we can further divide each of the combined rows into an A row and a B row, carefully allowing A to expand step by step from one combined row to the next. Since the width of the combined row is constant, if A expands, B automatically contracts.

Relationship of Unit Forms and Structures in a Gradation Design

A gradation design can be obtained in one of the following ways: gradational unit forms in a repetition structure; repetitive unit forms in a gradation structure; and gradational unit forms in a gradation structure.

It should be noted that either the unit forms or the structure or both could be in gradation. A repetition structure is flexible enough to contain most kinds of gradational unit forms, whereas a gradation structure may have many restrictions.

In a gradation structure, the structural subdivisions can range from very big to very small, or very narrow to very wide. They change both in shape and size, making accommodation of more complex kinds of unit form difficult.

Notes on the Exercises

Figures 46a, b, c, and d exemplify the use of gradational unit forms (circles in this case) in a repetition structure. Compare these with figures 17d and f, which feature repeated circles in a gradation structure. Figures 47a through h exemplify the use of gradational unit forms (in this case a stylized alphabet) in a gradation structure. While the latter problem represents a new departure, the former is closely linked with all the problems in preceding chapters, with the circle as a recurring motif.

46

a b

c d

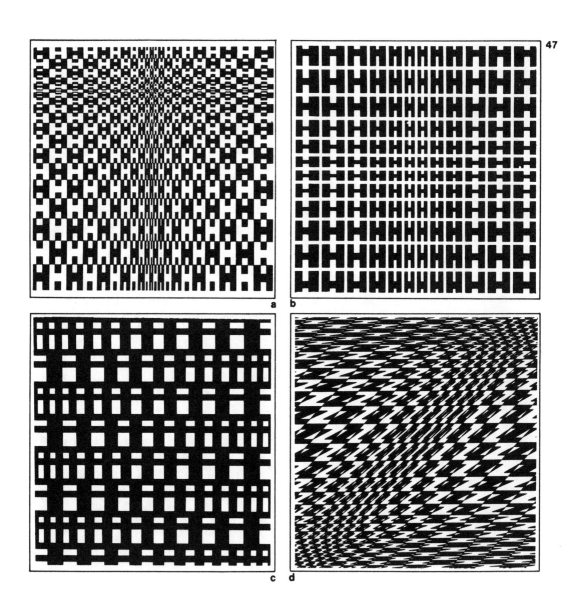

47

e   f

g   h

86

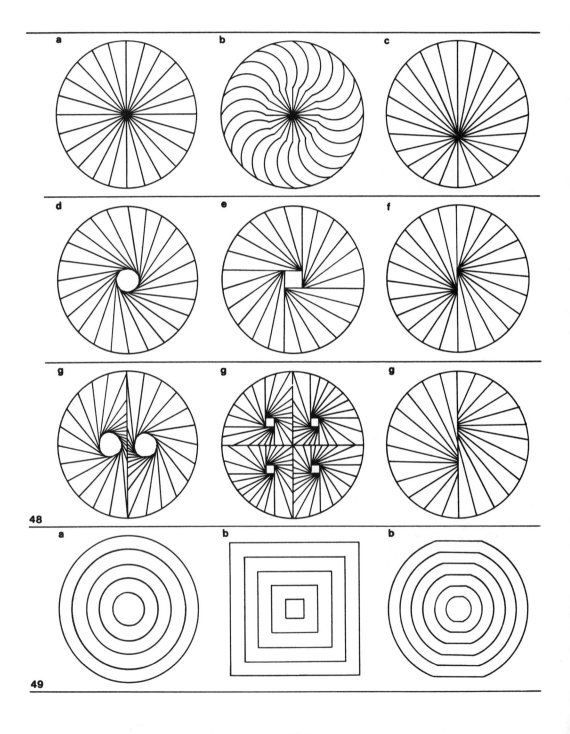

48

49

CHAPTER 7: RADIATION

Radiation may be described as a special case of repetition. Repeated unit forms or structural subdivisions which revolve regularly around a common center produce a pattern of radiation.

Radiation is a common phenomenon in nature. Look at the flowers in bloom and you can always discover radiation patterns in the arrangements of their petals. Dropping a stone on calm waters generates concentric ripples, which also suggest a kind of radiation. In an abstract way, the sun radiates light rays; so do most luminous objects.

Radiation can have the effect of optical vibration that we find in gradation. The repetition of unit forms or structural subdivisions around a common center has to go through a gradation of directions. Therefore, a radiation may also be called a special case of gradation. Sometimes the division between a gradation pattern and a radiation pattern is rather vague, as in the case when the climax of a gradation pattern is located in the center.

A radiation pattern arrests the attention immediately. It is very useful when a powerful, eye-catching design is required.

Characteristics of a Radiation Pattern

A radiation pattern has the following characteristics, which help to distinguish it from a repetition or gradation pattern:

(a) It is generally multi-symmetrical.

(b) It has a very strong focal point, which is usually located at the center of the design.

(c) It can generate optical energy and movement from or towards the center.

The Radiation Structure

A radiation structure consists of two important factors, the interplay of which establishes all the variations and complexity:

Center of radiation — This marks the focal point around which unit forms are positioned. It should be noted that the center of radiation is not always the physical center of the design.

Directions of radiation — This refers to the directions of structural lines as well as the directions of the unit forms.

For the sake of convenience, three main kinds of radiation structure may be distinguished: centrifugal, concentric, and centripetal. Actually, the three are very much interdependent. The centrifugal radiation structure may require a concentric structure to help in the placement of its unit forms. The centripetal usually needs a centrifugal structure to guide its construction. The concentric must have a centrifugal structure to determine its structural subdivisions.

The Centrifugal Structure

This is the commonest kind of radiation structure. In it, structural lines radiate regularly from the center or its vicinity in all directions.

(a) **The basic centrifugal structure** — This consists of straight structural lines radiating from the center of the pattern. All the angles formed by the structural lines at the center should be equal. (Fig. 48a)

(b) **Curving or bending of structural lines** — The straight structural lines in (a) can be curved or bent regularly as desired. When bending occurs, the positions where the structural lines start to make an abrupt turn are determined by a shape (usually a circle, the center of which coincides with the center of the radiation pattern) which is superimposed upon the structural lines. (Fig. 48b)

(c) **Center of radiation in off-center position** — The center of radiation is often also the physical center of the design, but it can be placed in an off-center position, as far as the edge or even beyond it. (Fig. 48c)

(d) **Opening up of the center of radiation** — The center of radiation can be opened up to form a round, oval, triangular, square, or polygonal hole. In this case, the structural lines do not radiate from the center of the hole but run as tangents to the circular hole or as extensions of the sides of the central triangle, square, or polygon. (Fig. 48d)

(e) **Multiple centers, by opening up of the center of radiation** — After the center of radiation has been opened up and a regular triangle, square, or polygon appears, each vertex of the triangle, square, or polygon can become a center of radiation. This means that if the polygon is a hexagon, there will be six centers of radiation. The design is divided into six sectors, with each sector its own center of radiation from which structural lines are radiated. (Fig. 48e)

(f) **Multiple centers, by splitting and sliding the center of radiation** — A center of radiation can be split into two by having half of the design radiate from one off-center position, and the remaining half from another off-center position, with the two centers on one straight line which passes through the physical center of the design. More centers can be created in similar fashion. (Fig. 48f)

(g) **Multiple centers or hidden multiple centers, by combining sections of off-center radiation structures** — Two or more sections of off-center radiation structures can be organized and combined to form a new radiation structure. The result is a multiple-center radiation whether the centers are visible or hidden. (Fig. 48g)

The Concentric Structure
In a concentric structure, instead of radiating from the center as in a centrifugal structure, structural lines surround the center in regular layers.

(a) **The basic concentric structure** — This consists of layers of equally spaced circles enclosing the center of the design which is also the common center of all the circles. (Fig. 49a)

(b) **Straightening, curving, or bending of structural lines** — The concentric structural lines as in (a) can be straightened, curved, or bent regularly, as desired. In fact, any single shape can be made into concentric layers. (Fig. 49b)

(c) **Shifting of centers** — Instead of having a common center, the circles can shift their centers along the track of a line, which may be straight, curved, bent, and possibly forming a circle, triangle, square, or any desired shape. Usually swirling movements result. (Fig. 49c)

(d) **The spiral** — A geometrically perfect spiral is very difficult to construct. However, a less perfect but still regular spiral can be obtained by dissecting the basic concentric structure and putting the sectors back again. Shifting of centers and adjusting of the radii of the circles can also produce a spiral. A spiral pattern generates strong centrifugal force, so it is halfway between a centrifugal and a concentric structure. (Fig. 49d)

(e) **Multiple centers** — By taking a section or a sector of a concentric structure and repeating it, sometimes with necessary adjustments, a concentric structure with multiple centers can be constructed. (Fig. 49e)

(f) **Distorted and/or hidden centers** — This can be created in the same way as described in (e), but instead of resulting in multiple

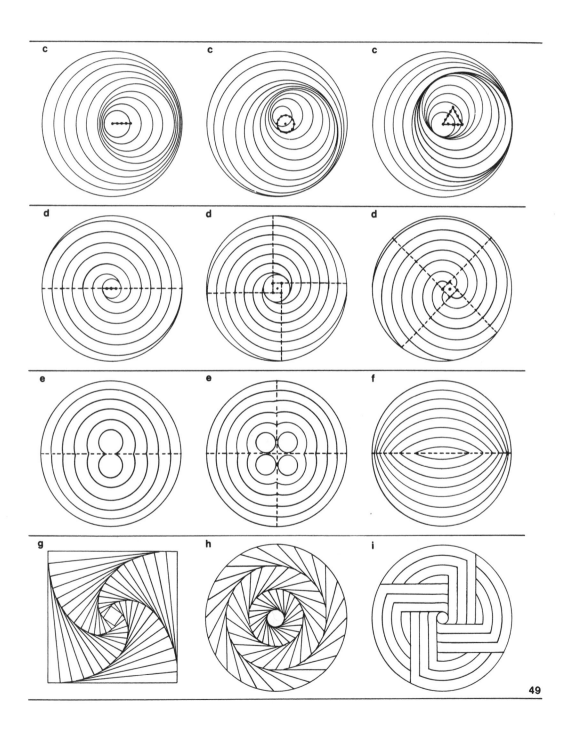

centers, the design may contain a distorted center, or several hidden centers. (Fig. 49f)

(g) **Gradual rotation of concentric layers** — If the concentric layers are not perfect circles but squares, polygons, or irregular shapes, they can be gradually rotated. (Fig. 49g)

(h) **Concentric layers with centrifugal radiations** — Centrifugal radiations can be constructed within each concentric layer. (Fig. 49h)

(i) **Reorganized concentric layers** — The concentric layers can be reorganized so that some of the structural lines can be bent and linked with other structural lines, resulting in interwoven patterns with one or more centers. (Fig. 49i)

The Centripetal Structure

In this kind of structure, sequences of bent or curved structural lines press towards the center. The center is not where all the structural lines will converge but where all angles or curves formed by the structural lines point towards.

(a) **The basic centripetal structure** — This consists of equal sectors within each of which are constructed equidistant lines parallel to the two straight sides of the sector, forming a series of angles progressing towards the center. (Fig. 50a)

(b) **Directional change of structural lines** — The parallel lines in the basic centripetal structure can change in direction, so that increasingly acute or obtuse angles are formed at the joining points of the structural lines. (Fig. 50b)

(c) **Curving and bending of structural lines** — The structural lines can be curved or bent regularly, creating complex changes within the pattern. (Fig. 50c)

(d) **Opening up of the center of radiation**

— By sliding the sectors of a centripetal structure, the center of radiation can be opened up and a triangle, square, polygon, or star shape can be formed. (Fig. 50d)

Superimposition of Radiation Structures

As pointed out earlier, the three kinds of radiation structure are interdependent. Unless the unit forms are just the structural lines themselves made visible, each kind of radiation structure generally requires another to produce fine structural subdivisions for the accommodation of unit forms. (Fig. 51a)

Superimposition in this way is just a practical necessity. Which kind of radiation structure will dominate during this superimposition depends on the shape and positioning of the unit forms.

Sometimes one radiation structure is superimposed upon another of the same type or a different type with a different purpose. The result is a complex composition, often producing interesting moiré patterns. (Fig. 51b)

Radiation and Repetition

A radiation structure may sometimes be superimposed upon a repetition structure. With the repetition structure remaining unchanged, the radiative structural lines may be shifted slightly so that the continuity of the radiative lines from one repetitive structural subdivision to the next is interrupted to provoke a sense of movement. (Figs. 52a and b)

A radiation structure may also be superimposed upon simple repetitive forms guided by an inactive repetition structure. (Fig. 52c)

Radiation and Gradation

Most of the radiation structures illustrated

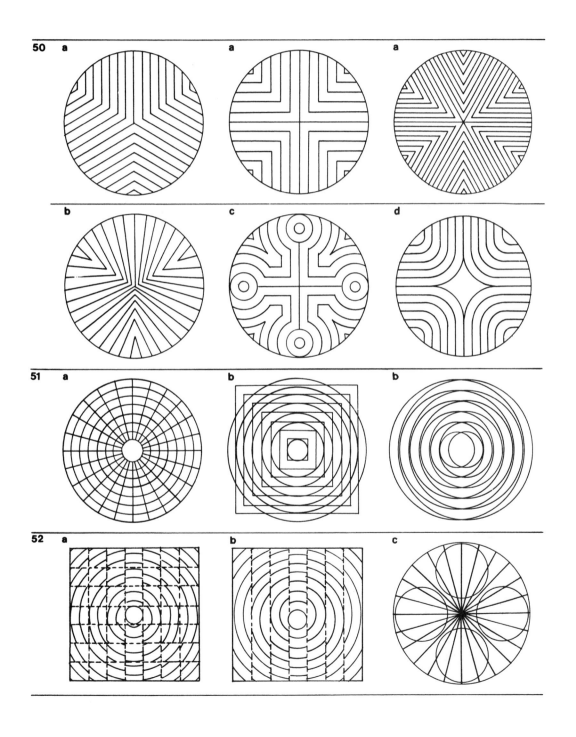

50 a   a   a

    b   c   d

51 a   b   b

52 a   b   c

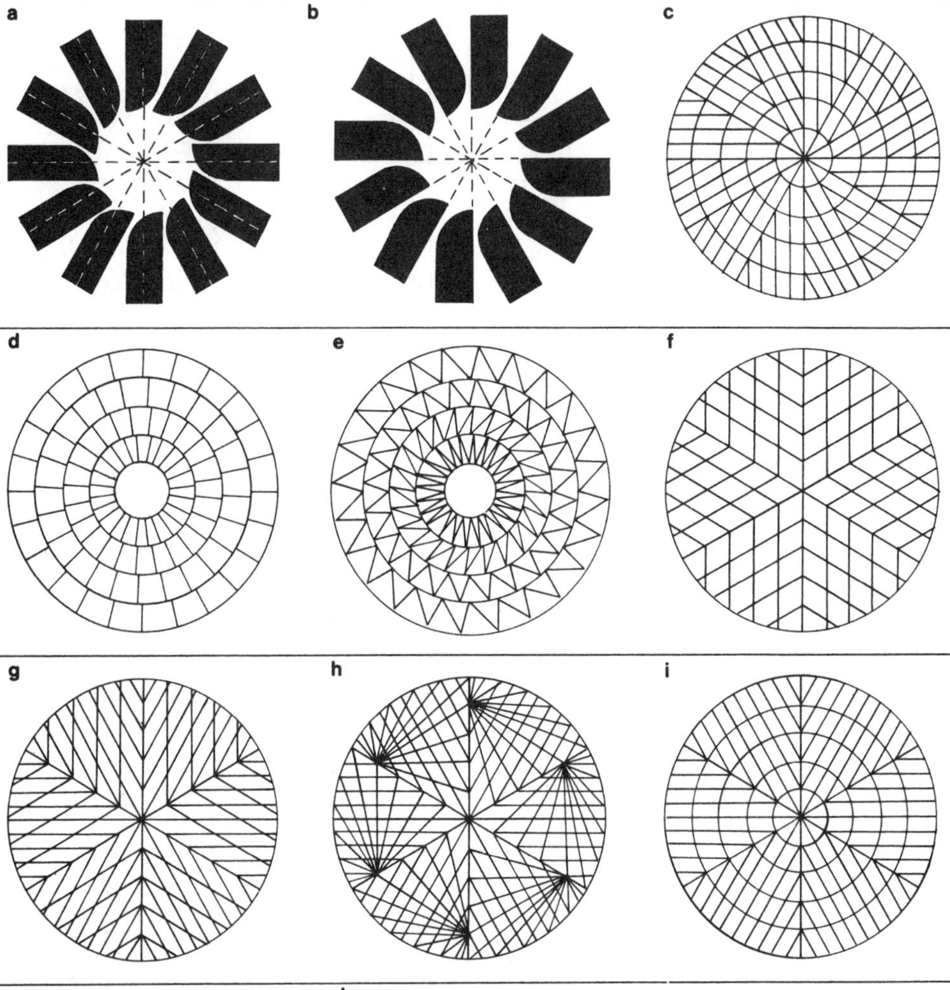

a

b

c

d

e

f

g

h

i

53

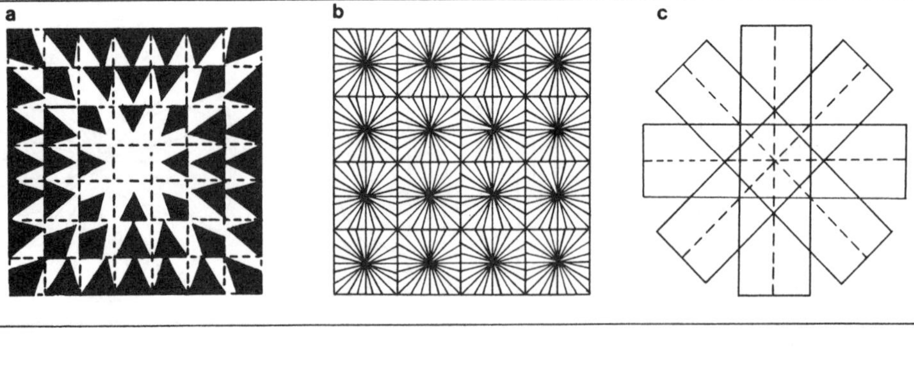

a

b

c

54

earlier in this chapter are constructed with repetitive angles and/or spacing. However, gradational angles and/or spacing may be used in a great many of the cases. (Figs. 55f and g)

A radiation structure may be superimposed on a gradation structure or a group of gradational unit forms in the same way as it is superimposed on a repetition structure or a group of repetitive forms.

Structural Subdivisions and Unit Forms

Structural subdivisions in a radiation structure are usually either repetitive or gradational, although they may also be similar to or plainly different from one another.

In a centrifugal structure, the subdivisions are generally repetitive in both shape and size. Unit forms fit these subdivisions in the same way that they fit those in a repetition structure, except that the subdivisions normally carry the unit forms in their directional rotation. The unit forms may conform to the directions of the subdivisions or maintain a constant angle to the axis of each subdivision. (Figs. 53a and b)

Within each of the subdivisions in a centrifugal structure, finer subdivisions can be constructed if desired. A sequence of parallel lines can be employed for the purpose, but there is virtually no limit to the ways of making further subdivisions. (Fig. 53c)

In a regular concentric structure, the subdivisions are in the form of a ring which can only accommodate unit forms of a linear nature. A centrifugal structure is usually required for making fine subdivisions, and each ring can be rotated variably, if necessary, so that the subdivisions in one ring do not have to align with those in the next ring. (Fig. 53d) Subdivisions obtained in this way are

generally repetitive within each ring, but gradational from the center towards outer rings. Unit forms fit these subdivisions in the same way as they fit those in a gradation structure. Of course it is also possible to subdivide each concentric ring in a different manner if desired. (Fig. 53e)

In a regular centripetal structure, the subdivisions are defined by sets of parallel lines which curl or bend towards the center. These can be further divided by superimposing sets of parallel lines, another centripetal structure, or a concentric structure. (Figs. 53f, g, h, and i)

Unit Forms in Radiation

We have spoken of unit forms in repetition, similarity, and gradation, and in each of these disciplines all the visual and relational elements can be considered. Radiation is a kind of discipline which involves structure only. If we have to speak of unit forms in radiation, it will be the concentric movement discussed under the heading of "Patterns of Gradation" in the chapter on gradation. Concentric movement creates a feeling of radiation, but basically it is a gradational use of unit forms. In planar rotation, the unit forms can be rotated in such a way that they all point to the physical center of the design. In planar progression, they can gradually move towards or away from the center from one concentric ring to the next. (Fig. 54a)

Unit forms can be designed as miniature radiation patterns which are arranged repetitively or gradationally in a repetition structure. The effect is still very much like radiation. (Fig. 54b)

Oversize Unit Forms

A unit form can sometimes be almost as big

as the entire radiation pattern itself, or its length or breadth can be comparable to the diameter of radiation. Such oversize unit forms can be rotated along a centrifugal structure, maintaining a fixed relationship to each of the structural lines. During rotation, one unit form will inevitably cross over several or all other unit forms, and careful manipulation of overlapping, interpenetration, union, subtraction, and intersection will produce exciting results. (Fig. 54c)

Irregular and Distorted Radiation

Any irregular departure from regular radiation structures can be made if desired. Irregularity can occur only in one section of a regular pattern, but the entire design can be created with a vague center and loosely scattered radiating elements or series of irregular concentric rings.

Photography and other mechanical means can be used to distort a regular radiation pattern. The pattern drawn or painted on paper can be photographed with a special lens, through a textured transparent screen or at an angle. It can also be curled, creased, folded, or crumpled, and then made into a flat picture by means of photography.

Notes on the Exercises

Figures 55a through n all illustrate radiation designs with unit forms more or less of a linear nature. In some examples the unit forms are just the structural lines made visible; in other examples they are designed to fit structural subdivisions.

No attempt is made here to group the examples into the three kinds of radiation structure discussed in this chapter, because although some are immediately distinguishable as this or that kind, most are a blending of the different kinds. It is strongly suggested that the examples should be carefully analyzed.

94

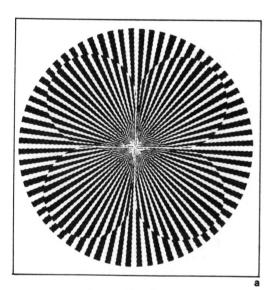

a

b

c

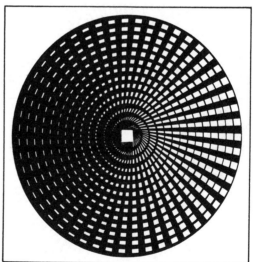

d

55

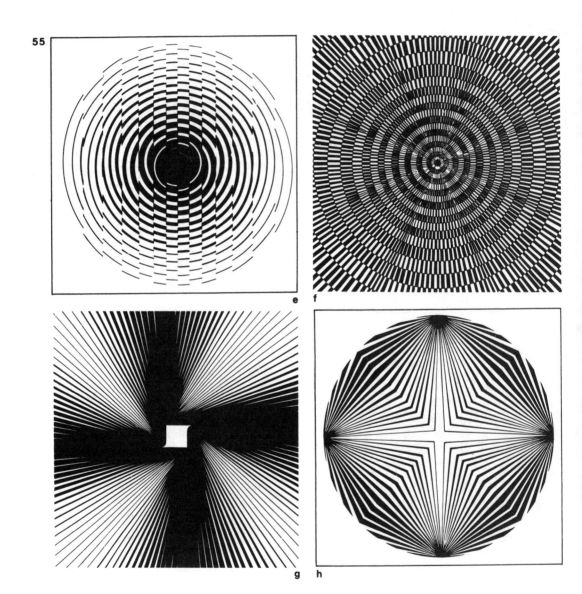

e

f

g

h

55

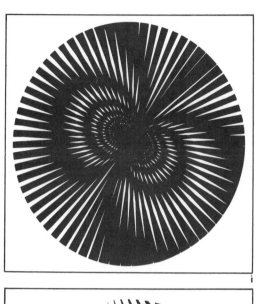

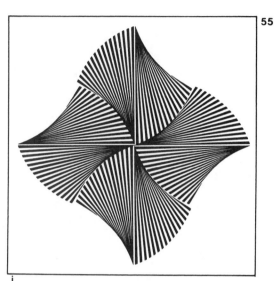

i

j

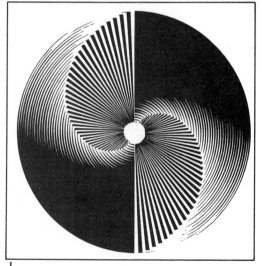

k

l

55

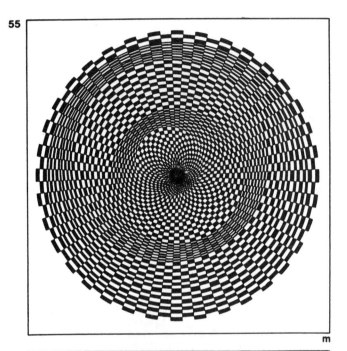

m

n

CHAPTER 8: ANOMALY

Anomaly is the presence of irregularity in a design in which regularity still prevails. It marks a certain degree of departure from the general conformity, resulting in slight or considerable interruption of the overall discipline. Sometimes anomaly is just a singular element among uniform organization.

Examples of anomaly around us are common: flowers among foliage, the moon in a starry night, cracks on a plain wall, an old church among modern skyscrapers.

In design, the use of anomaly has to be of genuine necessity. It must have a definite purpose, which may be one of the following:

(a) **To attract attention** — When anomaly is used sparingly, it tends to stand out and attract immediate attention. Center of interest can be created if anomaly happens only within a restricted area of the design.

(b) **To relieve monotony** — Plain regularity can be monotonous. Anomaly is able to generate movement and vibration. Anomalous areas in this case should be scattered either casually or systematically all over the design.

(c) **To transform regularity** — One kind of regularity can be transformed into another. Here anomaly is just a change of discipline.

(d) **To break down regularity** — Regularity can be completely broken down into disorder in one or more areas. Anomaly seems to be more violent in this case, but the unity of the design should be maintained.

These purposes will be discussed further when anomaly among unit forms and anomaly within structures are dealt with separately.

Anomaly among Unit Forms

Regularity exists among unit forms when they are related to each other under a certain kind of discipline, which may be repetition, similarity, or gradation. However, if we consider all the visual and relational elements, the relationship of various unit forms can be rather complex. Unit forms may be repetitive in all aspects, but they may also be repetitive only in certain elements and gradational in the remaining elements.

When anomaly is introduced among unit forms, any regularity that may exist within each of the visual and relational elements should be carefully examined. An anomalous unit form does not have to be different in every way from the general regularity. It can deviate in just one or two elements and conform to the general regularity in all other elements.

Anomaly is comparative. One anomalous unit can be more anomalous than another. Anomaly can be so subtle that it is barely noticeable, or it can be extremely prominent. Anomalous unit forms can maintain a certain kind of regularity among themselves, or they can be quite different among themselves.

Anomalous unit forms can attract attention in one or more of the following ways: (a) the anomaly is prominent; (b) all anomalous unit forms appear within a restricted area; (c) there are only a few of these anomalous unit forms (or there is only one). Concentrated anomaly normally becomes the center of interest in a design. (Fig. 56a)

Anomaly relieves monotony when the anomalous unit forms appear quite frequently, scattering over a wide area. They can be fairly indistinct, occurring as minor distortions or transfigurations of the regular unit forms. Their placement in the design can be orderly or casual, generating movements

56

a

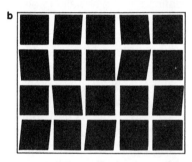

b

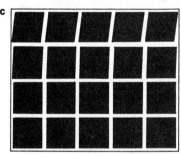

c

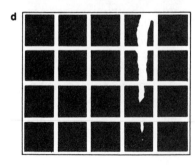

d

57

a

b

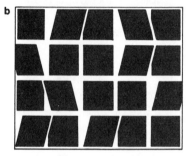

c

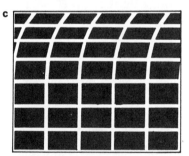

d

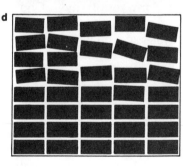

and adding accentuations. (Fig. 56b)

Regularity can be transformed from one kind to another when anomalous unit forms also establish a kind of regularity among themselves. Such anomalous unit forms are not just related to each other regularly, but are also arranged regularly. This is like merging or annexing two different groups of regular unit forms. The minority group is an anomaly in terms of the majority, but sometimes such distinction may be rather vague. (Fig. 56c)

Regularity can be broken down when unit forms in one or more areas appear to be torn, cracked, fractured, or dissolved. This can be more effective if the structure is also disrupted. (Fig. 56d)

Anomaly within Structures

The regular structures are those of repetition, gradation, and radiation. Similarity structures are less regular, but still maintain a certain degree of regularity.

Anomaly within a regular structure occurs when structural subdivisions in one or more areas of the design change in shape, size, or direction, become dislocated, or fall into complete disorganization. This marks one further step towards informality, but the structure is still a formal one apart from the anomalous areas.

Obviously unit forms are contained in structures of this nature. In areas where structural anomaly occurs, unit forms can be affected in one or more of the following ways:

(a) Their visual elements remain unaffected, but they may be forced to shift in position or direction, possibly crossing over adjacent structural subdivisions or unit forms.

(b) Their visual elements remain unaffected, but the anomalous structural lines, being active in this case, may trim off portions of the unit forms which are not totally confined within their respective subdivisions.

(c) They may be distorted as the subdivisions are distorted, but their relationship with the subdivisions remains consistent.

(d) They may become anomalous while maintaining a kind of regularity among themselves.

(e) They may become anomalous variously.

Structural anomaly can attract attention when it happens quite noticeably within a restricted area. Even if all the visual elements of the unit forms stay unchanged, structural anomaly stretches or squeezes space which easily draws the eye to focus on. (Fig. 57a)

Monotony in plain regularity can be relieved with frequent occurrence of anomalous structural subdivisions distributed in an orderly way or casually all over the design. This causes interesting variations of blank space and positioning of unit forms, the shapes and/or sizes of which may or may not be affected. (Fig. 57b)

The area or areas of anomaly may be just another kind of structural regularity different from the general discipline. Transformation of regularity can lead to exciting semi-formal compositions. (Fig. 57c)

Breakdown in a regular structure means that discipline is completely destroyed in one or more areas of anomaly. Structural lines get entangled, subdivisions distorted or dislocated, or the structure partially disintegrates. (Fig. 57d)

Notes on the Exercises

The uses of anomaly are shown in figures 58a, b, c, d, e, f, g, h, i, and j. Unit forms in these exercises are mainly of a linear nature. There is no restriction as to how general regularity dominates the design and how anomaly is introduced. Please note the effect of anomaly in each of the examples.

58

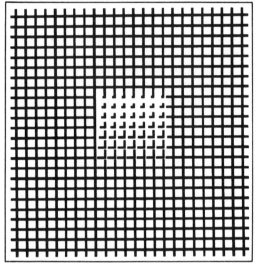

a

c

b

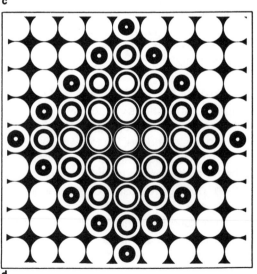

d

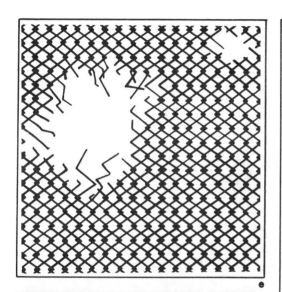

e

58

g

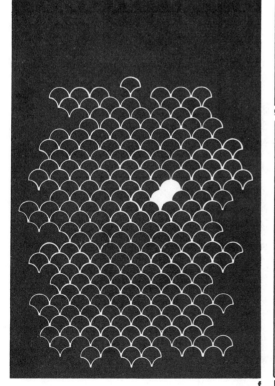

f

h

58

i

j

CHAPTER 9: CONTRAST

Contrast happens all the time, although its presence may be overlooked. There is contrast when a form is surrounded by blank space. There is contrast when a straight line meets a curve. There is contrast when one form is much bigger than another. There is contrast when vertical and horizontal directions coexist.

We experience all sorts of contrasts in our daily life. The day is in contrast with the night; a flying bird is in contrast with the sky; an old chair is in contrast with a modern sofa.

Contrast ranges far beyond commonly acknowledged opposites. It is quite flexible: it may be mild or severe, vague or obvious, simple or complex. Form A may appear contrasting to form B, but when form C is brought in, forms A and B may appear similar rather than contrasting to one another, and both of them can be contrasting to form C in varying degrees.

Contrast is just a kind of comparison whereby differences are made clear. Two forms can be found similar in certain aspects and different in other aspects. Their differences become emphasized when contrast takes place. A form may not look big when it is seen alone, but may appear gigantic against tiny forms next to it.

Contrast, Regularity, and Anomaly

Anomaly exists in regularity as irregular elements. There is contrast between anomaly and regularity because regularity is the observation of, whereas anomaly is the departure from, a certain kind of discipline. However,

contrast exists also within regularity itself.

Unless the design is nothing but a solidly and uniformly colored flat surface, there is always contrast between occupied and unoccupied space. In the arrangement of unit forms which are repetitive in shape, size, color, and texture, contrasts of position and/or direction may take place. Unit forms themselves may consist of contrasting elements in one way or another. All the contrasting elements can be woven together in the design as intrinsic parts of the regularity.

Regularity does not necessarily make a good design, although it may guarantee a certain degree of harmony. The same group of unit forms used in a repetition structure can be a dull design in the hands of one designer, but an exciting design in the hands of another. Proper use of contrast in the relational elements can make the difference.

Contrast of Visual and Relational Elements

Let us examine the use of contrast in respect of each of the visual and relational elements:

(a) **Contrast of shape** — Contrast of shape is quite complicated because a shape can be described in a multiplicity of ways. There is contrast between a geometric shape and an organic one, but two geometric shapes can be in contrast if one is angular but the other non-angular. Other common cases of contrast of shape are: curvilinear/rectilinear, planar/linear, mechanical/calligraphic, symmetrical/asymmetrical, beautiful/ugly, simple/complex, abstract/representational, undistorted/distorted, etc. (Fig. 59a)

(b) **Contrast of size** — Contrast of size is straightforward. Big/small contrast is seen among planar forms, whereas long/short contrast is seen among linear forms. (Fig. 59b)

(c) **Contrast of color** — Detailed discussions

59

a

b

c   d

e

f

g

h

60   a   b   c   d

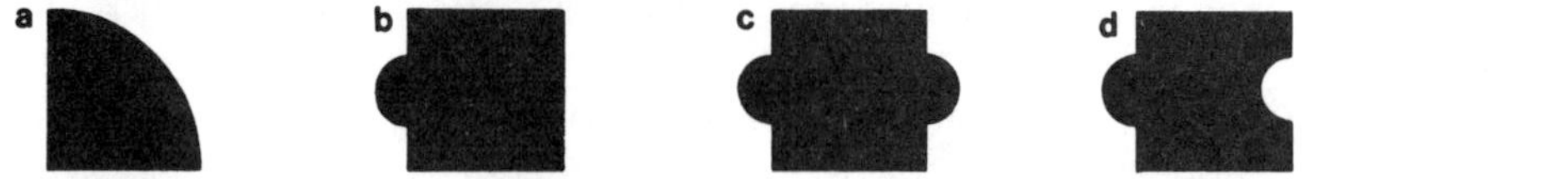

61   a

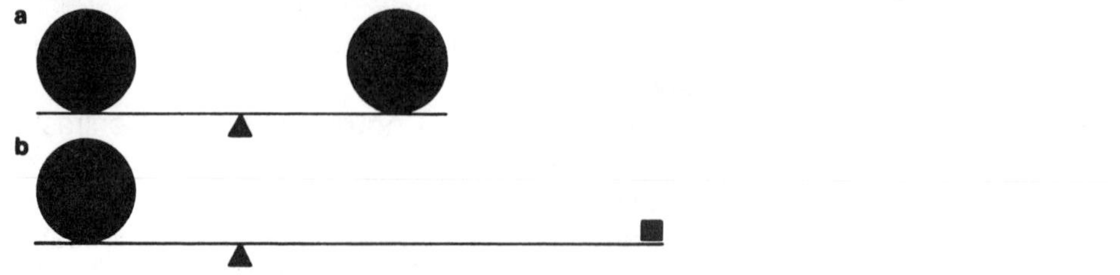

b

of color contrasts are beyond the scope of the present book, but some common cases can be mentioned here: light/dark, brilliant/dull, warm/cool, etc. (Fig. 59c)

(d) **Contrast of texture** — Texture will form the subject of a later chapter. However, some typical cases of textural contrasts are: smooth/rough, fine/coarse, even/uneven, matt/glossy, etc. (Fig. 59d)

(e) **Contrast of direction** — Any two directions meeting each other at an angle of 90 degrees are in maximum contrast. Two forms directly facing each other create a directional contrast of quite a different nature, because they are not unparallel, although one of them has been rotated a full 180 degrees. (Fig. 59e)

(f) **Contrast of position** — The position of a form is recognized as related to the frame of reference, the center, the structural subdivision that contains it, the structural lines nearby, or another form. The common positional contrasts are: top/bottom, high/low, left/right, central/off-center. (Fig. 59f)

(g) **Contrast of space** — Space will also form the subject of a later chapter. When space is considered as a flat plane, contrasts are perceived as occupied/unoccupied or positive/negative. Blank space can be seen as congested or expansive, and can have contrasts of shape and size if it is read as a negative form. When space is considered as illusory, forms may appear to advance or recede, to be near or far, flat or three-dimensional, parallel or unparallel to the picture plane, etc., in spatial contrast with one another. (Fig. 59g)

(h) **Contrast of gravity** — There are two types of gravitational contrasts: stable/unstable and light/heavy. Stability or instability may be due to the shape itself, or due to conformity to or deviation from either verticality or horizontality. A stable form is static, whereas an unstable form suggests movement. Lightness or heaviness of a form may be due to the use of color, but is also affected by shape and size. (Fig. 59h)

Contrasts within a Form

It is common for individual forms or unit forms to contain contrasting elements which may help to make them look more interesting. Sometimes contrast exists without being noticed, but a designer should be sensitive of its presence. Effective use of contrast is of paramount importance in designing.

To sharpen our awareness of contrasts within a form, we now take four forms and examine them carefully:

Figure 60a is composed of three edge lines, two straight lines of the same length being part of a square, and a curved line being part of a circle. There is a contrast of shape (angular/non-angular).

Figure 60b is composed of a square and a circle. The circle is obviously much smaller than the square. So there is not just a contrast of shape (angular/non-angular), but also a contrast of size (big/small).

Figure 60c is composed of one square and two circles. The circles are small in size, as in figure 60b. So there is a contrast of shape as well as a contrast of size, and then there is also a contrast of position (left/right) between the two small circles.

Like figure 60c, figure 60d is composed of one square and two circles, but in a different way. There is a contrast of shape as well as a contrast of size and a contrast of position. Furthermore, there is a contrast of space (positive/negative), because one circle is united to the square, but the other circle is subtracted from it.

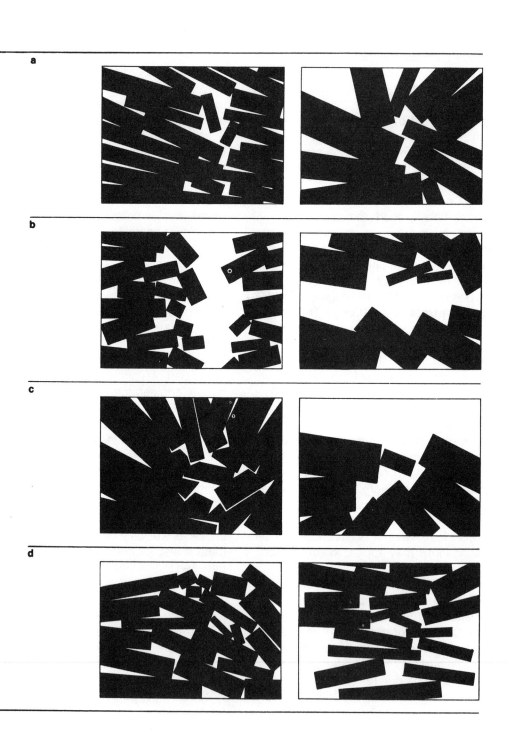

a

b

c

d

The Contrast Structure

Manipulation of contrasts of the relational elements can establish a contrast structure. This kind of structure is completely informal, with strict regularity excluded as far as possible.

As we have already seen, a formal structure (repetition, gradation, or radiation) consists of regularly constructed structural lines or subdivisions which guide the organization of unit forms into a definite order. An informal structure has no structural lines, and unit forms are positioned freely. Balance is to be maintained in both cases, but the kind of balance in each case is different. To illustrate this, balance in a formal structure is like distributing two equal weights equidistantly from the fulcrum (fig. 61a), whereas balance in an informal structure is like distributing two unequal weights at unequal distances from the fulcrum, with the lighter weight farther away, the heavier weight nearer by, with careful adjustments (fig. 61b).

In a contrast structure, unit forms are seldom repetitive in both shape and size but are in a loose relationship of similarity. They may have more than just one kind, but usually there is one kind that dominates. Among the two or more kinds of unit forms, contrasts of shape, size, and/or color may exist.

No definite rules can be established in the organization of a contrast structure. Shapes and sizes of unit forms are adjusted as felt necessary. Similarity is sought, not just among each of the visual elements, but among the relational elements as well in order to maintain a sense of unity, with occasional contrasts to produce tension and visual excitement.

We will now see how each relational element can be manipulated in a contrast structure:

(a) **Direction** — Most of the unit forms may have similar directions. Contrasting directions are used to provoke agitation. We can also arrange the unit forms in all sorts of directions, creating varying degrees of contrast among them. (Fig. 62a)

(b) **Position** — Unit forms can be positioned towards opposite borders of the frame of reference, creating tension in between. (Fig. 62b)

(c) **Space** — The encounter of positive and negative unit forms (resulting in subtraction) is a way of producing spatial contrast. Space can be pushed and squeezed by unit forms which are thrust against each other. It can also be left void, in contrast with congested areas. (Fig. 62c)

(d) **Gravity** — Unit forms dropping from high to low positions, or stacking from low to high positions, can suggest a gravitational pull. Stable and unstable unit forms, static and moving unit forms, or heavy and light unit forms can be put together in effective contrast of gravity. (Fig. 62d)

Dominance and Emphasis

Two factors should be considered in a contrast structure:

Dominance of majority — Dominance is gained by one kind of unit form which occupies more space in a design than other kinds. These unit forms, as distinguished from all others by shape, size, color, texture, direction, position, space, and/or gravity, are in a majority because they are spread over a wider area. Dominance of majority helps to pull the design together into an integrated whole.

Emphasis of minority — Dominance of majority does not necessarily put the minority into oblivion. On the contrary, the minority often gets emphasized and demands greater attention. It is like an anomaly, which is more readily seen.

63

a

b

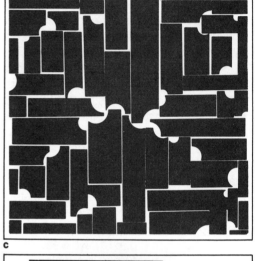

c

d

e

f

Dominance of majority and emphasis of minority normally work together in a contrast structure. Even if there is only one kind of unit form in the design, various relational elements can be manipulated to create dominance and emphasis. Dominance of majority is like the heavier weight, closer to the fulcrum, and emphasis of minority like the lighter weight, farther away from the fulcrum, establishing a balance as illustrated in figure 61b.

Notes on the Exercises

Figures 63a, b, c, d, e, and f are all examples of contrast structures. There are two kinds of unit form used: one kind is rectilinear, the other kind curvilinear. The two kinds are in contrast of shape and sometimes of size as well. They meet each other, creating new shapes by union or subtraction. Both kinds are allowed to change in shape within a certain range of similarity, and in size even more flexibly. Note the use of contrast in each of the examples.

64

65

CHAPTER 10: CONCENTRATION

Concentration refers to a way of distribution of unit forms which may be thickly gathered in certain areas or thinly scattered in other areas of a design. The distribution is usually uneven and informal, sometimes with one place of thickest gathering or thinnest scattering which becomes the center of interest.

In our environment, the city is a typical example of concentration. Buildings and people crowd around the heart of every city, while they are gradually thinned down towards the outskirts.

Essentially concentration is quantitative organization. Here the designer is concerned with the quantity of unit forms producing rhythmic accentuations or dramatic tensions by varying from one place to the next. Contrast is involved, but it is a contrast of less and more rather than a contrast of visual or relational elements.

Concentration of Unit Forms in Formal Structures

The effect of concentration can be created even within formal structures without changing the rigid structural discipline. Movement of unit forms is much restricted by the structural subdivisions which also govern the area occupied by each unit form and the directions of arrangement, but concentration can be made via one of the following ways:

Frequent absences — As we have seen as early as Chapter 2, when the unit form is of the same color as the ground, it can disappear without affecting the general discipline.

Thus frequent absences can result in uneven distribution of unit forms, leading to concentration in certain places in a design. The pattern of absences can be irregular or quite regular, depending on how much regularity the designer chooses to maintain in the design. (Fig. 64a)

Positional changes — Positional changes of unit forms inside active structural subdivisions can increase or decrease the proportion of occupied space as against unoccupied space. The effect of concentration occurs when there is more occupied space in one area surrounded by more unoccupied space in other areas. Directional changes can sometimes produce the same results. Regular gradational changes should be avoided in such cases. (Fig. 64b)

Quantitative changes — If the size of unit forms is rather small, one structural subdivision can house several of them conveniently. In this way actual quantitative changes can be made with some structural subdivisions containing one or none, others containing two or more unit forms. The effect of concentration can be achieved, but the structural subdivisions should be active, otherwise the structure would show no effect at all in the final design. Again, regular gradational changes should be avoided if we are after a concentration design and not a gradation design. (Fig. 64c)

We should note that among the different types of formal structure, the repetition structure provides the greatest flexibility for the effect of concentration. Both gradation and radiation structures, owing to their intrinsic qualities, have a predetermined area (or areas) of concentration, departure from which would be difficult if not impossible.

When there is more than just one kind of

unit form in a design, concentration of one kind and dispersion of another (or others) can produce effects of dominance and emphasis.

In concentration, each visual or relational element can be considered separately. For instance, in a repetition structure the unit forms can be repetitive in all elements except color, which may be distributed concentratively.

The Concentration Structure

When a formal structure is not used, unit forms can be freely organized to achieve the effect of concentration. This produces a concentration structure which is entirely informal. Sometimes a formal structure may be used just to provide some guidelines for the distribution of unit forms. Concentration structures of this kind can be said to be semi-formal.

The kinds of concentration structures are suggested as follows:

(a) **Concentration towards a point** — This means that the unit forms crowd around a pre-established conceptual point in a design. The density reaches the maximum where the point lies and gradually thins down in surrounding areas. The effect is a sort of informal radiation, and more so if the directions of the unit forms are arranged radiatively. The number of pre-established points can range from one to many which may be guided by a formal structure. The degree of concentration towards each point can be uniformly similar, alternatively similar, vaguely gradational, or all different. (Fig. 65a)

(b) **Concentration away from a point** — This is the reverse of (a), with blankness or extreme scantiness in the immediate areas surrounding the conceptual point. (Fig. 65b)

(c) **Concentration towards a line** — This means that the unit forms crowd around a pre-established conceptual line in a design.

Maximum density occurs along the line. The line can be straight or of any simple shape. When more than one pre-established line is used, they may be structural lines of a formal structure. Concentration towards a line approaches the effect of gradation. (Fig. 65c)

(d) **Concentration away from a line** — This is the reverse of (c), with blankness or extreme scantiness in the immediate area of the line. (Fig. 65d)

(e) **Free concentration** — This means that the unit forms are grouped freely with varying density and scantiness in the design. Organization is completely informal here, very much as in a contrast structure. Contrast of less and more prevails, but it should be carefully handled to create visual subtlety and/or drama. (Fig. 65e)

(f) **Over-concentration** — This means that the unit forms are grouped densely over the entire design, or over a rather wide area of the design, with or without gradual transition at the edges. If the unit forms are of similar size and grouped quite evenly, the result of over-concentration can become a similarity structure wherein each unit form occupies a similar amount of space. (Fig. 65f)

(g) **Deconcentration** — This is the reverse of (f). Here the unit forms never get concentrated in any place, but are thinly scattered over the entire design, or over a rather wide area. The scattering can be even, uneven, subtly rhythmical, or vaguely gradational. A similar structure can result if the unit forms, of similar size, are scattered quite evenly. (Fig. 65g)

Unit Forms in Concentration Structures

The effect of concentration is better achieved if all the unit forms are of relatively small size so that a large quantity of them can be used to build up the density desired

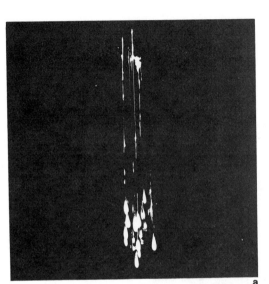

a

66

b

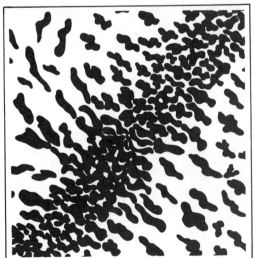

c

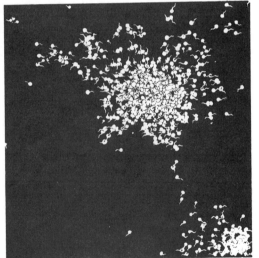

d

66

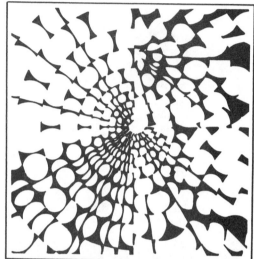

e

f

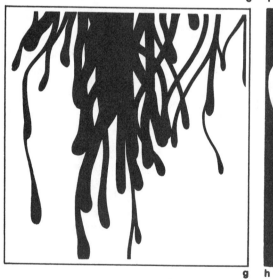

g

h

at suitable places. Size thus becomes the first element to be considered and shape only secondary. If the size of unit forms is generally large and its variation covers a wide range, the result may be a contrast structure rather than a concentration structure.

The shapes of the unit forms do not have to be all of one kind. Two or more kinds can be used, and the unit forms of each kind, among themselves, may be used in repetition or in similarity. If the shapes show a sense of direction, they can be arranged so that their directions may be repetitive, gradational, radiative, or just random.

Notes on the Exercises

Figures 66a, b, c, d, e, f, g, and h all exemplify the use of concentration structure. The unit forms are mostly organic, with variations in shape and size within a moderate range of similarity. It should not be difficult for us to recognize which kind of concentration structure is used in each exercise.

118

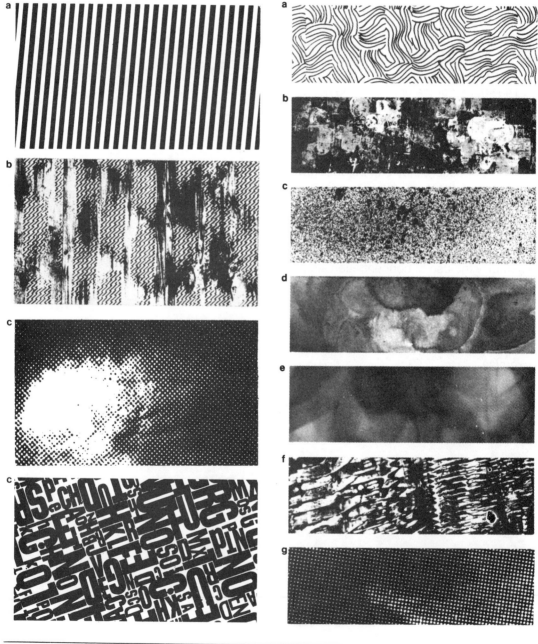

CHAPTER 11: TEXTURE

Texture is one visual element which has been mentioned frequently but never fully discussed in the preceding chapters. This is because the exercises are limited to uniform black and white surfaces, and the use of texture has been completely excluded. Texture, however, has unique aspects which are essential in certain design situations and should not be overlooked.

Early in Chapter 1, it was pointed out that texture refers to the surface characteristics of a shape. Every shape has a surface and every surface must have certain characteristics, which may be described as smooth or rough, plain or decorated, matt or glossy, soft or hard. Although we generally regard a flat painted surface as containing no texture at all, actually the flatness of the paint is a kind of texture, and there is also the texture of the material on which the shape is created.

Nature contains a wealth of textures. For instance, each kind of stone or wood possesses a distinct texture which an architect or an interior designer may choose for specific purposes. The piece of stone or wood may also be finished in a multiple of ways for diverse textural effects.

Texture may be classified into two important categories: visual texture and tactile texture. Appropriate texture adds richness to a design.

Visual Texture
Visual texture is strictly two-dimensional. As the term implies, it is the kind of texture that is seen by the eye, although it also may evoke tactile sensations. Three kinds of visual textures can be distinguished:

Decorative texture — This decorates a surface, and remains subordinate to shape. In other words, the texture itself is only an addition which can be removed without much affecting the shapes and their interrelationships in the design. It can be hand-drawn or obtained by special devices and can be rigidly regular or irregular, but it generally maintains a certain degree of uniformity. (Fig. 67a)

Spontaneous texture —This does not decorate a surface, but is part of the process of visual creation. Shape and texture cannot be separated, because the marks of texture on a surface are also shapes at the same time. Hand-drawn and accidental forms frequently contain spontaneous texture. (Fig. 67b)

Mechanical texture — This does not refer to texture obtained with the aid of mechanical drawing instruments such as the ruler or compasses. It refers to texture obtained by special mechanical means, and as a result, the texture is not necessarily subordinate to shape. A typical example of this kind of texture is the photographic grain or screen pattern we often find in printing. Mechanical texture can also be found in designs created by typography, and in computer graphics. (Fig. 67c)

The Making of Visual Texture
Visual texture can be produced in various ways. Some common techniques are suggested as follows:

(a) **Drawing, painting** — These are the simplest methods of producing visual texture. Minutely drawn or painted patterns can be constructed of densely gathered, tiny unit forms in rigid or loose structures for the surface decoration of any form. Spontaneous texture can be obtained with freely hand-drawn lines or brushstrokes. (Fig. 68a)

69

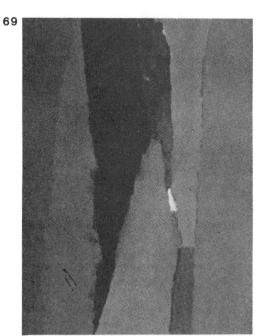

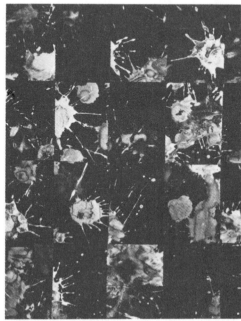

a   b

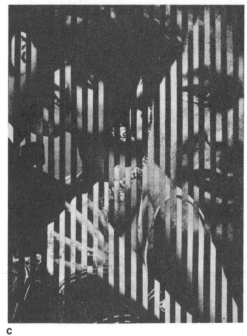

b   c

(b) **Printing, transferring, rubbing** — A carved pattern or a rough surface can be inked and printed on another surface to create a visual texture which may be decorative or spontaneous depending on how the technique is handled. Hand-painted images on one surface can be transferred to another surface when the paint is still wet. Rubbing with pencil or any suitable medium on soft and thin paper over a rough surface also produces textural effects. (Fig. 68b)

(c) **Spraying, spilling, pouring** — Liquid paint, diluted or evaporated to any desired consistency, may be sprayed, spilled, or poured onto a surface. Spontaneous texture is often obtained, but carefully controlled spraying can produce decorative texture as well. (Fig. 68c)

(d) **Staining, dyeing** — An absorbent surface may be stained or dyed to obtain a kind of visual texture. (Fig. 68d)

(e) Smoking, burning—A surface can be smoked over a flame to obtain a kind of texture. Sometimes burnt marks may also be utilized. (Fig. 68e)

(f) Scratching, scraping—A painted or inked surface can be scratched or scraped with some kind of hard or sharp tool to gain in texture. (Fig. 68f)

(g) Photographic processes—Special darkroom techniques can add interesting texture to photographic images. (Fig. 68g)

Collage

A direct way of using visual texture in a design is collage, which is a process of pasting, gluing, or fixing pieces of paper, fabric, or other flat materials onto a surface. Such materials may fall into three main groups according to whether images are present or important. The term "image" here refers to any printed, photographic, painted, or intentional or accidental forms or marks on the surface of the materials.

Materials without images —These materials are evenly colored or of uniform texture. The shapes of the cut or torn pieces are the only shapes to appear in the design. Examples of such materials are paper or fabric with solid color or minute patterns which spread rather regularly all over the surface, printed sheets of crowded, small type, selected areas from photographs or surfaces containing spontaneous texture with all contrasts minimized. (Fig. 69a)

Materials with images — These materials, such as paper or fabric printed with uneven patterns or treated with spontaneous texture, photographs with strong tonal or color contrasts, printed sheets of large type or large and small type, etc., contain images of considerable prominence. Such images are used abstractly in the collage, regardless of any representational or literal content. They are seen as forms which are as important as, and sometimes even more important than, the shapes of the cut or torn materials. (Fig. 69b)

Materials with essential images — Images on the materials are essential when they have a definite representational content or when the images have to maintain their identity and are not to be destroyed during the process of the collage. In this case they are more important than the cut or torn shapes of the materials, and the collage is thus of a different nature. Materials with representational significance are commonly photographs which can be dissected and rearranged or combined with other photographs for dramatic purposes or special effects. Materials with abstract images can be dissected and re-arranged in the same way, resulting in transformations or distortions without rendering the original images unrecognizable. (Fig. 69c)

Tactile Texture

Tactile texture is a kind of texture that is not only visible to the eye but can be felt with the hand. Tactile texture rises above the surface of a two-dimensional design and approaches a three-dimensional relief.

Broadly speaking, tactile texture exists in all types of surfaces because we can feel them. This means all kinds of paper, however smooth, and all kinds of paint and ink, however flat, have their specific surface characteristics which can be discerned by the sense of touch. In two-dimensional design, we can say that a blank area or a solidly printed or painted area contains no visual texture, but there is always the tactile texture of the paper and the ink or paint.

To narrow down its scope, we can limit our discussion to the kinds of tactile texture specially created by the designer for the purpose. This means the materials have been specially shaped or arranged, or combined with other materials, to form a composition, or the materials have undergone special treatment, resulting in new textural sensations. Thus we can have three distinct kinds of tactile texture:

Available natural texture — The natural texture of the materials is maintained. The materials, which may be paper, fabric, branches, leaves, sand, strings, etc., are cut, torn, or used as they are, and pasted, glued, or fixed onto a surface. No effort is made to hide the identity on the materials.

Modified natural texture — The materials are modified so that they are not the same as usual. For instance, paper is not pasted flat but creased or crumpled, or it can be stippled, scratched, embossed. A piece of

sheet metal can be folded, hammered, or drilled with tiny holes. A piece of wood can be carved. The materials are slightly transformed, but not beyond recognition. (Fig. 70a)

Organized texture — The materials, usually in small bits, chips, or strips, are organized into a pattern which forms a new surface. The textural units may be used as they are or modified, but they must be small or cut into small pieces. Examples of these are seeds, grains of sand, chips of wood, leaves cut into very narrow strips, paper twisted into tiny balls, pins, beads, buttons, strings or threads to be woven, etc. The materials may sometimes be identifiable, but the new surface sensation is much more dominant. (Fig. 70b)

All kinds of tactile texture can be transformed into visual texture by the photographic process.

Light and Color in Tactile Texture

The play of light upon a tactile texture may be very interesting. Certain materials may reflect or refract light, with fascinating results. The tactile quality of rough surfaces is usually emphasized by strong side-lighting.

Some designs may have been conceived with light modulation as an essential element. In this case, the textural units are usually long and thin, projecting from the surface of the support material, so that shadows are rather linear, forming intricate patterns.

However, it should be pointed out that both light and shadow are visual, not tactile, because they have nothing to do with the sense of touch. Programmed lighting and changing relationships of the light source and the design can produce kinetic light patterns, but still the effect is a pure visual sensation.

Color can also play an interesting role in

tactile texture. The natural color of the materials can be maintained, but a coat of color can create a different feeling, at least rendering the materials less immediately recognizable, giving them less of an available natural texture but more of a modified natural texture. Diverse materials on a surface can resemble each other if they are all coated with the same color.

When there is more than one color on a surface, the colors will form a pattern which is visual. Sometimes the visual pattern can dominate over the sensation provoked by the tactile texture.

Notes on the Exercises

Figures 71a, b, c, d, e, f, g, and h all show the use of printed type to form textural patterns. Single characters of large type or lines of small type from printed matter have been specially cut and arranged so that blank spaces are eliminated as far as possible. Type of the same size and weight can be grouped to form a uniform texture, while a gradational texture can be created with type of varying size and weight.

Some of the examples were done by gathering and arranging type to form a uniform or gradational texture on a thin sheet of paper. This was later cut into pieces for final organization into a structured pattern.

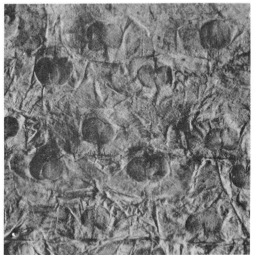

70

a

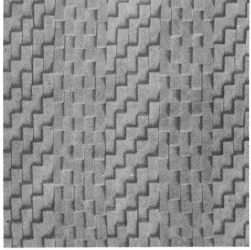

b

71

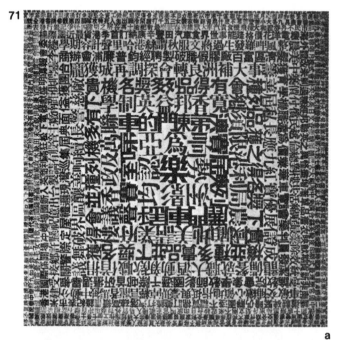

a

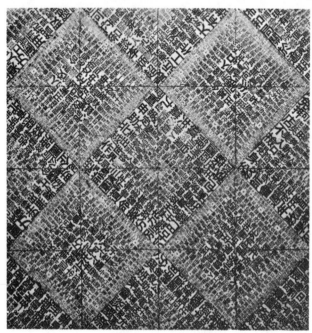

b

c

71

e

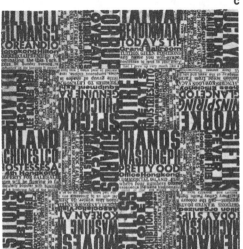

d

f

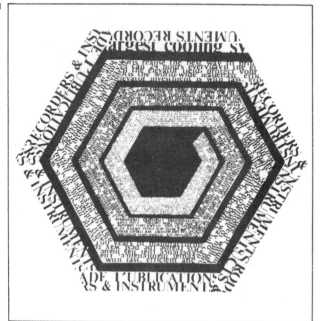

g

h

CHAPTER 12: SPACE

Space, like texture in the preceding chapter, has been mentioned in almost every chapter but has never been fully discussed. The nature of space is rather complex because there are many ways space can be viewed. Space may be positive or negative, flat or illusory, ambiguous, or conflicting. Each of these aspects will be carefully examined here.

Positive and Negative Space

Positive space is what surrounds a negative form, and negative space is what surrounds a positive form. Positive and negative forms were discussed in Chapter 2 (fig. 8). All positive forms contain positive space, but positive space is not always perceived as a positive form. Similarly, all negative forms contain negative space, but negative space is not always perceived as a negative form. This is because positive space can be a background for negative forms and negative space for positive forms, and backgrounds are not normally recognized as forms which usually exist in a certain degree of isolation.

Of course, positive (or negative) space completely or nearly isolated by negative (or positive) forms can be identified as positive (or negative) form, but such forms are generally very much hidden unless we consciously look for them. If they are found frequently and regularly, then the figure-ground relationship is reversible: at one moment we find positive forms and negative space, at another moment we find negative forms and positive space. (Fig. 72a)

Flat and Illusory Space

Space is flat when all the forms seem to lie on the picture plane and be parallel to it. The forms themselves should be flat too, and appear equidistant from the eye, none nearer and none farther. It is possible, however, that we can feel the space surrounding the forms to be very deep, leaving all the forms floating on the picture plane.

In a flat space situation, forms can meet one another by touching, interpenetration, union, subtraction, intersection, coinciding, or just be in detachment, but they can never meet by overlapping. (Fig. 72b) Overlapping suggests that one form is nearer to our eyes than another, thus rendering the space illusory to some extent. (Fig. 72c) Variations in shape, size, color, and texture may also destroy the flatness of space, but this does not always happen.

Space is illusory when all the forms seem not to lie on or be parallel to the picture plane. Some forms may appear to advance, some to recede, some to present their frontal views, and some to show their oblique views. The forms themselves may be flat or three-dimensional. The design area opens up like a window or a stage where the forms are displayed in varying depths and/or at different angles. (Fig. 72d)

Flat Forms in Illusory Space

Forms are considered flat when they have no apparent thickness. Flat forms in illusory space are like forms made of thin sheets of paper, metal, or other materials. Their frontal views are the fullest, occupying the largest area. Their oblique views are narrowed, and occupy less area. The following are some common ways flat forms can be used in illusory space:

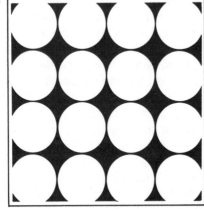

(a) **Overlapping** — When one form overlaps another, it is seen as being in front of or above the other. The flat forms may have no appreciable thickness at all, but if overlapping occurs, one of the two forms must have some diversion from the picture plane, however slight the diversion may be. (Fig. 73a)

(b) **Change in size** — Increase in size of a form suggests that it is getting nearer, whereas decrease in its size suggests that it is farther away. The greater the range of change in size present in the design, the deeper is the illusion of spatial depth. (Fig. 73b)

(c) **Change in color** — On a white background, darker colors stand out much more than lighter colors, thus appearing closer to our eyes. On a very dark background, the reverse is true. If both warm and cool colors are present in a design, generally the warm colors appear to advance whereas the cool ones recede. (Fig. 73c)

(d) **Change in texture** — Coarser textures normally appear closer to our eyes than finer textures. (Fig. 73d)

(e) **Change in view** — A form is in full frontal view when it is parallel to the picture plane. If it is not parallel to the picture plane, we can only see it from a slanting angle. Change in view is a result of spatial rotation (see Chapter 6, section on spatial gradation), creating illusory space though not a very deep one. (Fig. 73e)

(f) **Curving or bending** — Flat forms can be curved or bent to suggest illusory space. Curving or bending changes their absolute frontality and affects their diversion from the picture plane. (Fig. 73f)

(g) **Addition of shadow** — The addition of a shadow to a form emphasizes the physical existence of the form. The shadow may be cast in front of or behind the form, linked to or detached from it. (Fig. 73g)

Volume and Depth in Illusory Space

All flat forms can become three-dimensional forms in illusory space with the suggestion of thickness, which just requires supplementary views added to the frontal view. As a three-dimensional form is not always seen in full frontality, there are many angles and points of view from which it can be seen and represented on a flat surface convincingly. (Fig. 74a)

There are isometric and other systems of projection in the representation of volume and depth. (Fig. 74b) There are also laws of perspective by means of which we can depict volume and depth with a surprising degree of realism. (Fig. 74c) If we have to represent a cube that has six equal edges meeting each other at right angles, simple systems of projection maintain the equality of the edges and angles to some extent, but perspective which gives a more convincing picture renders most of the equal elements unequal.

When a series of cubes is to be represented with one behind another, no decrease in size of the cubes is shown with the various systems of projection, but a gradational decrease in size is shown with perspective. (Fig. 74d)

Plane Representation in Illusory Space

Volume is contained by planes which can be represented in various ways:

(a) **Outlined planes** — Planes can be outlined, and the designer may choose any thickness of line for his purpose. Outlined planes in illusory space are usually represented as opaque planes: we cannot see what is behind them. If they are represented as transparent planes, then they may become more like spatial frames. (Fig. 75a)

(b) **Solid planes** — These are planes

a

b

c

d

e

f

g

73

a

74

without ambiguity. Solid planes, if they are of the same color, can be used as flat forms to suggest illusory depth, but it is difficult for them to work together to suggest volume. Solid planes with color variations can represent volume with great effectiveness. (Fig. 75b)

(c) **Uniformly textured planes** — A uniformly textured plane is distinguishable from another which it adjoins or overlaps even if the texture of the two planes is the same. This is because the textural pattern of one plane does not have to spread continuously to the plane adjacent to it. Certain kinds of texture have strong directional feeling which can give emphasis to planes that is not seen frontally but sideways. Densely spaced parallel lines of the same width or regular dot patterns can form textural planes which provide many possibilities for the designer. (Fig. 75c)

(d) **Gradationally colored or textured planes** — Gradationally colored or textured planes have a different effect in the creation of spatial illusion. They suggest light and shadow patterns or metallic sheens on surfaces, thus enhancing realism to some extent. They are particularly effective in the representation of curved surfaces. (Fig. 75d) Textured planes in perspective should be depicted in such a way that the textural patterns are also seen in perspective. Such textured planes are not uniform but gradational and even radiative (radiating from the vanishing points).

Fluctuating and Conflicting Space
Space fluctuates when it appears to advance at one moment and recede at another moment. We have already mentioned a kind of simple fluctuating situation when we discussed positive and negative space and reversible figure-ground relationships earlier in this chapter (fig. 72a). A more dynamic fluctuating

situation is illustrated in figure 76a, which can be interpreted either as a shape that is seen from above or as a shape seen from below. Both interpretations are valid. Spatial fluctuation creates interesting optical movements.

Conflicting space is similar to fluctuating space yet intrinsically different. Fluctuating space is ambiguous, because there is not a definite way whereby we can interpret the spatial situation, but conflicting space provides an absurd spatial situation which seems impossible for us to interpret at all. In conflicting space, we feel we are definitely looking down if we only see one part of the design, and we feel we are definitely looking up if we only see another part of the design. However, when the design is seen as a whole, the two visual experiences are in serious conflict with each other and cannot be reconciled. The situation is absurd because it does not exist in reality. Somehow it evokes a strange visual tension which offers many interesting possibilities for artists and designers. (Fig. 76b)

Notes on the Exercises
Various types of illusory space are depicted in figures 77a, b, c, d, e, f, g, and h. The planes are constructed of regular line patterns, some repetitive, some gradational.

If we review all the exercises illustrated in this book, we can, in fact, discover more examples depicting illusory space. Figure 26f suggests a solid sphere. Figures 47g and h both show curved surfaces; figures 55b and j appear to be reliefs, and there are still more.

The exercises, from Chapter 3 to the present chapter, represent a journey the reader has made. He will see that the earlier exercises generally have greater restrictions, demanding more specific unit forms,

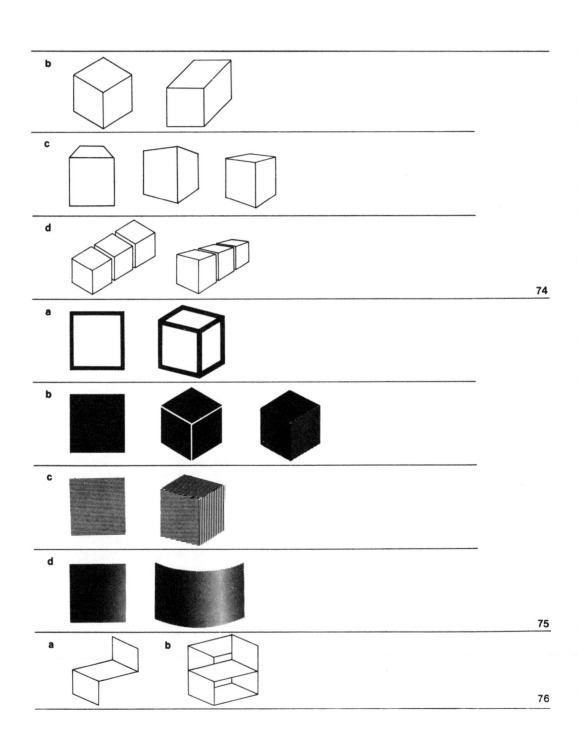

b

c

d

74

a

b

c

d

75

a   b

76

a
b
c
d

77

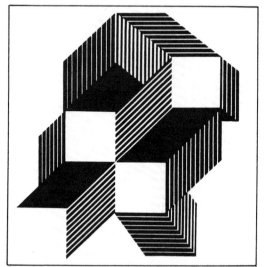

e

f

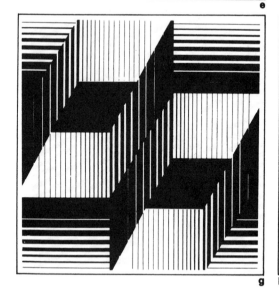

g

h

TWO-DIMENSIONAL FORM

TWO-DIMENSIONAL FORM

PART I
ASPECTS OF FORM

FORM

Broadly speaking, all that is visible has form. Form is everything that can be seen—everything with shape, size, color, and texture that occupies space, marks position, and indicates direction. A created form can be based on reality—recognizable—or abstract—unrecognizable. A form might be created to convey a meaning or message, or it could be merely decorative. It might be simple or complex, harmonious or discordant.

In a narrow sense, forms are self-contained, positive shapes that occupy space and are distinguishable from a background.

Three-Dimensional Form

Because we live in three-dimensional space, our experience of form is primarily three-dimensional. A three-dimensional form is one that we can walk toward, away from, or around; it can be viewed from different angles and distances. If it is within reach, we might touch or even handle it.

A three-dimensional form is not necessarily stationary. A living creature can be described as a three-dimensional form that runs, flies, swims, or moves part of its body. A man-made three-dimensional form can consist of moving, movable, or modular elements. Three-dimensional forms interact with other three-dimensional forms in the environment.

Two-Dimensional Form

Form and Shape

Man's writings, drawings, paintings, decorations, designs, and doodles are of shapes and colors that can be perceived as two-dimensional forms.

Natural surfaces that display textures and patterns are also sometimes perceived as two-dimensional forms. We can, however, regard two-dimensional forms essentially as a human creation for the communication of ideas, the recording of experiences, the expression of feelings and emotions, the decoration of plain surfaces, or the conveyance of artistic visions.

Two-dimensional forms consist of points, lines, and/or planes on a flat surface.

Our visual experiences of the three-dimensional world influence our perception of two-dimensional forms. A shape against an empty background appears to be surrounded by a void. Volume and thickness can be added to a shape, which can be rotated in space to exhibit different views.

The terms *shape* and *form* are often used synonymously, but their meanings are not the same. A shape is an area easily defined with an outline. A shape that is given volume and thickness and that can exhibit different views becomes a form. Forms display some depth and volume—characteristics associated with three-dimensional figures, whereas shapes are forms depicted at particular angles, from particular distances. A form can therefore have many shapes.

Figures 1 through 4 show the same leaf form in a variety of shapes.

139

140

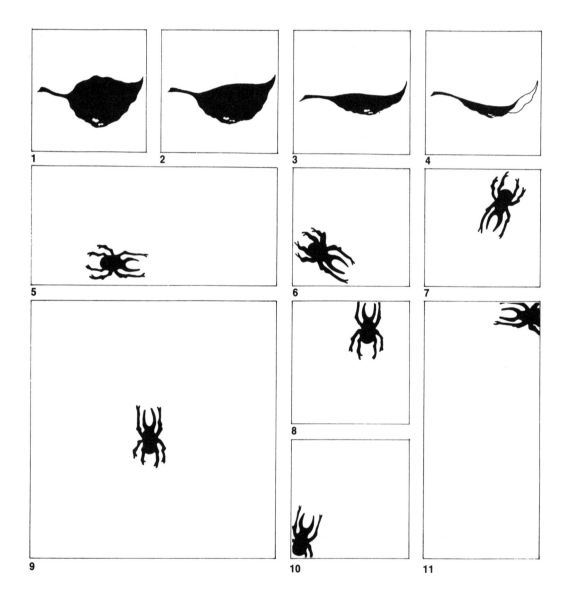

Frame of Reference

Form and Space

A design normally begins as an area that is bound by four edges at right angles to one another. These edges constitute the *frame of reference,* which has a shape of its own.

Within the frame of reference, a form or numerous forms can be introduced. A *figure-ground* situation thus emerges; forms are seen as *figures,* and the space behind forms and the space between them and the frame of reference as *ground* or *background* in the resulting *composition.* A composition is the visual effect that is generated by the interaction of figures and ground.

Furthermore, the frame of reference provides scale—we get a sense of the *size* of forms—and establishes the *positions* and *directions* of elements.

Figures 5 through 11 feature the same form (and the same shape) in different compositions. Notice how different compositions result from different frames of reference (figs. 5–8); how compositions look smaller when the frame of reference is large (fig. 9) and how it can be cropped by the frame of reference when the form moves partially beyond its boundary (figs. 10, 11).

Form is *positive space,* space that is occupied. Unoccupied space surrounding a form is known as *negative space.* Positive space is seen as a positive shape (fig. 12). When negative space is surrounded with positive shapes, it becomes a negative shape (fig. 13).

A shape is perceived as a flat form when it shows no thickness, fully faces the viewer, and suggests no depth. This is the effect created by pasting a shape cut from thin paper on another piece of paper. When one shape overlaps another, some depth is created (fig. 14). When the same shape is shown curled, folded, or flipped, a form of considerable depth is introduced (figs. 15–17). The same shape can be displayed at different sizes in the same composition; a sequence of receding forms suggests infinite depth (fig. 18).

A shape that is given thickness or volume transforms a flat, two-dimensional space within the frame of reference into space of appropriate depth (fig. 19). Flat and voluminous forms, shallow and deep spaces, produce different visual illusions, which must be considered when creating two-dimensional designs.

141

THE VISUALIZATION OF FORM

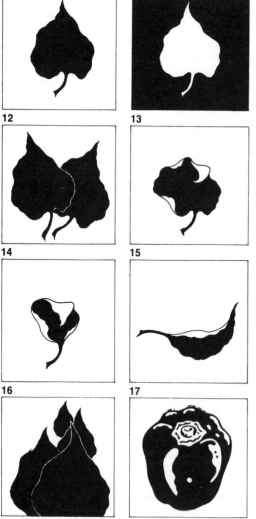

12

13

14

15

16

17

18

19

As a form takes shape on a two-dimensional surface, it can be depicted in a number of different ways without a change in its size, color, position, or direction.

Visualizing a form requires the application of points, lines, and planes that describe its contours, surface characteristics, and other details. Each method of treatment results in a different visual effect, although the general shape of the form remains the same.

20

Visualization with Lines

Visualization with Planes

A line is created by moving an appropriate tool across a surface by hand. It is easy to visualize a form constructed with lines. It is somewhat like drawing, except that solid lines of uniform breadth might be used in design creation.

An outline is the most economical expression of basic visual information (fig. 20). If a fine line does not achieve the visual impact desired, a much bolder line could replace it (fig. 21).

Within the outline details can be introduced that provide descriptive information and strengthen the connections and divisions of elements, the apparent volume and depth, and the spatial sequence from foreground to background of the form (fig. 22).

A form can also be visualized with primary and secondary lines to clarify its structure; in this case, lines of two or more uniform breadths may be used (fig. 23).

The shape outlined in figure 20 can be painted black to create a continuous flat plane. The result is a silhouette—the simplest expression of a form (fig. 24).

Black and white areas can be easily reversed; a black shape on a white background becomes a white, or negative, shape on a black background (fig. 25).

A shape that is achieved with one continuous plane is usually void of details. Negative lines (white lines on the solid black plane) can be used to introduce details. Negative lines separate a large plane into smaller planes (fig. 26).

143

21

22

23

24

Visualization with Lines and Planes

25

Lines are used to create seemingly light shapes, whereas planes create heavy shapes. Lines and planes used together allow light and heavy areas to coexist within a shape; details can be introduced where necessary. This manner of visualization is particularly suitable for adding light and shade to enhance the effect of volume in a form (fig. 27).

144

26

27

Visualization with Points

Visualization with Texture

Repeated points can be arranged to outline a form (fig. 28). Points can also be grouped as a plane to suggest a form (fig. 29). When used to create planes, points produce texture.

Texture can be created with points, short lines, long lines, or any combination of these. Texture can be shown as a regular pattern, or as an irregular pattern, with slight variations in the shape or size of similar elements (figs. 30, 31).

Texture generally adds visual variations to planes and surface characteristics to forms. Texture can also be applied in light-dark modulations to establish volume (fig. 32).

145

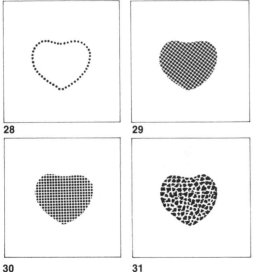

28

29

30

31

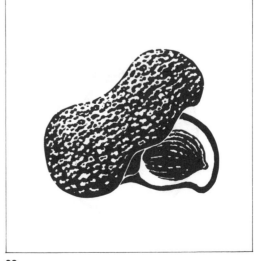

32

TYPES OF FORMS

Representational Forms

Forms can be broadly classified according to their particular contents.

A form that contains a recognizable *subject* communicates with viewers in more than purely visual terms. This is called a *representational* form. When a form does not contain a recognizable subject, it is considered *nonrepresentational* or abstract.

A representational form can be rendered with photographic realism or with some degree of abstraction—as long as it is not so abstract as to make the subject unrecognizable (fig. 33). If the subject cannot be identified, the form is nonrepresentational.

Sometimes the subject of a representational form is fantastic. The form, however, will present a transformed reality, one that suggests volume and space, so the fantastic subject conveys a kind of reality to the viewer (fig. 34).

146

33

34

Natural Forms

Man-made Forms

Representational forms can be further classified according to subject matter. If the subject is something found in nature, the form can be described as a *natural* form (fig. 35).

Natural forms include living organisms and inanimate objects that exist on the earth's surface, in the oceans, or in the sky.

Man-made forms are representational forms that are derived from objects and environments created by man (fig. 36). They can feature buildings, furniture, vehicles, machines, tools, household products, toys, apparel, or stationery, to name a few possibilities.

147

35

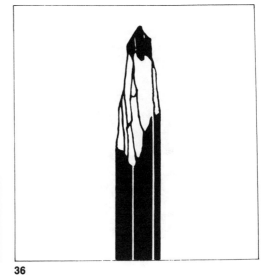

36

Verbal Forms

Abstract Forms

Written language consists of characters, letters, words, and numerals that make precise visual communication possible. A form based on an element of written language is a a *verbal* form (fig. 37).

A verbal form is representational in that it depicts a recognizable idea, rather than something that exists in a material sense.

An abstract form lacks a recognizable subject (fig. 38). It could be the designer's intention to create a form that represents nothing. This form could have been based on a subject that has become obliterated after excessive transformation, or it could have been the result of experimentation with materials that led to unexpected results.

An abstract form expresses a designer's sensitivity to shape, color, and composition without relying on recognizable elements.

148

37

38

TYPES OF SHAPES

Calligraphic Shapes

The same form, whether representational or abstract, can be expressed in different shapes. This does not mean that it must be seen from different views, angles, and distances, or that it must be moved or transformed; the different *approaches* possible in visual creation produce different results.

One approach is to draw the shape freehand in a somewhat *calligraphic* manner. Another approach is to create an *organic* shape by reducing a shape to all smooth curves. A third approach is to use only straight lines, circles, or arcs to establish a *geometric* shape.

The movement of the hand, the drawing tool, the medium, and the drawing surface are apparent in a calligraphic shape. The tool is generally a pen, pencil, or brush, whose particular characteristics are apparent in the finished form (fig. 39).

149

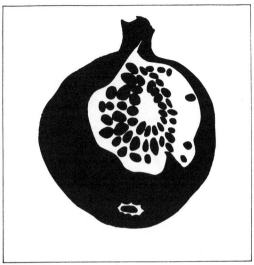

39

Organic Shapes

Geometric Shapes

An organic shape displays convexities and concavities with softly flowing curves. It also includes points of contact between curves (fig. 40).

When visualizing a form as an organic shape, all pen lines and brushstrokes should be controlled to minimize traces of hand movements, and the recognizable effects of particular tools.

A geometric shape relies on mechanical means of construction. Straight lines have to be drawn with rulers, circles and arcs with compasses. Sharpness and precision must prevail. All traces of hand movements or tools should be eliminated as much as possible (fig. 41).

150

40

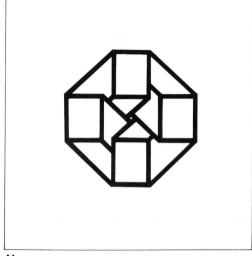

41

PART II
DESIGNING A FORM

DESIGN AND FORM

Singular Forms

Design is the entire composition of which form is the most conspicuous part. Sometimes all visual elements in a design are collectively referred to as form, but it is more common that clearly defined shapes are taken as forms, which constitute the composition.

Designing a form can be a process separate from designing a composition, although one affects the other considerably. It is often useful to see a form first in isolation and then as an element among other elements. A designer should explore extensively the numerous options for shaping a form.

If a composition consists of only one form, it is called a *singular* form. A composition with a singular form does not have a conglomerate of smaller, clearly distinguishable forms (fig. 42).

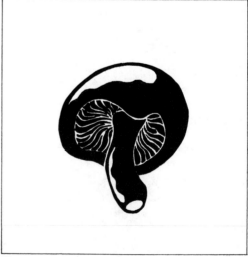

42

Plural Forms

Compound Forms

When a form is repeated in a composition, it is called a *plural* form.

The *components* of a plural form might vary slightly, but must be closely associated, overlapped, interlocked, or joined in order for them to be read as one image in the composition (fig. 43).

Different forms can be united to create a *compound* form (fig. 44).

A plural can become a compound form by adding an element that is different in form.

153

43

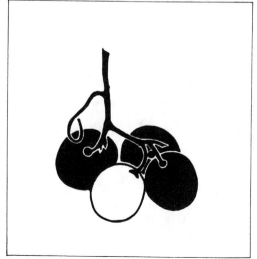

44

Unit Forms

Superunit Forms

A form used repeatedly in a composition is a *unit* form (fig. 45).

Unlike the components of a plural form, unit forms are individual elements that do not constitute a larger form. Unit forms are often used in patternlike designs.

Two or more unit forms can be grouped together and then repeated in a design. Each group is considered a *superunit* form (fig. 46).

A superunit form is different from a plural form in that the elements of a plural form combine to produce a single shape; a superunit form can be a loosely packed group of unit forms.

154

45

46

CREATING GEOMETRIC SHAPES

Straight Lines

Forms can be designed either as geometric or as organic shapes. Generally speaking, natural forms are more easily adapted to organic shapes, whereas man-made and abstract forms are more easily expressed as geometric shapes.

Geometric shapes are created using straight lines and circles. The nature of geometry demands careful planning in order for lines to meet at a certain angle, for one arc to flow into another, to divide space equally, and to establish a regular pattern.

A straight line is the shortest distance between two points.

A straight line with breadth displays weight in addition to length and direction (fig. 47).

As a line becomes heavier, its endings become more and more prominent, displaying shape characteristics of their own (figs. 48, 49).

Used as an edge to a plane, a line divides positive and negative space or distinguishes one plane from another (fig 50).

155

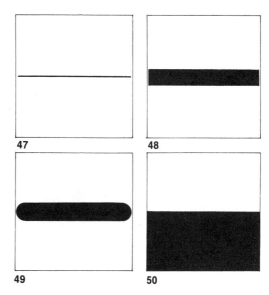

47   48

49   50

Circles

Arcs

A circle is established with a fixed center and radius. Only its circumference is visible after the circle is drawn.

Described as a linear shape, the circle is an unbroken line that encloses space. This unbroken line can also acquire breadth (figs. 51, 52). It separates the space it surrounds from the space surrounding it.

As a planar shape, the circle displays a maximum area within a minimum boundary without angularity or direction (fig. 53).

A fragment of a circle, part of its circumference, forms an arc (fig. 54).

An isolated arc is visualized as a linear shape of definite breadth, whose endings might be shaped (figs. 55–57).

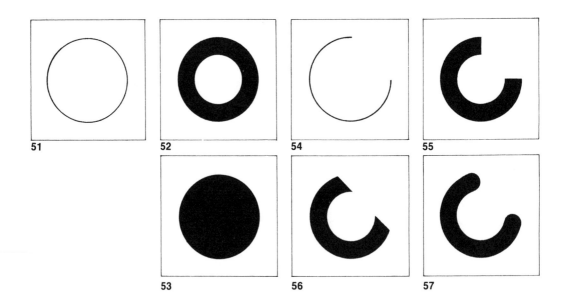

51

52

54

55

53

56

57

Relating Straight Lines

Two straight lines can be brought together in numerous ways by changing their positions and/or directions. Two lines can touch, join, or overlap (figs. 58–61). Lines can be joined end to end or end to edge (figs. 59, 62). Bold lines with curved endings require special treatment (figs. 63–66).

Bold lines can overlap, forming a negative shape in the overlapped area (fig. 67).

Parallel bold lines can touch or join without creating one continuous line (figs. 68, 69).

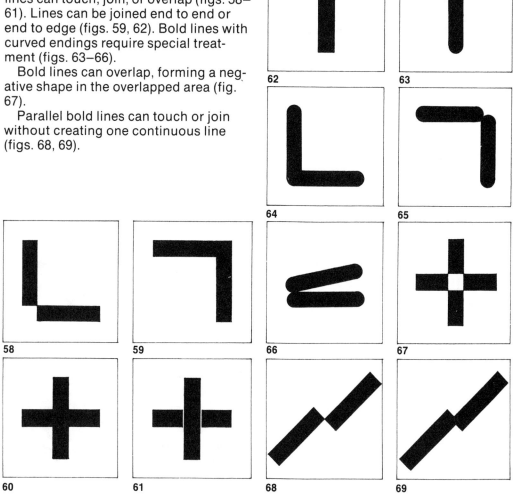

62

63

64

65

58

59

66

67

60

61

68

69

Relating Circles

Circles can touch, join, overlap, or interlock (figs. 70–73). Boldly drawn circum-
ferences can lead to more variations
(figs. 74–79).

Circles of different sizes can be superimposed, with larger ones containing
smaller ones (figs. 80, 81).

158

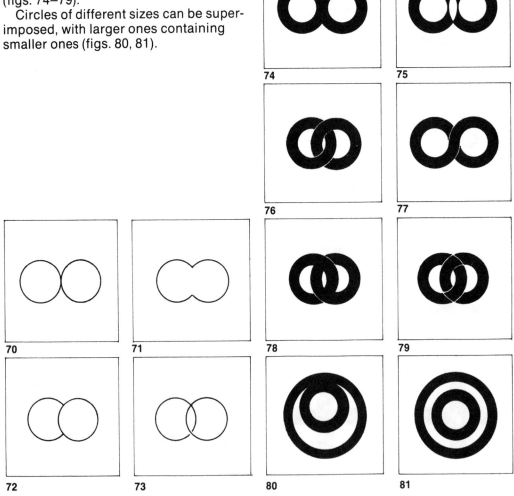

74

75

76

77

70

71

78

79

72

73

80

81

Relating Arcs

Two arcs can touch, join, overlap, or interlock (figs. 82–86). Arcs that are joined can produce an enclosed space or a winding curve (figs. 87, 88). The end of arcs can vary to achieve different effects (figs. 89, 90). Arcs of different sizes can be arranged with or without connecting their endings (figs. 91, 92).

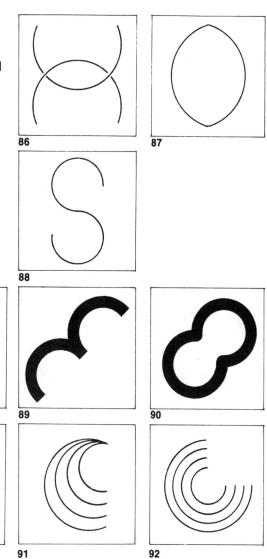

86

87

88

82

83

89

90

84

85

91

92

Relating Straight Lines, Circles, and Arcs

Straight lines, circles, and arcs can be made to relate in a multitude of ways by manipulating their breadths, their endings, their ending-to-ending joints (figs. 93, 94), their ending-to-edge joints (fig. 95), their edge-to-edge joints (fig. 96), the way they overlap (fig. 97), the way they interlock (fig. 98), the way they interpenetrate (fig. 99), the way they interweave (fig. 100), their continuities (figs. 101, 102), and their enclosures (figs. 103, 104).

160

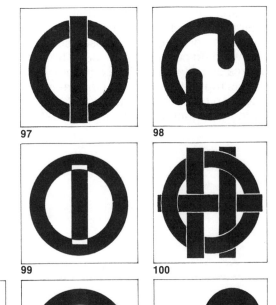

97

98

99

100

93

94

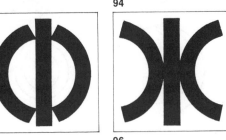

95

96

101

102

103

104

Angles and Pointed Tips

When two lines meet, they form an *angle.* Angles are measured in degrees. Angles of 30, 45, 60, 90, and 120 degrees are considered regular angles. Figures 105 through 109 show shapes constructed of straight lines at regular angles.

The endings of two arcs, or of one arc and one straight line, can also be joined, displaying a pointed tip. Just as angles can be acute or obtuse, the place where two lines meet to form an angle (the pointed tip) can be sharp or blunt (figs. 110–14).

Angles and tips in a shape can be rounded by using tiny arcs (figs. 115, 116).

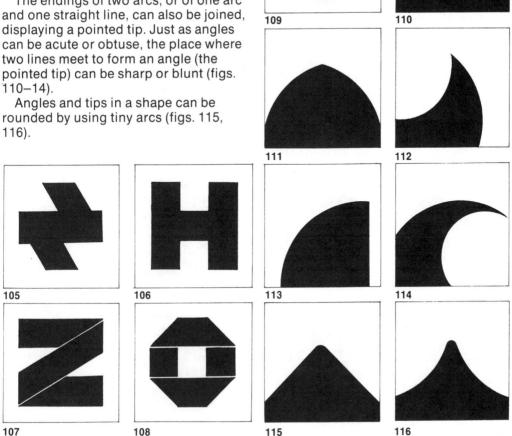

109

110

111

112

105

106

113

114

107

108

115

116

161

The Addition of Planes

The space enclosed by lines can be filled with solid color to form a plane. Two planes can be combined, or added, whether or not they are of the same shape or size (figs. 117–120).

Planes might overlap or intersect with other planes, while the shape of an individual plane maintains its separate identity (figs. 121–24). Shapes thus created are less seen as singular forms, but more as plural or compound forms (see page 17).

Two planes that have been combined might have some common edges, which result in a shape without easily discernible components (figs. 125, 126).

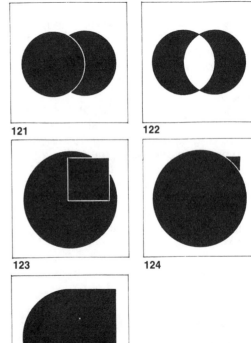

121

122

123

124

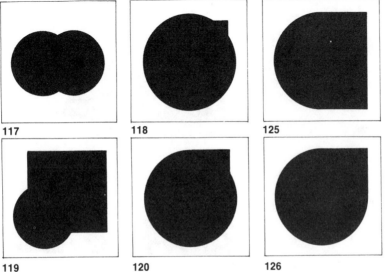

117

118

125

119

120

126

The Subtraction of Planes

The Interpenetration of Planes

When a negative plane overlaps a positive plane, space appears to have been subtracted from the positive plane. The resulting shape shows a missing portion where the negative plane merges with the background (figs. 127, 128). Sometimes subtraction leads to loose parts (fig. 129).

A smaller negative plane can be completely contained within a larger positive plane (fig. 130).

Two planes can create a transparent effect by forming a negative shape within an overlapped area (figs. 131, 132). Negative shapes might become positive when overlapped within a design that includes the interpenetration of more than two planes (fig. 133).

163

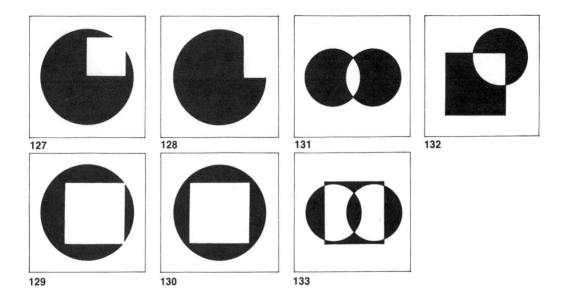

127

128

131

132

129

130

133

The Multiplication of Planes

The same plane can be *multiplied,* or used repeatedly without change in shape or size. Each plane is thus seen as a component of a plural form.

A plane that is multiplied can produce separate planes (fig. 134), planes that touch (fig. 135), planes that are joined (fig. 136), planes that overlap (figs. 137, 138), planes that interpenetrate (fig. 139), planes that combine positive and negative shapes (fig. 140).

164

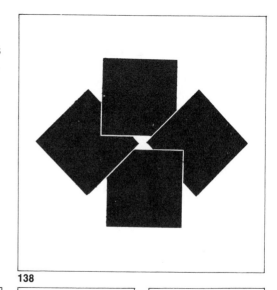

138

134

135

139

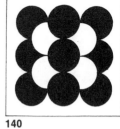

140

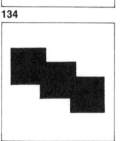

136

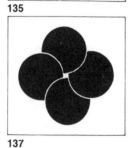

137

The Division of Planes

A plane can be divided into equal or unequal parts. Negative lines can be introduced with gaps between dissected shapes (figs. 141, 142). The slight displacement of dissected shapes can lead to interesting effects, but the original shape of the plane must remain recognizable (fig. 143).

Dissected shapes can touch, join, overlap, or interpenetrate (fig. 144).

143

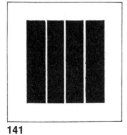

141

142

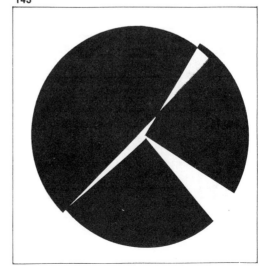

144

Varying the Size of Planes

A plane can be enlarged gradually, or dilated. Smaller planes can then be placed within larger planes concentrically, or with slight variations in the direction or position of elements (figs. 145, 146). Alternate positive and negative shapes might be overlapped (fig. 147).

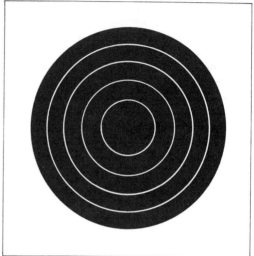

146

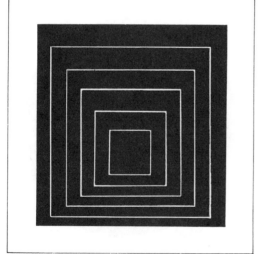

145

147

The Transformation of Planes

Planar shapes (or flat forms) can be rotated gradually to achieve transformation. The transformed shapes can then be superimposed (fig. 148). In addition, the size of shapes can be altered to suggest receding and advancing elements in space (fig. 149).

As with size variations, alternate positive and negative shapes might be overlapped (fig. 150).

149

148

150

167

Folding Planes

Establishing Volume

A plane can be manipulated to form a round or pointed corner where it is made to fold. Folding might expose the reverse side of a shape, which can then be visualized in outline (figs. 151, 152). A negative line can indicate a sharp fold (fig. 153).

A shape can be thickened along one or more of its edges to establish volume. The combination of lines and planes helps to distinguish the frontal plane from the side planes in a shape (figs. 154, 155).

Volume can be presented with the frontal plane turned obliquely or laterally (figs. 156, 157).

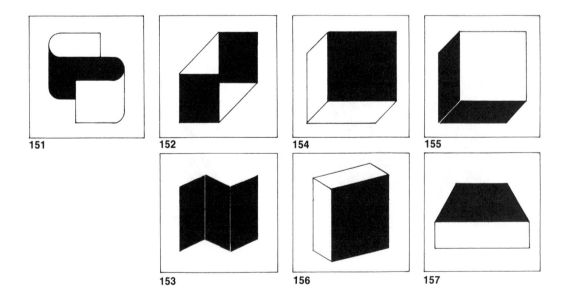

151

152

154

155

153

156

157

Regularity

Most geometric shapes are regular, or have components with consistent or orderly positions and directions. Shapes should be positioned at predetermined distances (fig. 158). The direction of shapes should be at predetermined angles, establishing fan, circular, or spiral patterns (fig. 159).

With two or four components, a shape might resemble a square (fig. 160). With three components, a triangular shape might result (fig. 161).

160

161

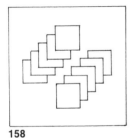

158

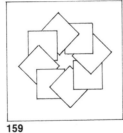

159

Deviation

Symmetry

Sometimes strict regularity produces a rigid composition, and some deviation is desirable. Deviation is effectively applied when one or more components change shape, size, position, or direction without seriously disrupting the original design (figs. 162–65).

Symmetrical shapes are regular shapes whose left and right halves are mirror images. An invisible straight line, an *axis,* divides the shape equally (fig. 166). A symmetrical shape can be positioned horizontally or on a slant (fig. 167).

170

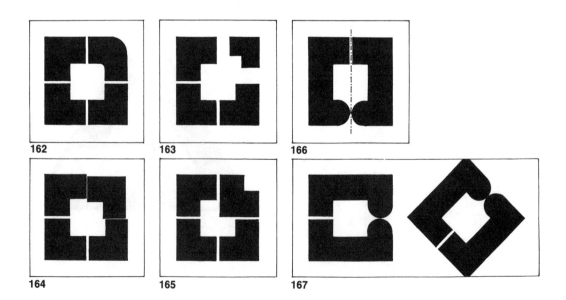

162

163

166

164

165

167

Asymmetry

Slight deviation can be introduced in a
symmetrical shape by shifting the two
halves out of alignment, by overlapping
the halves, or by adding some variation
to one of the halves (figs. 168–70).

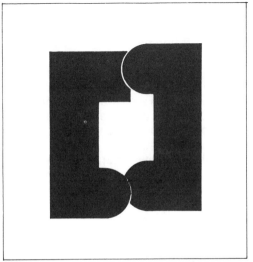

169

168

170

CREATING ORGANIC SHAPES

C and S Curves

Organic shapes are formed of smoothly flowing curves with imperceptible transitions or projecting connections. The curves are usually hand drawn, but drawing instruments, such as French curves or flexible curves, are sometimes used. Straight lines are rarely present. A shape created with curves and straight lines exhibits geometric as well as organic characteristics.

Although simplicity is generally desirable, an organic shape can display intricate details.

A line that flexes in a single direction results in a *C curve* (fig. 171). The other type of curve, an *S curve,* is produced when a line is flexed in two directions (fig. 172). The S curve is actually two C curves joined from opposite directions.

Both C and S curves can be presented as small or large loops (figs. 173, 174).

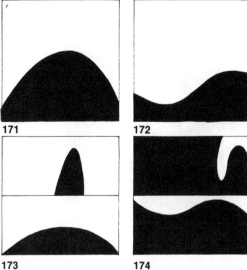

171

172

173

174

Shapes with Pointed Tips

Shapes with Rounded Tips

Two curves that meet can either establish a continuous flow or a pointed tip. Pointed tips can be seen either as projecting from the body of a shape (fig. 175), or as inverted toward it (fig. 177).

Tips that are blunt (figs. 175, 177) can be sharpened by extending the curves near their junction (figs. 176, 178).

Any projecting or inverted tip can be rounded by smoothing the point (figs. 179, 180).

This rounded tip can be exaggerated with a prominent ending (figs. 181, 182).

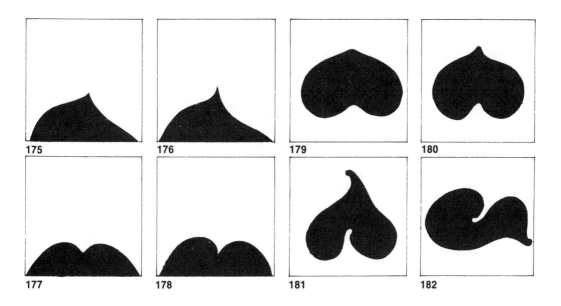

175

176

179

180

177

178

181

182

The Joining and Linking of Shapes

The Splitting, Tearing, and Breaking of Shapes

Two shapes that overlap (fig. 183) can be partially joined (fig. 184).

Two separate shapes (fig. 185) can be linked with protrusions (fig. 186).

A shape (fig. 187) can be split partially or completely into two or more shapes, while the overall image remains intact (figs. 188, 189). The split components might be manipulated to introduce slight variations if desired.

The tearing and breaking of shapes result in ragged edges, which introduce some irregularity (fig. 190).

174

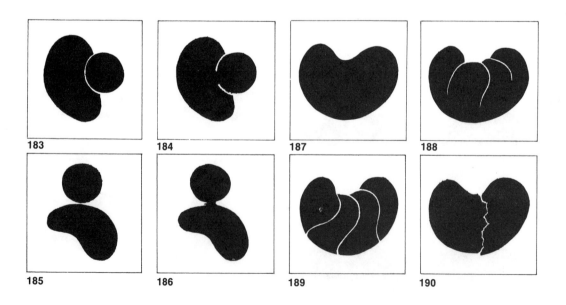

183

184

187

188

185

186

189

190

Cutting and Removing Parts of Shapes

The Curling and Twisting of Shapes

A portion, or portions, of a shape can be cut and removed, altering its edge (fig. 191), or producing negative shapes (figs. 192, 193). Cut edges might be left ragged to suggest a forced break (fig. 194).

A shape can be treated as a soft plane that curls to reveal the bottom or back of the shape (fig. 195).

A shape can also be distorted by twisting it and narrowing its middle (fig. 196).

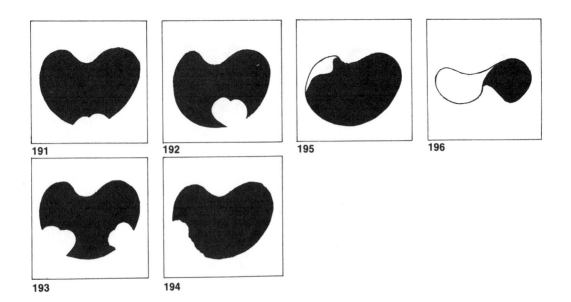

191

192

195

196

193

194

The Rippling and Creasing of Shapes

The Inflation and Deflation of Shapes

The excessive curling of a shape leads to ripples (fig. 197).

Creases created by curling and rippling a shape can be given sharp edges (fig. 198). Creasing can be effected only halfway down the shape (fig. 199).

A shape can be inflated to considerable fullness (approaching a circle) without an obvious increase in size (fig. 200). It can also be deflated, or contracted, becoming crinkled, without an obvious decrease in size (figs. 201, 202).

176

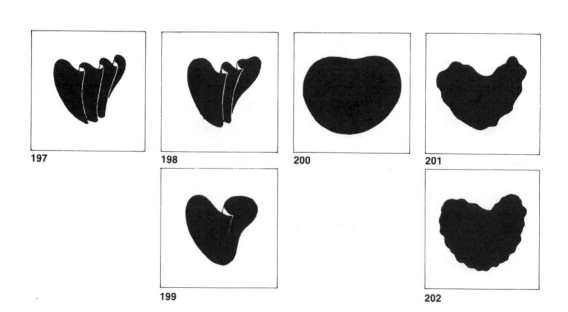

197

198

200

201

199

202

The Metamorphosis and Deformation of Shapes

The Proliferation of Shapes

A shape can *metamorphose*—be affected by internal growth in one or more specific areas (fig. 203). It can be *deformed* as if it is being acted upon by some external force that is squeezing, pulling, or pushing it (figs. 204–6).

Multiple use of a shape is called *proliferation* (fig. 207). The size and shape of overlapped or superimposed, proliferated elements can vary (figs. 208–10).

177

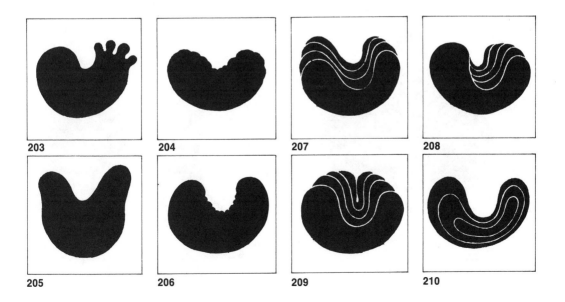

203

204

207

208

205

206

209

210

Symmetrical Expression

Symmetry can be introduced in an organic shape. To achieve strict symmetry, a mirror image can be created of components on either side of an invisible axis (fig. 211). The axis, however, can become a C- or S-shaped curve, and the components can be appropriately adjusted for a symmetrical expression (fig. 212).

Further manipulations of the resultant shape can also be introduced (fig. 213). Components can vary slightly without destroying the symmetry of the structure (fig. 214).

178

212

211

213

214

VARIATIONS OF A FORM

Internal Variation

A form, whether abstract or representational, geometric or organic, can be developed into different configurations. The designer can thus examine all possible variations before deciding on one.

Illustrations on the next few pages feature a variety of L-shaped forms (fig. 215).

One way to change the shape of a form is to change the internal area from a solid plane (fig. 215) to an empty space. The form might have a fine or a bold outline (figs. 216, 217).

The form can be split into two or more stripes (fig. 218), covered with a texture or pattern (fig. 219), layered (fig. 220), or given other details (fig. 221).

179

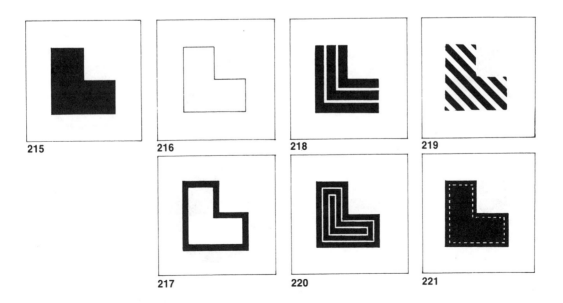

215

216

218

219

217

220

221

External Variation

Extension

The two basic ways to vary a form externally are with corner (fig. 222) and edge variations (fig. 223).

    Sometimes internal variations lead to external variations, or vice versa. The combined external-internal variations can establish interesting results (figs. 224, 225).

A form can be extended with a border or concentric layers (fig. 226). Creating a frame of a certain shape (fig. 227), adding a shape to serve as background (fig. 228), or introducing subsequent layers (fig. 229) can also be used as extensions.

180

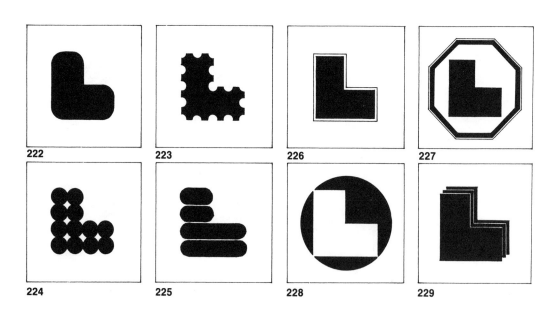

222

223

226

227

224

225

228

229

Superimposition

Transfiguration

Other forms can be superimposed on a given form without obliterating its general shape (figs. 230–32).

A form can be *transfigured* by changing a portion of the form or the entire form to something representational (figs. 233–35).

181

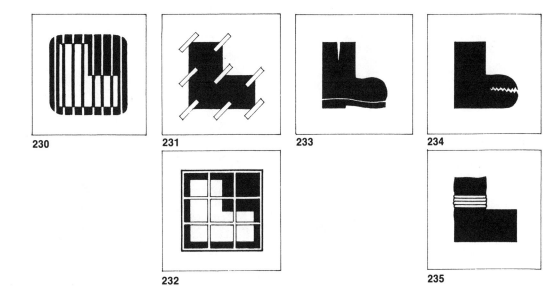

230

231

233

234

232

235

Dislocation

Distortion

A form can be dissected or broken into two or more parts and then dislocated (figs. 236–38).

The simplest way to distort a form is to change the proportion of its height and width. This can be done by using a superimposed square grid as a guide (fig. 239). A grid of decreased height or narrower width is then drawn to map out a distorted shape (fig. 240).

Diagonal distortion, circular distortion, or any other distortion can be effected in a similar manner (figs. 241, 242).

182

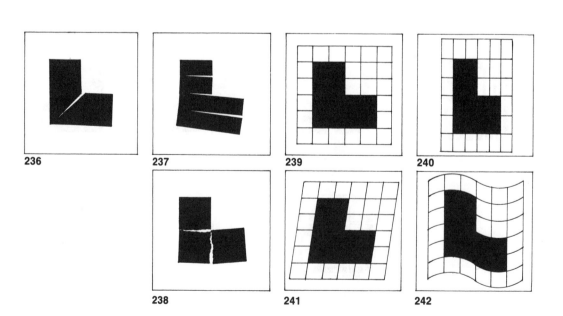

236

237

239

240

238

241

242

Three-Dimensional Manipulation

A form can be regarded as a three-dimensional plane that might bend, fold, or be seen from different angles and distances (figs. 243–46).

When thickness is added to a form, it acquires volume (fig. 247). It can be rotated in space, displaying a different shape (fig. 248). It can also be made to appear transparent (fig. 249).

An extension to a form can approximate shadows or reflections cast on water (figs. 250–52).

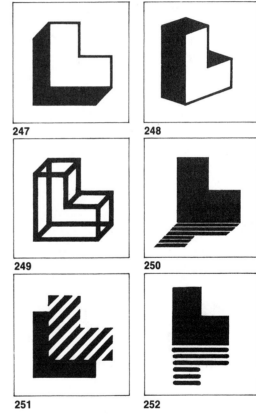

247

248

249

250

183

243

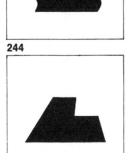

244

251

252

245

246

Further Developments

All the previously mentioned methods of developing a form can be combined, producing many more possible configurations (figs. 253–58).

257

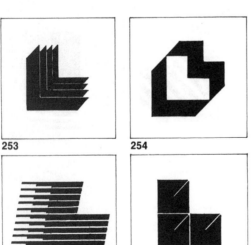

253

254

255

256

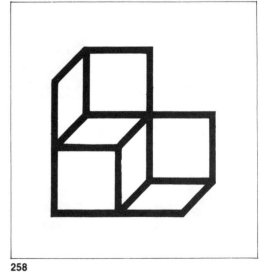

258

184

PART III
REPRESENTATIONAL
FORMS

FORMS AND SUBJECTS

Observing Natural Forms

Most representational forms capture the basic characteristics of shapes and avoid subjects with unusual, less familiar details. For instance, a leaf can be depicted as a shape representing leaves of most deciduous trees, or it can be depicted as a shape representing one particular tree. It is rare, however, that a leaf of an unusual shape is chosen as the subject for a design.

Various ways of designing a form have been suggested in Part II, and these can be applied to the design of representational forms. It should first be decided whether to present a form as a geometric shape or as an organic shape, and how abstract it could be and still satisfy design goals. A preliminary search into a range of specimens is often desirable, so that their particularities can be compared and general features extracted. Drawing a selected specimen or two is necessary for achieving a thorough understanding of the subject.

Natural forms are diverse, but possess the same basic structural characteristics determined by natural laws governing their growth. It is helpful to observe and identify the environmental forces that affect the shapes of natural forms. The shapes of the components of natural forms and how they work together structurally should then be examined.

186

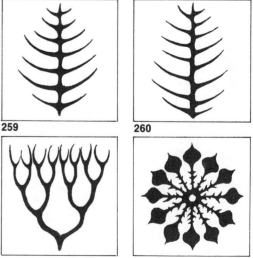

259

260

261

262

Branching and Fanning

Spirals and Undulations

A common feature in the structures of plants and animals is the existence of a backbone or central columnar shape with elements that *branch* bilaterally (fig. 259) or in an alternating pattern (fig. 260). Branching can also take the form of a splitting—one element splits into two, two into four, and so on (fig. 261).

When more than two elements branch, a *fanning* pattern can result. Fanning can extend 360 degrees, with rotating elements emerging from one central point (fig. 262), or surrounding a large open center (fig. 263).

Linear shapes in nature are seldom linear in the geometric sense. These natural shapes actually curl slightly or prominently in one or more directions.

If a linear shape proceeds as a C curve, winding around a center in graduated swirls, a *spiral* is formed (fig. 264). Suggesting three dimensions, a conical (fig. 265) or tubular shape can be created (fig. 266).

If it proceeds as an S curve, narrow or wide *undulations* result (figs. 267, 268). Undulations can form a grooved shape or chain to suggest a third dimension (figs. 269, 270).

187

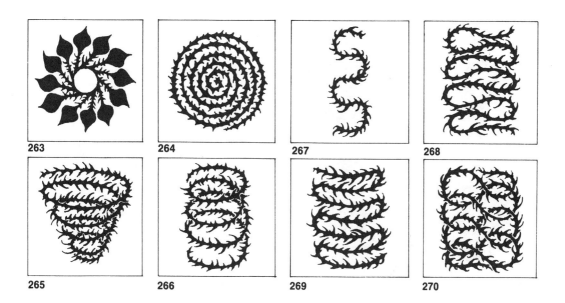

263

264

267

268

265

266

269

270

Affinity and Unity

Observing Man-made Forms

Elements within a particular natural form —cells, sections, or layers that make up a surface—usually display *affinity* (figs. 271, 272). These elements are not strict repetitions, but vary individually or progressively to conform to an overall shape and structure. There might be several types of elements, with affinity among elements of the different types.

Affinity establishes *unity*. Unity is also established by fitting elements tightly together (fig. 273). Transitions create a smooth flow between elements (fig. 274).

Man-made forms are either crafted with tools by hand or manufactured with machines. Generally, tools and machines are efficient at creating straight lines, flat surfaces, right angles, circles, and cylinders. This explains why most man-made forms display a geometric configuration. Organic shapes are sometimes introduced as decorations, or for ergonomic reasons.

The nature of its materials and the assembly of its parts are important considerations when observing a man-made form. It is also important to study the form from different viewpoints.

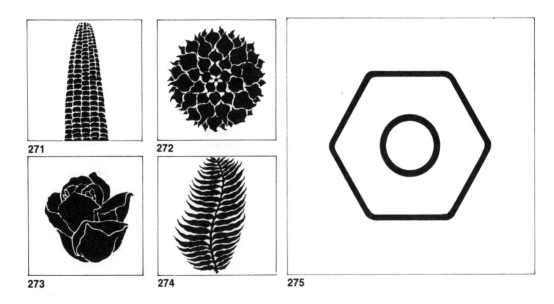

271

272

273

274

275

Materials and the Assembly of Parts

Plans, Elevations, and Perspectives

Materials can be thin sheets or solid masses, soft or hard, transparent or opaque, light or heavy. Materials used to fabricate man-made forms can be singular or can be parts that are assembled.

Parts can be assembled by fitting them, bonding them, or joining them with springs, pivots, or hinges, which allow for movement.

Man-made forms are often conceived as *plans* and *elevations.* Viewing the form from above establishes its plan (fig. 275). Viewing it from the front and sides establishes its elevations (figs. 276, 277). Plan and elevation studies are the basic ways of visualizing a man-made form.

The form is then studied from different viewpoints, or *perspectives* (fig. 278). It must be noted that most planes are distorted when seen in perspective.

189

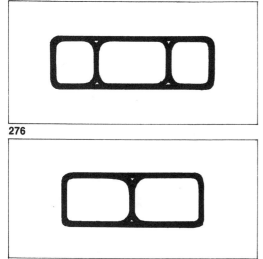

276

277

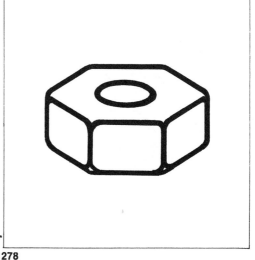

278

SELF-CONTAINED COMPOSITIONS

Establishing Singular Forms

Designing with representational forms can begin with a series of self-contained compositions—singular forms, plural forms, and/or compound forms that are established without a frame of reference. These might then be contained within specific frames of reference to help define spatial relationships.

To create a *singular form,* the chosen subject is first studied from different viewpoints with drawings and sketches. One drawing (fig. 279) is then selected and used as the basis for design development. Consideration is given to aspects of aesthetics as well as communication. The singular form can be visualized as one solid plane (fig. 280), planes displaying details (fig. 281), lines (fig. 283), the combination of lines and planes (figs. 282, 284, 285), or a textured shape (fig. 286).

190

279

280

281

282

283

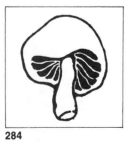

284

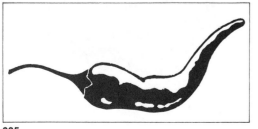

285

286

Establishing Plural Forms

Repeating a singular form establishes a *plural form* (fig. 287). The singular forms, now components, could vary externally and/or internally (fig. 288). They could touch, overlap, join, or remain separate. Joining representational forms can result in a rather unnaturalistic, yet interesting design (fig. 289). Separate forms must be adjacent, with one intruding the semienclosed space of the other if they are to be considered plural (fig. 290).

Two or more components can be arranged in accordance with the following concepts:

    a. *translation*—varying the positions, but not the directions, of components (fig. 291)

    b. *rotation*—varying the directions, with minimal change in position, of components (figs. 292–95)

    c. *reflection*—creating components as mirror images (figs. 296–98)

    d. *dilation*—increasing the size of superimposed or adjacent components (fig. 299)

Positions of components are also effected with rotation and reflection and frequently with dilation. Positional changes in such cases should be kept to a minimum.

Components can also be grouped randomly, or using a combination of the concepts described above (figs. 300–306).

287

288

289

290

291

292

293

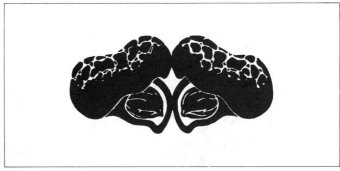

296

294

295

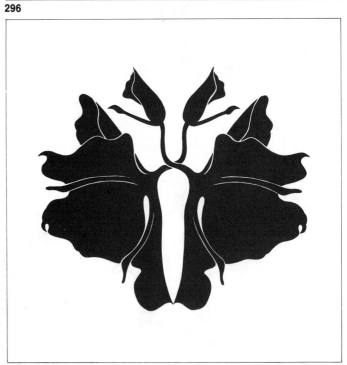

297

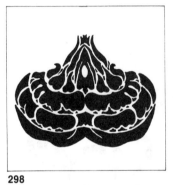

298

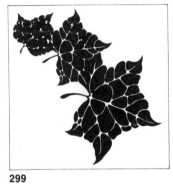

299

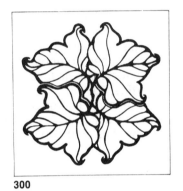

300

301

302

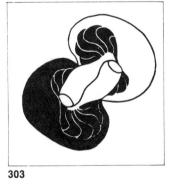

303

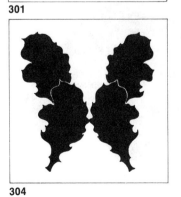

304

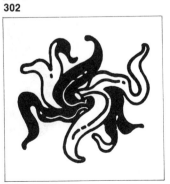

305

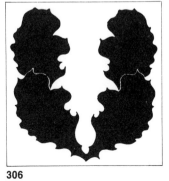

306

Establishing Compound Forms

A compound form is established with dissimilar components, or with similar *and* dissimilar components. Used in a self-contained composition, a compound form can be taken as a singular form (figs. 307–9).

Plural forms can be based on compound forms, producing more intricate designs (figs. 310–14).

307

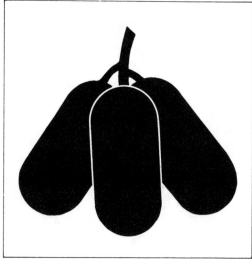

308

309

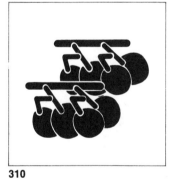

310

311

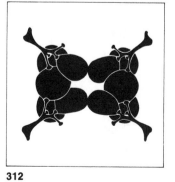

312

313

314

COMPOSITIONS WITH REPETITION

Two-way Continuance

Singular, plural, or compound forms can be applied as unit or superunit forms in repetition within a definite frame of reference. Their regular arrangement could establish a *formal* composition—all elements are organized in a kind of mathematical order.

Repetition involves reproducing the same shape in a design as well as placing the shapes at intervals, which can be determined with lines forming an invisible structural grid.

The simplest composition with repetition involves the arrangement of unit or superunit forms as two-way continuance, resulting in *rows* that can extend vertically, horizontally, or at any given angle (figs. 315, 316).

The row does not have to be straight. It can be crooked or curved. Unit forms can display a change of direction regularly within the row if desired.

315

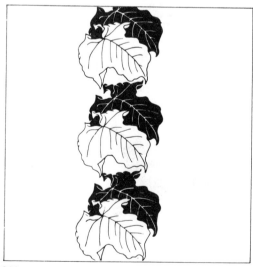

316

Four-way Continuance

When rows of unit or superunit forms are repeated regularly, four-way continuance is achieved (fig. 317).

Compositions with four-way continuance create a patternlike design (figs. 318–27). If a space is not completely filled, the composition becomes less formal (figs. 328, 329).

318

317

319

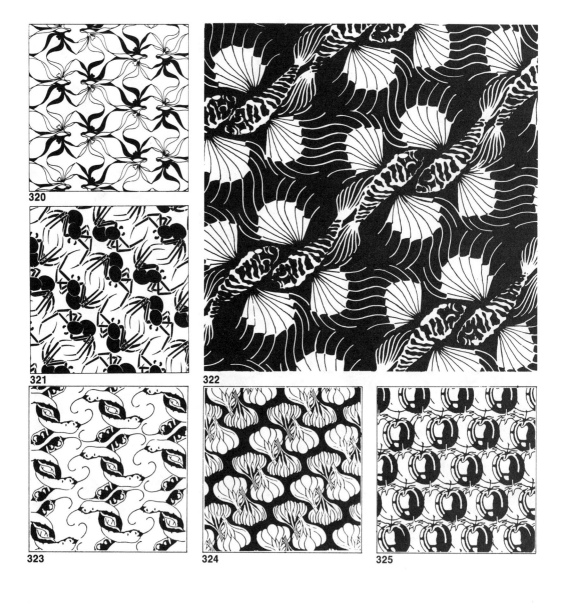

320

321

322

323

324

325

326

327

328

329

Six-way Continuance

A structural grid can comprise triangles to guide the placement of unit forms. This produces a six-way continuance, with shapes grouped as triangles or hexagons. If each unit form consists of a head and a tail, it is interesting to observe that the heads will meet at one point and the tails will meet at another point, in an alternating manner (figs. 330–34).

202

331

330

332

Development and Variations of the Repetition Structure

333

Unit forms can be photocopied (or traced) and cut out to explore all possible repetitions. A form can also be traced and then flipped over to obtain a mirror image (fig. 335). Superunit forms created this way can relate to each other in a different pattern of repetition, resulting in regular, but not monotonous, compositions (figs. 336–41). Isolated background shapes can be changed from white to black to achieve variations (figs. 342–44).

The structural grid can can be made visible as actual lines of definite breadth, or made to become edges of spatial cells, embellishing the unit or superunit forms (figs. 345–47).

203

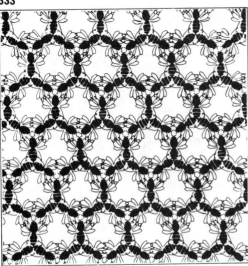

334

335

336

337

338

339

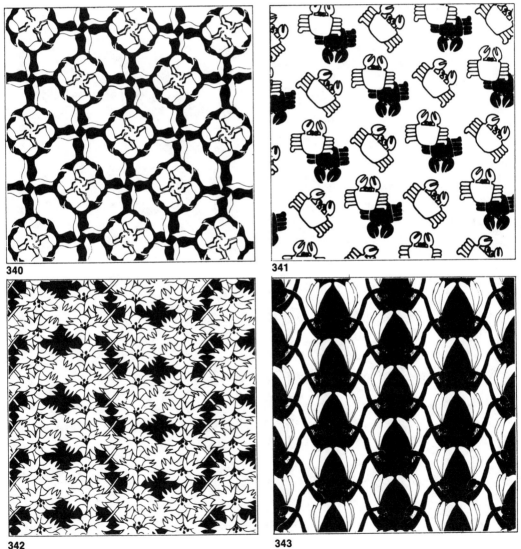

340

341

342

343

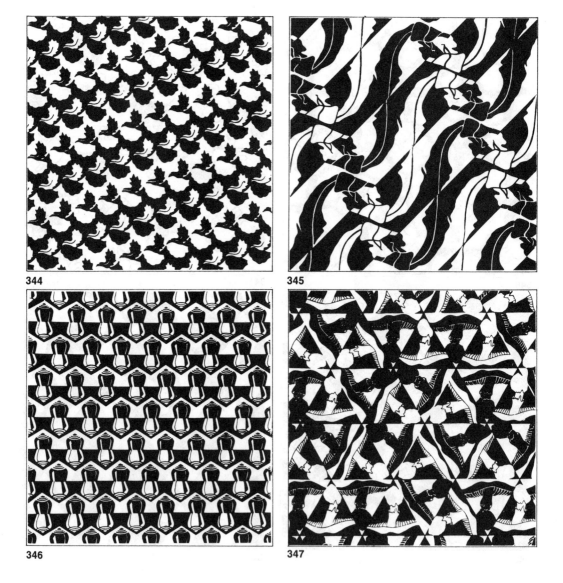

344

345

346

347

COMPOSITIONS WITH RADIATION

Full and Segmentary Radiation

The repetition of unit or superunit forms around a common center results in *radiation,* which is a technique used in formal compositions.

The basic structural grid for a design with radiation has a *center of reference* —the meeting point of all radiating lines, or the point around which structural lines revolve. Radiation normally features lines that converge near the center, with space between lines increasing as they move away from the center.

Structural lines guide the placement of unit or superunit forms that are directly linked to or equidistant from the center of reference.

The 360-degree rotation of unit or super-unit forms results in full radiation. The center of reference could be the point at which lines converge, either exactly, overlapping, or at some regular distance from the center of reference. The angle of rotation for each form must be consistent to establish regularity (fig. 348).

Rotating forms less than 360 degrees results in segmentary radiation (fig. 349). The fan or arc effect that results admits considerable background space near the center of radiation.

207

348

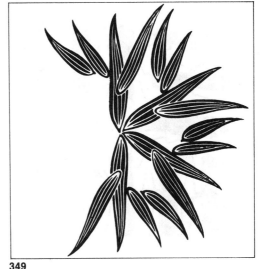

349

Rotation and Translation

A superunit form composed of trans-
lated unit forms can be rotated to
achieve radiation (fig. 350).

Rotated unit forms displaying radiation can be used as a superunit form for
translation in a repetition structure (figs.
351, 352).

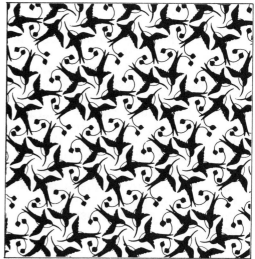

351

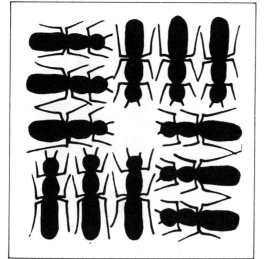

350

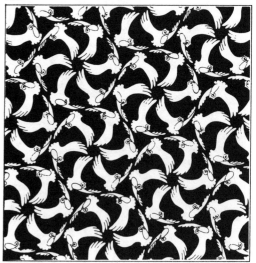

352

Rotation and Reflection

Rotation and Dilation

A full radiation might be cropped and joined to its mirror image on the other side of the cropped edge, which functions as an axis for reflection (fig. 353).

Dilated forms can be used instead of forms of uniform size. Slight variations of shape can be introduced during dilation if desired. These forms can be rotated to achieve a segmentary radiation, and then reflected or rotated again to achieve full radiation (figs. 354, 355).

Dilated forms in rotation can result in a spiral arrangement, a kind of radiation (fig. 356).

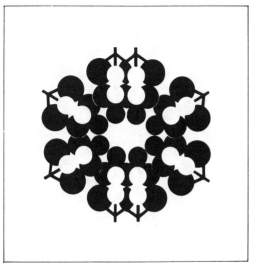

353

354

The Interception of Active Structural Lines

After establishing radiation, a composition could be superimposed with structural lines, making parallel or concentric subdivisions that intercept the forms. The interception could result in the dissection and partial dislocation of forms (figs. 357–61).

355

356

357

358

359

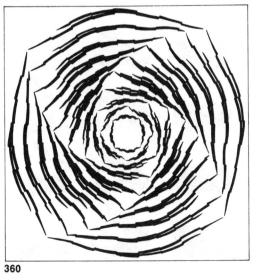

360

361

COMPOSITIONS WITH GRADATION

Gradation of Shape

Gradation refers to the systematic altera- tion of the shape, size, position, direc- tion, or proportion of a form. The forms produced by these changes are then arranged in sequence, with smooth tran- sitions between forms.

Unit forms in gradation can be posi- tioned according to a regular repetition structure with gradual variations. Unit forms can also be positioned with increasing or decreasing density.

Gradation of shape can be achieved by varying a form internally and/or exter- nally.

External without internal variation is achieved by adding to or subtracting from the form (fig. 362). Creating inter- nal without external variations requires more prominent gradations. In most cases, shape gradations affect the exter- nal and internal aspects of a form (fig. 363). Any form can be changed to any other form with the appropriate number of shape gradations.

212

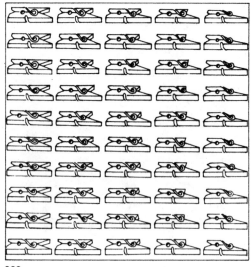

362

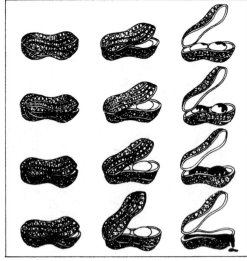

363

Gradation of Size

Gradation of Position

Size can be altered by enlarging or reducing forms arranged in sequence (usually in repetition). The transition could move from light to heavy rhythms, from heavy to light, or in an alternating fashion (fig. 364).

This is possible in a repetition structure with active structural lines that intercept and partially crop forms. The height of forms decreases as they are gradually moved down along the structural line (fig. 365).

213

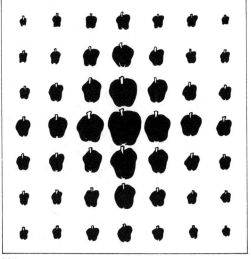

364

365

Gradation of Direction

Rotating a form from left to right on a flat surface, while maintaining its shape, effects a change in direction (figs. 366, 367). It can also change direction if it is rotated from front to back in three-dimensional space; different views are seen as different shapes (figs. 368, 369).

Figure 370 features directional changes from left to right and from front to back, as well as gradations of shape and size.

367

366

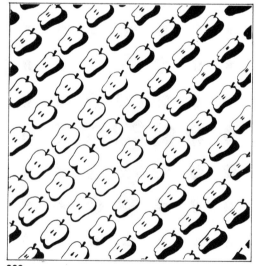

368

Gradation of Proportion

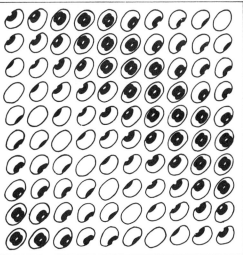

369

The narrowing and widening of subdivisions in a gradation structure might demand the narrowing and widening of forms. Forms altered this way are affected by gradation of proportion, which involves considerable shape distortions (figs. 371–73).

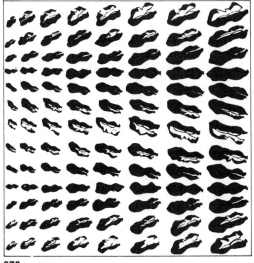

370

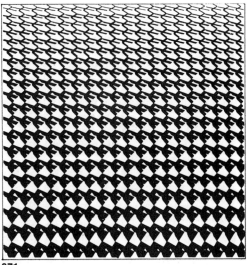

371

COMPOSITIONS WITH SIMILARITY

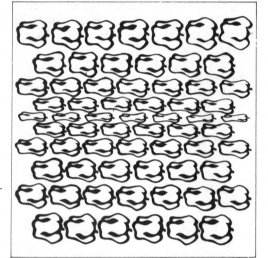

372

If the shape, size, color, or texture of unit forms in a composition varies slightly, they are not part of a strict repetition, but are more loosely, or *similarly,* related.

Similarity can also describe the placement of unit forms; the similar arrangement of unit forms might resemble a repetition, radiation, or a gradation structure.

373

374

216

375

376

377

378

379

380

Similarity and Repetition

Similarity and Radiation

The visual effect of close similarity is much like that of repetition. Similarity is achieved when a form is repeated with slight external and/or internal variations (figs. 374, 375). Forms in nature are never strict repetitions; no two leaves on the same tree are identical.

Similarity can also be established by rotating a form and displaying different views (fig. 376).

A formal structure can comprise similarly related forms that are not arranged in any sequence, introducing an element of informality to the design (figs. 377–79).

A more informal design is achieved when the similarly related forms are distributed with similar density (fig. 380).

Rotated similar forms on a flat surface can be grouped regularly or freely to suggest radiation (figs. 381, 382).

381

382

Similarity and Gradation

**COMPOSITIONS WITH
CONCENTRATION**

The arrangement of unit forms can proceed from dense to sparse in moderately
smooth transitions to suggest gradation
(fig. 383).

Figure 384 illustrates this effect, but
also features superimposed structural
lines that intercept and crop the unit
forms.

Concentration is the gathering of unit
forms in particular areas of a composition. This establishes rhythmic movements, often creating a center of interest
and subordinate accents.

Concentration can be associated with
natural phenomena—fleeting clouds,
splashing water, falling leaves, migrat-
ing birds.

383

384

Points of Concentration

A point in a composition can mark the densest concentration of unit forms. Density could gradually give way to the sparse placement of elements; loose elements could activate otherwise blank space (figs. 385, 386).

When there is more than one point of concentration, densities at the different points should vary, allowing one point to emerge as the center of interest. In dense areas, voids become prominent; a void is often the center of interest in a composition with tightly packed elements (fig. 387).

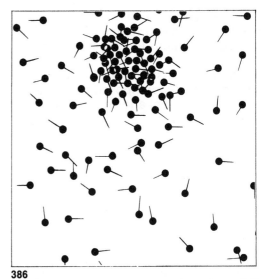

386

385

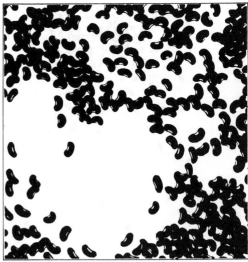

387

Linear Concentration

A concentrated area in a design can be linear, forming a band, with or without loose elements nearby (figs. 388–90).

Unit forms within the band could vary in density (fig. 391). A composition could contain more than one band (fig. 392).

389

388

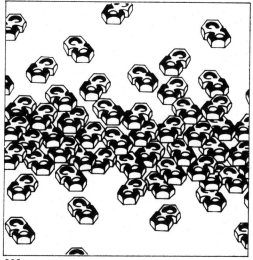

390

Planar Concentration

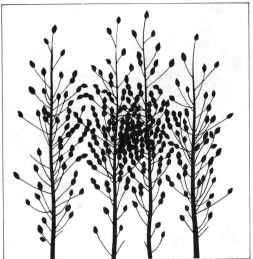

Unit forms can be brought together as a plane of almost even density. The plane could be an isolated shape within the frame of reference or could partially extend beyond it (fig. 393).

222

391

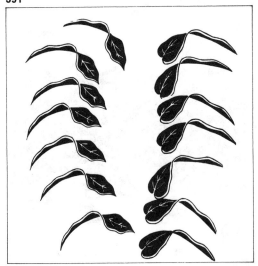

392

393

COMPOSITIONS WITH CONTRAST

Contrast of Appearance

Contrast is used to suggest visual distinctions. Increased contrast enhances visibility. Decreased contrast assimilates elements in a composition. In most cases, contrast is used intuitively by the designer, but it can be consciously applied to effect comparisons and to establish a center of interest.

Contrast can refer to the appearance, placement, or quantity of forms.

Contrast can be applied to one or more aspects of a form's appearance—its shape, size, color or texture.

Contrasting shapes can differ externally or internally, or have different basic shapes (figs. 394, 395). Contrast can be introduced by relating large and small forms (figs. 396–99).

In a black-and-white design, a planar form and a linear form establish contrasting tones (figs. 400–402). Contrast of texture happens when some forms display fine details and others are plainly visualized forms (figs. 403–5).

223

394

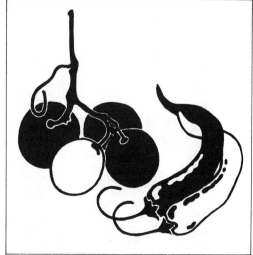

395

224

396

397

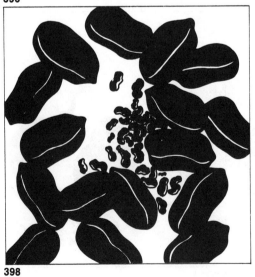

398

399

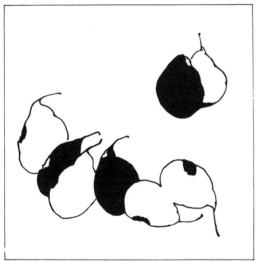

400

401

402

403

Contrast of Placement

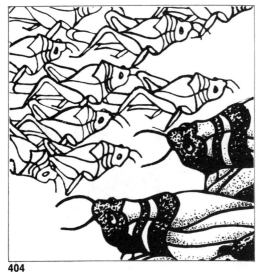
404

Contrast of placement refers to the position, direction, and spatial relationships of forms.

Contrast of position refers to the arrangement of forms within the frame of reference (figs. 406, 407).

Forms arranged in conflicting directions establish contrast (figs. 408, 409). Contrast of direction can also be achieved by rotating forms and presenting different views (fig. 410).

Overlapping forms suggest depth (fig. 411). Forms of varying sizes suggest relative distances (fig. 412).

226

405

406

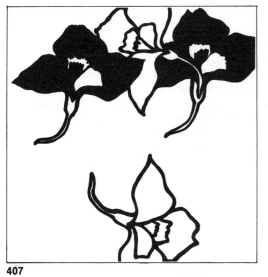

407

408

409

410

Contrast of Quantity

411

Contrast of quantity refers to the density and sparseness of elements in a composition when only one type of unit form is used (fig. 413).

Contrast of quantity as mass and void can be arranged as forms surrounding a blank area, or as forms gathered closely with a surrounding void (figs. 414, 415).

If two types of unit forms are used, fewer instances of one form can be contrasted with many instances of another (figs. 416–19).

412

413

414

415

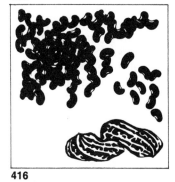

416

417

418

419

COMPOSITIONS WITH ANOMALY

Anomaly in Shape

The combination of regular and irregular elements in a design establishes *anomaly.* Because regular elements are more numerous than irregular ones, anomaly also features contrasting quantities.

Anomaly can be introduced only in formal compositions with a repetition, radiation, or a gradation structure. The strict regularity of the composition makes a slight irregularity prominent.

Anomaly can be effected with the variation of shape, size, color, texture, position, or direction. An anomalous element usually marks the center of interest. Several anomalous elements can acccentuate different aspects of the design. Anomalous elements introduced too frequently lose their distinction as such and are seen as another set of unit forms.

The presence of a form different in shape from the unit forms introduces an anomaly. The shape can be completely different, or have only external and/or internal variations (figs. 420–22).

420

Anomaly in Size

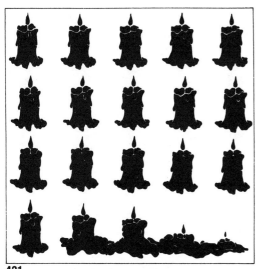

421

A particularly large or small form among unit forms of the same size introduces another type of anomaly. Fitting a large form into the composition might require the removal of some smaller unit forms (fig. 423).

422

423

Anomaly in Color

Anomaly in Texture

One unit form can be changed from a planar shape to a linear shape to introduce anomaly in ''color'' to a black-and-white design (fig. 424).

When one or more unit forms display texture or more details, anomaly in texture results (fig. 425).

232

424

425

Anomaly in Position and Direction

One or more unit forms can be dislocated in a composition, achieving anomaly in position and/or direction (figs. 426–28).

427

426

428

THREE-DIMENSIONAL DESIGN

THREE-DIMENSIONAL DESIGN

CHAPTER 1: INTRODUCTION

The Two-dimensional World

What is a two-dimensional world? The two dimensions are length and breadth. They co-establish a planar surface, on which flat visible marks can be displayed, that has no depth except for an illusory kind. The marks have no thickness and can be either abstract or representational. The surface and the marks taken together reveal a two-dimensional world which differs completely from the world of our day-to-day experience.

The two-dimensional world is essentially a human creation. Drawing, painting, printing, dyeing, or even writing are activities which directly lead to the formation of the two-dimensional world.

Sometimes we may see three-dimensional things two-dimensionally, such as a view we enjoy just because of its sheer pictorial beauty. Today, with the progress of technology, a camera readily transforms everything in front of its lens into a flat picture, and television instantly transmits moving images to a defined surface. Textural marks on smooth natural materials such as stone, wood, etc. also suggest two-dimensional imagery. It is, however, through the human eye that the two-dimensional world gains its significance.

The Three-dimensional World

We live, in fact, in the three-dimensional world. What we see in front of us is not a flat picture with length and breadth only, but an expanse with physical depth, the third dimension. The ground underneath our feet stretches all the way to the distant horizon. We can look straight ahead, look back, look to the left, look to the right, look up, and look down. What we see is a continuum of space in which we are enveloped. There are many objects nearby which we can touch, and objects farther away which are also tangible if we try to reach for them.

Any object that is small, lightweight, and close to us can be picked up and turned around in our hands. Each movement of the object displays a different shape because the relationship between the object and our eyes has changed. If we walk straight ahead into a scene (this is not possible in the two-dimensional world), not only will the objects in the distance gradually become bigger, but their shapes will also change, for we will see more of certain surfaces and less of others.

Our understanding of a three-dimensional object can never be complete at a glance. A view from one fixed angle and distance may be deceptive. A circular shape first seen from some distance away may on closer examination turn out to be a sphere, a cone, a cylinder, or any shape which has a round base. To understand a three-dimensional object, we

237

may have to view it from different angles and distances, and piece the information together in our minds for a complete grasp of its three-dimensional reality. It is through the human mind that the three-dimensional world gains its significance.

Two-dimensional Design

Two-dimensional design refers to the creation of a two-dimensional world with conscious efforts of organization of the various elements. Casual marking such as doodling on a flat surface may have chaotic results. This may be far from two-dimensional design, the main objective of which is to establish visual harmony and order, or to generate purposeful visual excitement.

Two-dimensional design is not within the scope of the present book, but some of its principles will be mentioned when relevant to our discussion.

Three-dimensional Design

Similar to two-dimensional design, three-dimensional design also aims at establishing visual harmony and order, or generating purposeful visual excitement, except that it is concerned with the three-dimensional world. It is more complicated than two-dimensional design because various views must be considered simultaneously from different angles, and much of the complex spatial relationships cannot be easily visualized on paper. Yet it is less complicated than two-dimensional design because it deals with tangible forms and materials in actual space, so that all the problems involving illusory representation of three-dimensional forms on paper (or any kind of flat surface) can be avoided.

Some people are inclined to think sculpturally but many others tend to think pictorially. These people may have some difficulties in three-dimensional design. Often they are so involved with the frontal view of a design they neglect other views. They may find internal structures of three-dimensional forms beyond comprehension, or be easily attracted by surface color and texture when volume and space are more important.

Between two-dimensional thinking and three-dimensional thinking, there is a difference in attitude. A three-dimensional designer should be capable of visualizing mentally the whole form and rotating it mentally in all directions, as if he had it in his hands. He should not confine his image to one or two views, but should thoroughly explore the play of depth and the flow of space, the impact of mass and the nature of different materials.

The Three Primary Directions

To start thinking three-dimensionally we must, first of all, know about the three primary directions. As mentioned earlier, the three dimensions are length, breadth, and depth. In order to obtain the three dimensions of any object, we must take measurements in the vertical, horizontal, and transverse directions.

Thus the three primary directions consist of a vertical direction which goes up and down, a horizontal direction which goes left and right, and a transverse direction which goes forwards and backwards. (Fig. 1)

For each direction we can institute a flat plane. In this way we can have a vertical plane, a horizontal plane, and a transverse plane. (Fig. 2)

Doubling such planes, the vertical plane now becomes the front and rear planes, the horizontal plane the top and bottom planes, and the transverse plane the left and right planes. With these, a cube can be constructed. (Fig. 3)

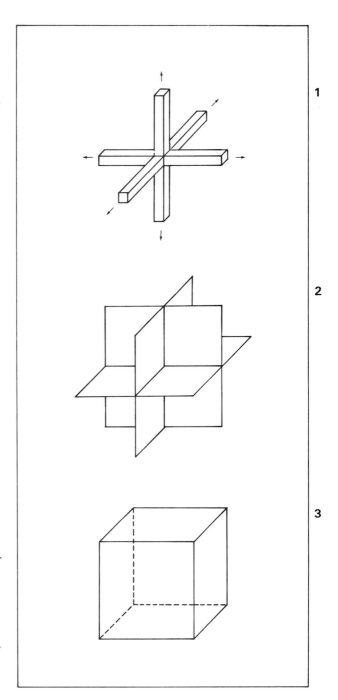

1

2

3

239

4

5

6

7

240

The Three Basic Views

Any three-dimensional form can be placed inside an imaginary cube with which three basic views can be established. (Fig. 4)

By projecting the form onto the top, front, and side planes of an imaginary cube, we can have:

(a) a plane view—view of the form as seen from the top; (Fig. 5)

(b) a front view—view of the form as seen from the front; (Fig. 6)

(c) a side view—view of the form as seen from the side. (Fig. 7)

Each view is a flat diagram, and these views together (occasionally supplemented by auxiliary and/or sectional views) provide the most accurate description of a three-dimensional form, although one needs to have some background knowledge of engineering drawing to be able to reconstruct the original form from these views.

Elements of Three-dimensional Design

In two-dimensional design, there are three sets of elements:

(a) the conceptual elements—point, line, plane, and volume;

(b) the visual elements—shape, size, color, and texture;

(c) the relational elements—position, direction, space, and gravity.

Conceptual elements do not exist physically, but are perceived as being present. Visual elements, of course, can be seen, and constitute the final appearance of a design. Relational elements govern the overall structure and internal correspondences of the visual elements.

All these elements are just as essential for three-dimensional design, although we will define them in a slightly different way, and add a set of constructional elements for practical reasons. The constructional elements are, in fact, concrete realizations of the conceptual elements and will be indispensable in our future discussions.

Conceptual Elements

A three-dimensional design can be conceived in the mind before it takes on physical shape. The design is thus defined by the following conceptual elements:

(a) point—a conceptual point indicates position in space. It has no length, breadth, or depth. It marks the two ends of a line, the single place where lines intersect, and the meeting of lines at a corner of a plane or the angle of a solid form. (Fig. 8)

(b) line—as a point moves, its path becomes a line. A conceptual line has length but no breadth or depth. It has position and direction. It de-

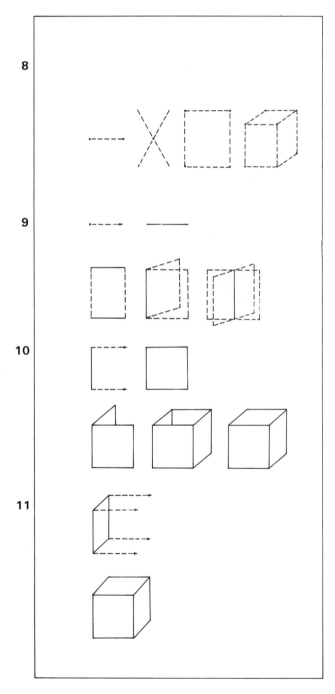

8

9

10

11

242

fines the border of a plane, and marks the place where two planes join or intersect each other. (Fig. 9)

(c) plane—the path of a line in motion (in a direction other than its own intrinsic direction) becomes a plane. A conceptual plane has length and breadth but no depth. It is bound by lines. It defines the external limits of a volume. (Fig. 10)

(d) volume—the path of a plane in motion (in a direction other than its own intrinsic direction) becomes a volume. A conceptual volume has length, breadth, and depth, but no weight. It defines the amount of space contained or displaced by the volume. (Fig. 11)

It is important to note that many of our three-dimensional ideas are first visualized on a flat piece of paper. We usually use a fine line to indicate the border of a plane or volume. This line is visual as it appears on the two-dimensional surface, but is conceptual when its only use is as a means of representing a three-dimensional form.

Visual Elements

Three-dimensional forms are seen differently from different angles and distances and under different lighting conditions. Therefore, we must consider the following visual elements to be independent of such variable situations:

(a) shape—shape is the outward appearance of a design

and the main identification of its type. A three-dimensional form can be rendered on a flat surface by multiple two-dimensional shapes, and we must be aware of this to be able to visually relate all such different aspects to the same form. (Fig. 12)

(b) size—size is not just greatness or smallness, length or brevity, which can only be established by way of comparison. Size is also concrete measurement, and can be measured on any three-dimensional form in terms of length, breadth, and depth (or height, width, and thickness) from which its volume can be calculated. (Fig. 13)

(c) color—color, or light and dark value, is what most clearly distinguishes a form from its environment, and it can be natural or artificial. When it is natural, the original color of the material is presented. When it is artificial, the original color of the material is covered up by a coat of paint, or transformed by treating with some other method. (Fig. 14)

(d) texture—texture refers to the surface characteristics of the material used in the design. It may be naturally unadorned or specially treated. It may be smooth, rough, matt, or glossy as determined by the designer. It may be small-scale texture that accents two-dimensional surface decoration or bolder texture that accents three-dimensional tactility. (Fig. 15)

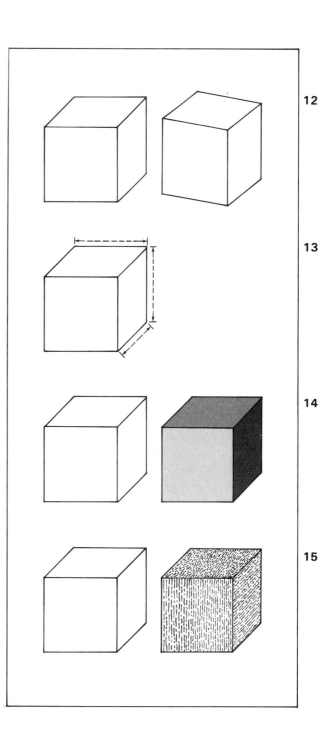

12

13

14

15

243

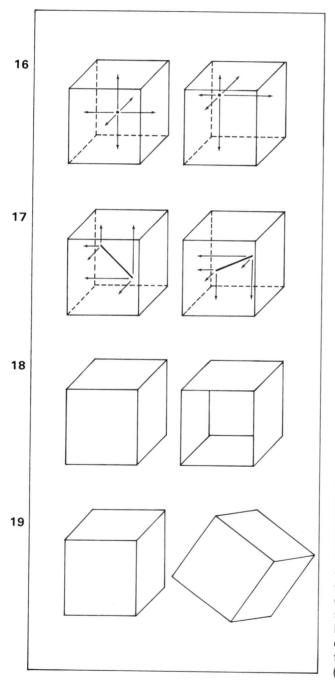

16

17

18

19

244

Relational Elements

Relational elements are more complicated in three-dimensional design than in two-dimensional design. Whereas in two-dimensional design a frame of reference is used, in three-dimensional design we can use an imaginary cube to establish the relationships.

(a) position—position must be ascertained by more than one of the three basic views. We have to know how a point is related to the front/rear, top/bottom, and side planes of the imaginary cube. (Fig. 16)

(b) direction—direction, too, should be seen from more than one view. A line could be parallel to the front/rear planes but oblique to all other planes of the imaginary cube. (Fig. 17)

(c) space—space here is, of course, actual and not illusory. It can be seen as positively occupied, unoccupied, or internally hollowed. (Fig. 18)

(d) gravity—gravity is real and has a constant effect on the stability of the design. We cannot have forms in mid-air without supporting, hanging, or anchoring them in some way. Some materials are heavy and some are light. The material used determines the weight of the form as well as its capacity to bear gravitational loads of other forms on top of it. All three-dimensional structures are subject to the laws of gravity and this means certain arrangements and positioning are just not possible. (Fig. 19)

Constructional Elements

Constructional elements have strong structural qualities and are particularly important for the understanding of geometric solids. These elements are used to indicate the geometric components of three-dimensional design:

(a) vertex—when several planes come to one conceptual point, we have a vertex. Vertices can be projected outward or inward. (Fig. 20)

(b) edge—when two nonparallel planes are joined together along one conceptual line, an edge is produced. Again edges may be projected outward or inward. (Fig. 21)

(c) face—a conceptual plane which is physically present becomes a surface. Faces are external surfaces which enclose a volume. (Fig. 22)

Ideally all vertices should be sharp and pointed, all edges should be sharp and straight, and all faces should be smooth and flat. In reality this depends on the materials and techniques, and certain minor irregularities are normally unavoidable.

Constructional elements can help to precisely define volumetric forms. For example, a cube has eight vertices, twelve edges, and six faces.

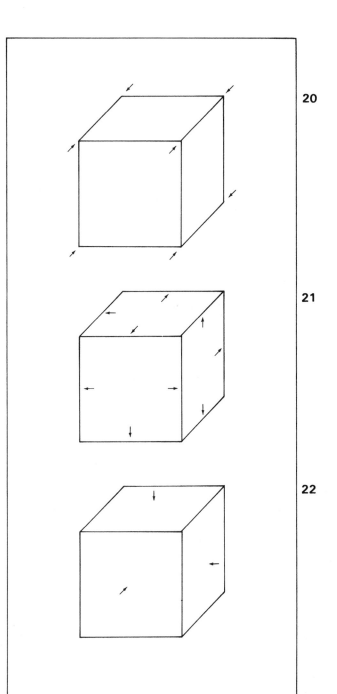

20

21

22

Form and Structure

Form is a term easily confused with *shape.* Earlier it was pointed out that a three-dimensional form can have multiple two-dimensional shapes when rendered on a flat surface (see Fig. 12). This means that shape is really only one aspect of form. When a form is rotated in space, each step of rotation reveals a slightly different shape, because a different aspect is seen by our eyes.

Form, then, is the total visual appearance of a design, although shape is its main identifying factor. We also identify form by size, color, and texture. In other words, all the visual elements are referred to collectively as form.

Structure governs the way a form is built, or the way a number of forms are put together. It is overall spatial organization, the skeleton beneath the fabric of shape, color, and texture. The external appearance of a form can be rather complex, while its structure is relatively simple. Sometimes the internal structure of a form may not be immediately perceived. Once this is discovered, the form can be better understood and appreciated.

Unit Forms

Smaller forms which are repeated, with or without variations, to produce a larger form are referred to as *unit forms.* Sometimes these repeated units are called *modules.*

A unit form may be made of even smaller components, which can be called *sub-unit forms.*

A larger unit may be made of two or more unit forms in a constant relationship that appears frequently in a design. They are called *super-unit forms.*

Repetition and Gradation

Unit forms can be used in exact repetition or in gradation.

Repetition means that the unit forms are identical in shape, size, color, and texture. Shape is the most important visual element of unit forms, so that we can have unit forms repeated in shape but not in size. Color and texture can vary if desired, but they are not within the scope of this book.

Gradation means transformation or change in a gradual, orderly manner. Here the sequential arrangement is very important, otherwise the order of gradation cannot be recognized.

We can have gradation in shape, with the shape changing slightly from one unit to the next, or gradation in size, with the units repeated or graduated in shape.

CHAPTER 2: SERIAL PLANES

Points determine a line. Lines determine a plane. Planes determine a volume.

A line can be represented by a series of points. (Fig. 23)

A plane can be represented by a series of lines. (Fig. 24)

A volume can be represented by a series of planes. (Fig. 25)

When a volume is represented by a series of planes, each plane is a cross section of the volume.

Serial Planes

Thus, to construct a volumetric form, we can think in terms of its cross sections, or how the form can be sliced up at regular intervals, which will result in serial planes.

Each serial plane can be considered as a unit form which may be used either in repetition or in gradation.

As mentioned, repetition refers to repeating both shape and size of the unit forms. (Fig. 26)

Gradation refers to gradual variation of the unit form, and it can be used in three different ways:

(a) gradation of size but repetition of shape; (Fig. 27)

(b) gradation of shape but repetition of size; (Fig. 28)

(c) gradation of both shape and size. (Fig. 29)

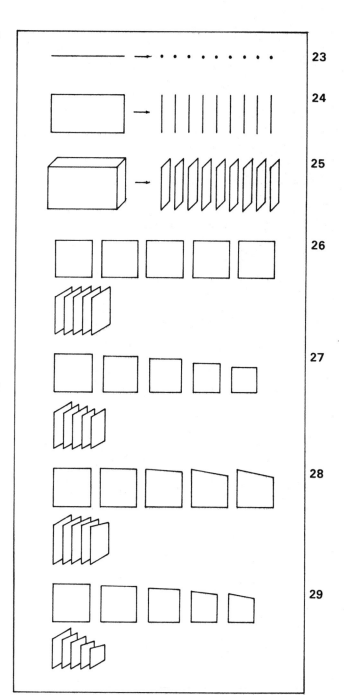

23

24

25

26

27

28

29

247

Dissection of a Cube

To illustrate a bit further, we can dissect a cube into a number of thin planes of the same thickness.

The simplest way is to dissect along the length, breadth, or depth, in parallel layers. As a result, a number of serial planes are obtained which are repeats in both shape and size (Fig. 30).

The same cube can also be dissected diagonally. There are many ways to do this. Our diagram here shows a kind of diagonal dissection resulting in serial planes with gradation of shape. Size is gradational too. The height remains constant, but the breadth increases or decreases gradually. (Fig. 31)

It should be pointed out that in dissection along the length, breadth, or depth all serial planes have squared edges. (Fig. 32)

In diagonal dissection, all serial planes have bevelled edges. (Fig. 33)

The edges may not be of much significance if the planes are extremely thin, but if they are thick, influences of the edges on the design should not be overlooked.

In arranging serial planes, the relational elements should be taken into consideration. The two main relational elements which must not be neglected are position and direction.

Positional Variations

Position has to do with, first of all, spacing of the planes. If no directional variations are introduced, all the serial planes will be parallel to one another, each following the next successively, with equal spacing between them.

Let us assume that all the planes are squares of the same size. If one plane follows another in a straight manner, then the two vertical edges of the planes trace two parallel straight lines, with a width the same as the breadth of the planes. (Fig. 34)

Spacing between the planes can be made narrow or wide, with different effects. Narrow spacing gives the form a greater feeling of solidity, whereas wide spacing weakens the suggestion of volume. (Fig. 35)

Without changing the spacing between the planes, the position of each plane can be shifted gradually towards one side or back and forth. This causes the volumetric shape to undergo various distortions. (Fig. 36)

Again without changing the spacing between the planes, the position of each plane can be shifted gradually upwards or downwards. This can be easily done if the planes are hung or supported in midair. (Fig. 37)

If the planes are placed on a baseboard, we can reduce the height of the planes to suggest the effect of their gradual sinking-in just by positional variation in a vertical manner. (Fig. 38)

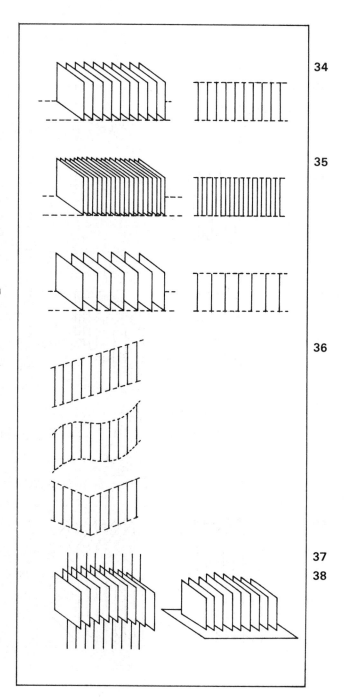

34

35

36

37

38

249

Directional Variations

Direction of the planes can be varied in three different ways:

(a) rotation on a vertical axis; (Fig. 39)

(b) rotation on a horizontal axis; (Fig. 40)

(c) rotation on its own plane. (Fig. 41)

Rotation on a vertical axis requires a diversion of the planes from parallel arrangement. Position is definitely affected, because every directional change simultaneously demands positional change.

The planes in this case can be arranged in radiation, forming a circular shape. (Fig. 42)

Or they can form a shape with curves left and right. (Fig. 43)

Rotation on a horizontal axis cannot be done if the planes are fixed on a horizontal baseboard. If they are fixed on a vertical baseboard, their rotation on a horizontal axis would be essentially the same as the rotation on a vertical axis described above.

Rotation on its own plane means that the corners or edges of each plane are moved from one position to another without affecting the basic direction of the plane itself. This results in a spirally twisted shape. (Fig. 44)

The planes can be physically curled or bent if desired. (Fig. 45)

Construction Techniques

Any kind of sheet material can be used for making serial planes. Acrylic sheets are excellent when a transparent effect is desired. Plywood boards can be used for construction in a very large scale. Most of the models shown in this chapter have been made of thick cardboard, which can be handled easily. The thickness of the cardboard ensures firm adhesion to the baseboard if there is one.

For cardboard construction, adhesives that give a quick, strong bond are the best. The serial planes should stand in a vertical position on the horizontal baseboard for maximum firmness and stability. Tilted planes are possible only when the materials and the bond are both extremely strong, and the joining edge of each plane is precisely bevelled. (Fig. 46)

For reinforcement purposes, additional plane(s) can be used next to the top or side edges of the planes. This is recommended only when those edges of the planes play a rather insignificant role in the final shape of the design. (Fig. 47)

Horizontally arranged serial planes demand a very strong bond if only one vertical board is used for attachment. (Fig. 48)

Normally two or more vertical boards should be used for horizontal serial planes. (Fig. 49)

A vertical supporting core can be used for horizontal serial planes of a free-standing shape if desired. (Fig. 50)

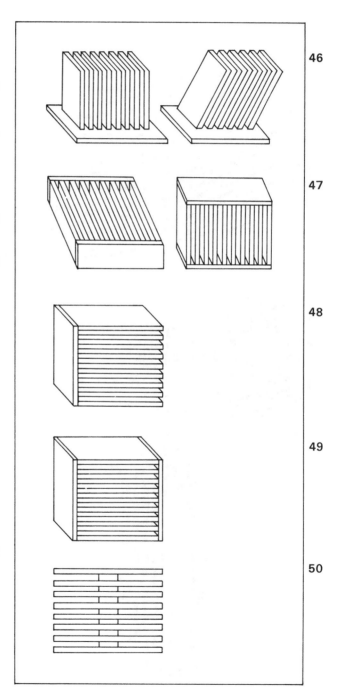

46

47

48

49

50

51

Figures 51 to 66 all illustrate the same design problem in projects by different students.

Figure 51—this is constructed of horizontal serial planes which are repeated both in shape and size. The planes are all parallel to one another with equal spacing in between, and they are anchored to two vertical planes.

Figure 52—here a number of repetitive vertical planes are placed around a common vertical axis. The result is a cylindrical shape.

Figure 53—the arrangement is similar to Figure 52. Here the serial planes increase gradually in height from the foreground to the background. The volumetric feeling of the form is not very strong because the spacing between planes is rather wide along the circumference of the shape.

52

54

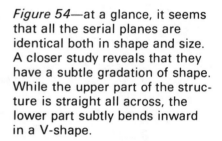

Figure 54—at a glance, it seems that all the serial planes are identical both in shape and size. A closer study reveals that they have a subtle gradation of shape. While the upper part of the structure is straight all across, the lower part subtly bends inward in a V-shape.

Figure 55—with a straight plane standing in the middle of the structure, all other planes are bent in increasingly sharper angles. The volumetric form suggested here is an emerging spherical shape.

55

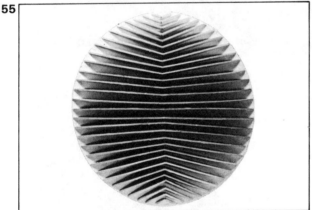

Figure 56—this shows the effective use of gradation of shape. Each plane is obtained by the combination of a positive rectangular shape and a negative circular shape. The former has a constant width but the latter grows bigger and bigger and moves gradually downward and forward. The straight edges of the rectangular shape remain straight at the front but those at the rear change gradually into sweeping curves to echo the negative circular shapes.

56

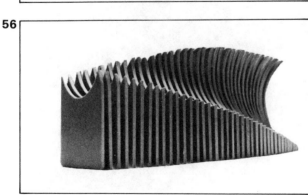

Figure 57—this is a triangular structure which is the result of gradation of both shape and size of the serial planes. The short, wide V-shaped planes at the two sides become tall and narrow towards the middle by gradation of size and shape.

Figure 58—circular planes of exactly the same size and shape have been used in this structure. The sinking-in effect of the planes on the backboard is due to positional variation. The two loops which make the general shape very much like the numeral 8 are the result of directional variation.

Figure 59—the use of gradation of shape is quite obvious here, and gives the feeling of planes emerging from or sinking into the baseboard.

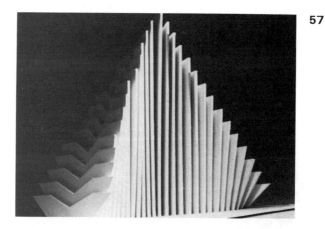

57

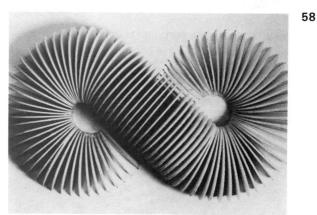

58

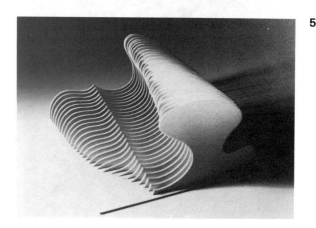

59

255

60

Figure 60—gradation of shape is used here in a rather complicated way. The form rises from the baseboard in high relief, but it splits up in the center to reveal another form within the deep concavity.

Figure 61—this is a free-standing form with a projecting semi-sphere in the front and another in the back. Both semi-spheres have a concave portion, inside of which a smaller semi-sphere is nested. The effect is similar to Figure 60.

Figure 62—the play of concavity and convexity here is the same as in Figure 60.

Figure 63—here the semi-spherical shape has been cut into two parts, and the shape of each part is further modified. A prominent negative shape now becomes the focal point of the design.

61

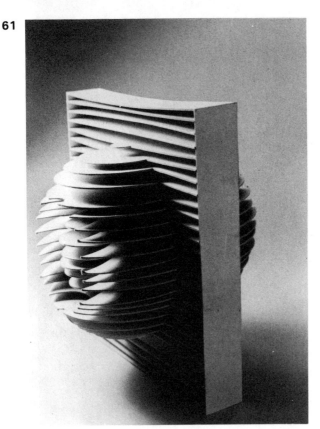

62

63

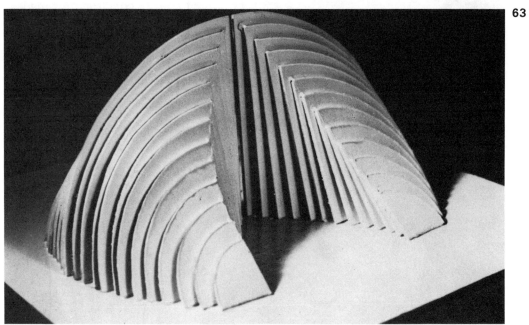

64

Figure 64—in this form, gradation of shape is used in combination with directional variation. Note the introduction of a negative shape which runs like a tunnel at the lower part of the design.

Figure 65—all the planes in this structure are repetitive in shape and size, but are arranged in a slightly zigzag manner by positional variation. This zigzag arrangement echoes the shapes of the planes themselves. The result is an interesting shape with faceted faces and identical front, rear, left, and right views.

65

Figure 66—this not only has identical views from four sides, but from top and bottom also. Each of the six views displays the letter X in the same shape and size. To construct this, negative shapes are introduced into square serial planes which are all repetitive in size. Some are repetitive in shape and some are graduated in shape.

66

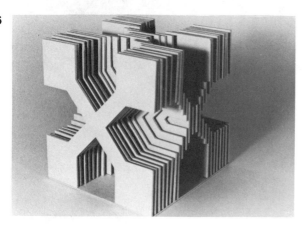

CHAPTER 3: WALL STRUCTURES

Cube, Column, and Wall

Starting with a cube, we can place a second cube above and a third cube below it. (Fig. 67)

Now we have a column of three cubes that can be extended in either direction to include any desired number of cubes. (Fig. 68)

The column can also be repeated left and right. When a number of columns are erected, one adjacent to another, we have a wall. The wall structure is basically two-dimensional. The cube has been repeated in two directions, first in the vertical direction and then in the horizontal direction.

Each cube is a spatial cell in the wall structure. These spatial cells are arranged two-dimensionally on a frontal plane. (Fig. 69)

All formal two-dimensional structures can become wall structures with the addition of some depth, and their structural sub-divisions can be made into spatial cells. (Fig. 70)

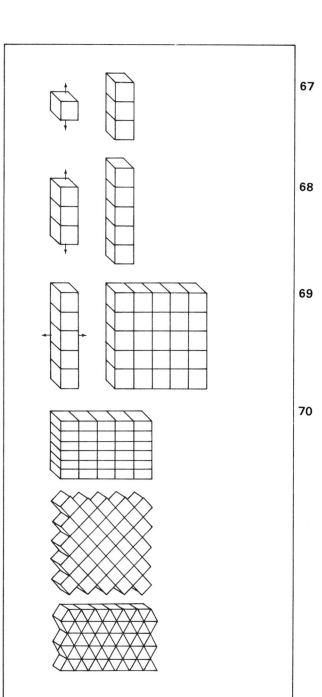

67

68

69

70

71

72

73

74

75
76

77
78

79
80

Spatial Cells and Unit Forms

To explore the various possibilities of making wall structures, we can first bend a strip of thin cardboard or glue four pieces of thick cardboard together to form a cube without the front and rear planes. (Fig. 71)

This is our simplest spatial cell. We can see through it and place a unit form inside. The unit form can be as simple as a flat plane used repetitively or with slight variations. (Fig. 72)

As a planar shape, the unit form can be positive or negative. (Fig. 73)

It can be a combination of two positive shapes or one positive and one negative. (Fig. 74)

Unit forms can be used in gradation of shape if desired. (Fig. 75)

Gradation of size can be effected by:

(a) enlarging or reducing proportionately; (Fig. 76)

(b) changing of width only; (Fig. 77)

(c) changing of height only; (Fig. 78)

If the unit form is a combination of two smaller shapes, size of one can be kept constant while size of the other varies. (Fig. 79) Or both shapes can vary in different ways. (Fig. 80)

Positional Variations of Unit Forms

Variations of positioning of the unit forms can be accomplished by:

(a) moving the shape forward or backward; (Fig. 81)

(b) moving the shape up or down; (Fig. 82)

(c) moving the shape left or right; (Fig. 83)

(d) reducing the height or width of the shape to suggest the feeling of its sinking into one of the enclosing planes. (Fig. 84)

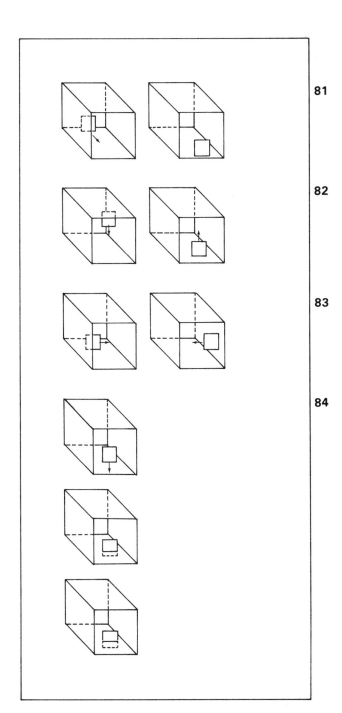

81

82

83

84

Directional Variations of Unit Forms

Inside each spatial cell, the unit form can be rotated in any direction desired. During each step of rotation, it will be seen differently from the front.

Let us observe the effects of rotating a square shape. In Figures 85 to 88, the first vertical column represents the front views, the second vertical column the side views, and the third vertical column the plane views.

Rotation on the shape's own plane does not change the shape at all in the front view. The side view of the shape is always a line. The plane view of the shape is also always a line. (Fig. 85)

Rotation along a vertical axis makes the square shape, in the front view, which becomes a narrower and narrower oblong that decreases finally to a line. In the side view it is first a line which gradually becomes a square. In the plane view, the shape remains a line of constant length that varies in direction. (Fig. 86)

Rotation along a horizontal axis is very similar to rotation along a vertical axis. The shape remains a line of constant length, not in the plane view, but in the side view. (Fig. 87)

Rotation along a diagonal axis leads to more complicated results. In the front view, the square is transformed into a diagonal line after a series of graduated parallelograms. Different shapes of parallelograms are also seen in the side and plane views. (Fig. 88)

85

86

87

88

262

Unit Forms as Distorted Planes

If greater three-dimensional effects are desirable, unit forms can depart from the character- istics of a flat plane. Two or more flat planes can be used for the construction of one unit form, or a simple flat plane can be treated in the following ways to become a unit form:

   (a) by curling; (Fig. 89)

   (b) by bending along one or more straight lines; (Fig. 90)

   (c) by bending along one or more curved lines; (Fig. 91)

   (d) by cutting and curling; (Fig. 92)

   (e) by cutting and bending. (Fig. 93)

Wall Structures Not Remaining Flat

When one spatial cell is placed on another, the flat frontality of the wall structure can be made slightly more three-dimensional by posi- tional variation. (Fig. 94)

   A similar effect can be obtained by varying the depths of the spatial cells. (Fig. 95)

   Directional variation in the ar- rangement of the spatial cells is possible but must be done with care, as too much rotation may make the side planes of the spatial cells too prominent.

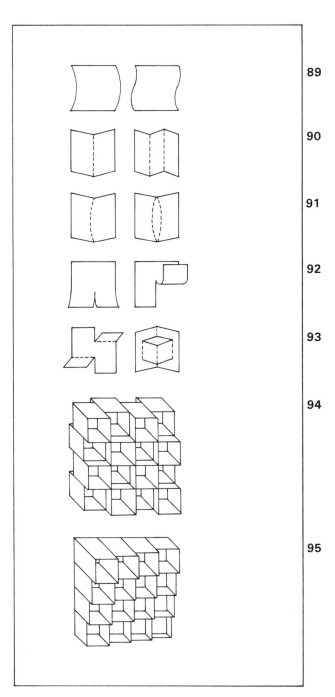

89

90

91

92

93

94

95

96

97

98

99

100

Modifications of Spatial Cells

Greater three-dimensional quality can be achieved by the modification of spatial cells.

Enclosing planes of the spatial cells can be trimmed so that some of the front edges are not perpendicular to the base or side planes. (Fig. 96)

The straight edges of the spatial cells can be changed to curvilinear edges. (Fig. 97)

The enclosing planes of the spatial cells can be constructed so they are not at right angles to one another. (Fig. 98)

The spatial cells can be so designed that they are part of the unit form structure. (Fig. 99)

The spatial cells can become the unit forms, or we can have unit forms to erect a wall structure without the use of spatial cells. (Fig. 100)

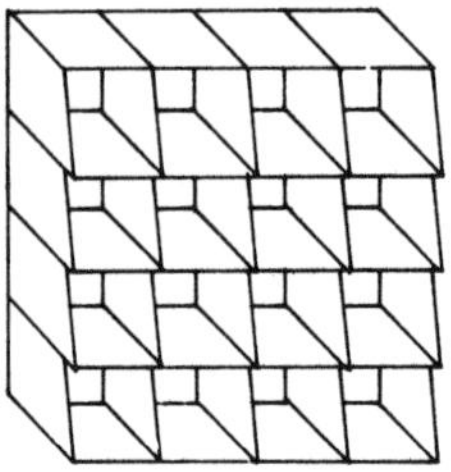

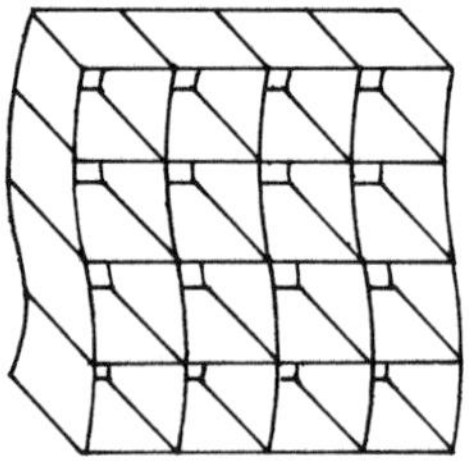

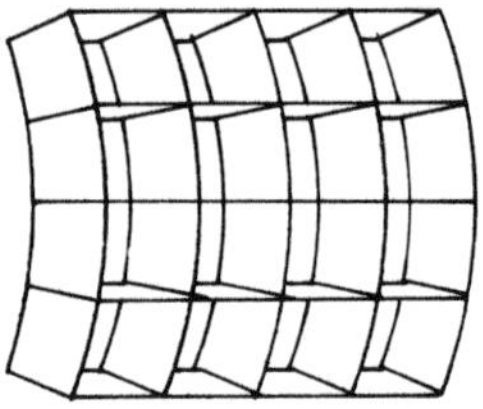

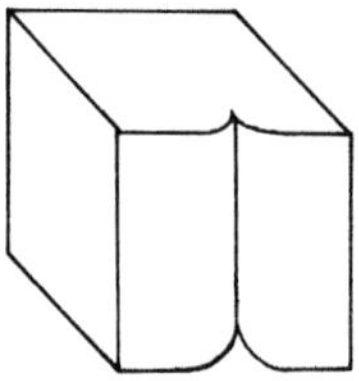

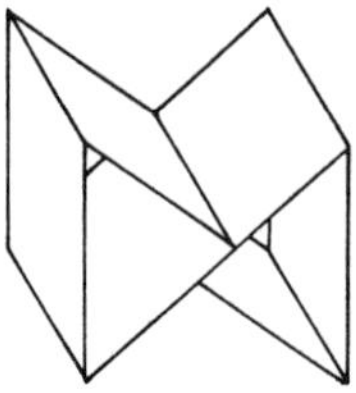

Figures 101 to 113 are examples of student projects solving the design problem of creating wall structures.

Figure 101—spatial cells here are arranged with slight positional variation. The linear unit forms are, in fact, part of the enclosing planes of the spatial cells which have been treated in a way similar to Figure 93.

Figure 102—unit forms are cut-out shapes from the enclosing planes of the spatial cells. They are interlocked in an interesting way. Spatial cells are made of cardboard cubes with top and bottom planes missing, and therefore they become parallelograms in the plane view when the side edges are pulled by the interlocking unit forms.

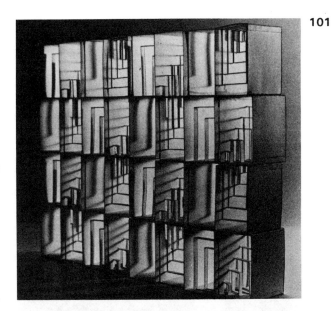

101

102

103

Figure 103—spatial cells here are specially constructed in a way very much like Figure 99. Triangular negative shapes are made on the curled planes. The result gives a tactile feeling of texture after the spatial cells have been repeated many times.

Figure 104—interpenetrating spatial cells are here arranged with some positional variation. The interpenetrated areas have been distorted by cutting and bending, but no separate unit forms are introduced in the spatial cells.

104

Figure 105—similar to Figure 101, unit forms here are strips cut and folded inward from the side planes of spatial cells. Some parts of the side planes have been removed. The whole design has a transparent effect with delicate linear elements.

Figure 106—spatial cells have been so greatly transformed that they become unit forms that are very linear in character. The depth of the design is shallow, but it contains a large number of tilted planes in various directions.

105

106

267

107

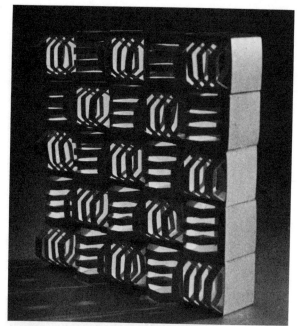

Figure 107—unit forms are placed in each spatial cell with slight projection from the front plane of the wall structure.

Figure 108—spatial cell and unit form are one and the same in this design. Triangular planes instead of square planes have been used in the construction.

108

Figure 109—again, the spatial cells also serve as the unit forms. The arrangement shows a gradation of cylindrical shapes. As contact between curved surfaces is rather restricted, the whole wall structure is quite flexible and can be curled at will.

Figure 110—the faceted surface of this structure has a relief effect. This is achieved by cutting, scoring and folding of flat continuous planes.

109

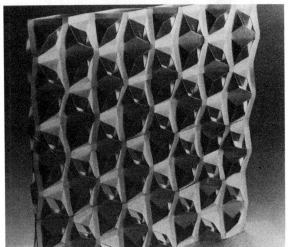

110

111

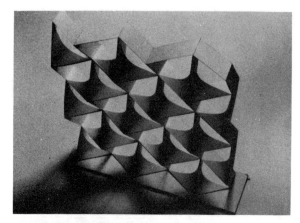

Figure 111—each spatial cell is triangular. The unit form inside it is a piece of curled plane joining two edges of the spatial cell.

Figure 112—a strip of thin cardboard is folded three times to form a spatial cell which is also the unit form. In folding, the beginning and the ending of the strip do not overlap, but instead the right edge of the beginning of the strip touches the left edge of the ending of the strip. This causes a slight twist of the planes in the resulting form.

112

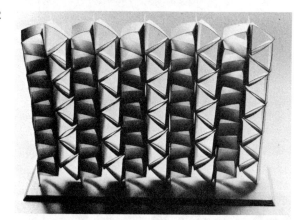

Figure 113—the spatial cells are cubical and arranged one directly above or adjacent to the next. The unit forms are made of curled strips of thin cardboard.

113

CHAPTER 4: PRISMS AND CYLINDERS

The Basic Prism and Its Variations

As we have seen in the last chapter, a number of cubes placed one directly above the other makes a column. This is actually also the shape of a prism.

A prism is a form with ends which are similar, equal, and parallel rectilinear figures, and with sides which are rectangles or parallelograms. For the sake of convenience, we can have a basic prism which has parallel square ends and rectangular sides that are all perpendicular to the ends. (Fig. 114)

From this basic prism, the following variations can be developed:

(a) the square ends can be changed to triangular, polygonal, or irregularly-shaped ends; (Fig. 115)

(b) the two ends can be non-parallel to one another; (Fig. 116)

(c) the ends do not have to be of the same shape, size, and/or direction; (Fig. 117)

(d) the ends do not have to be flat planes; (Fig. 118)

(e) the edges do not have to be perpendicular to the ends; (Fig. 119)

(f) the edges do not have to be parallel to one another; (Fig. 120)

(g) the body of the prism can be curved or bent; (Fig. 121)

(h) the edges of the prism can be curved or bent. (Fig. 122)

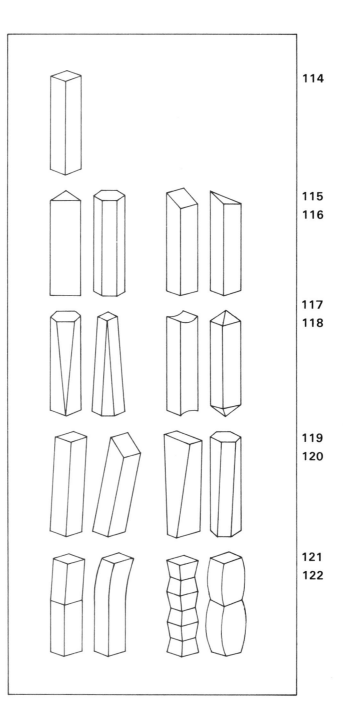

114

115
116

117
118

119
120

121
122

271

123

124

125

126

272

127

The Hollowed Prism

If the prism is not of solid material, but constructed of cardboard, then variations and transformations can be even more complicated.

Let us make a hollowed prism by using one sheet of thin cardboard which is scored, folded, and glued together. The ends of this prism are open, without covering planes. (Fig. 123)

Ends, edges, and faces of this prism can all be treated in special ways.

Treatment of the Ends

The ends of the hollowed prism can be treated in one or more of the following ways:

(a) the ends may be covered up, but instead of using a flat continuous plane for each end, we can have planes containing negative shapes; (Fig. 124)

(b) the edges or faces near the two ends can be cut into different shapes, and the resulting loose pieces can be curled or folded if necessary; (Fig. 125)

(c) the ends can be split into two or more sections; (Fig. 126)

(d) a specially designed shape can be formed on or attached to the ends. (Fig. 127)

Treatment of the Edges

Treatment of the edges usually affects the faces as well. Diversion from parallel edges not only changes the rectangularity of the shapes of the faces, but sometimes leads to warped or faceted faces which can be very interesting. Ends of the prisms may also be affected.

Our illustrations here show the following treatments:

(a) nonparallel straight edges; (Fig. 128)

(b) wavy edges; (Fig. 129)

(c) chain of rhombic shapes along the edges; (Fig. 130)

(d) circular shapes developed along the parallel straight edges; (Fig. 131)

(e) intersecting edges; (Fig. 132)

(f) complicated pattern scored on the surface of the thin cardboard before it is folded to form a prism. Some of the lines of the pattern are also the edges of the prism. (Fig. 133)

Other edge treatments may be just simple subtraction or addition of shapes along the edges.

In subtraction, negative shapes are introduced along the edges.

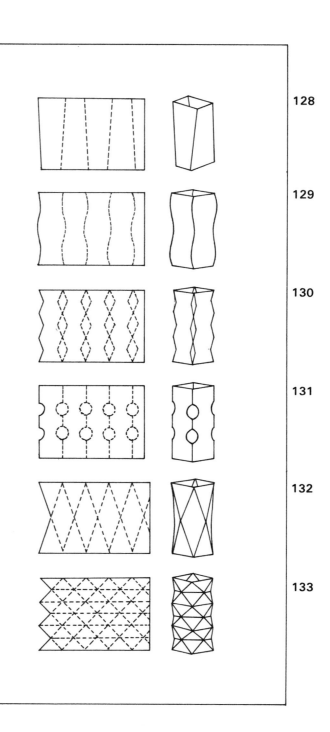

128

129

130

131

132

133

273

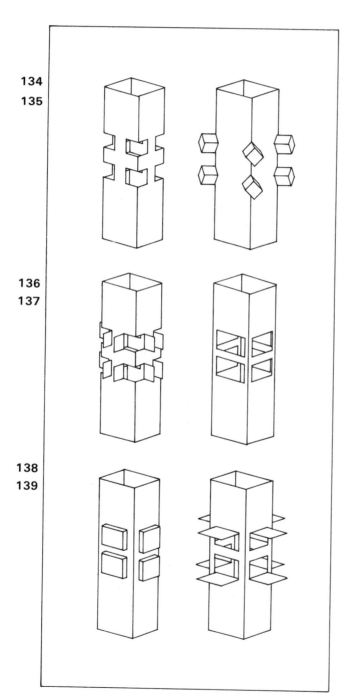

134
135

136
137

138
139

As each edge is the joining of two faces, negative shapes are made by cutting away some parts of both of these adjacent faces. (Fig. 134)

In addition, separately made shapes are attached to the edges. Such shapes may cover or intrude a little bit on the adjacent faces unless the shapes are strictly planar in nature. (Fig. 135)

It is possible to have lines cut and scored or shapes partially cut along the edges and on the adjacent faces. By bending such shapes inwards (or sometimes outwards as well) without detaching them, a play of positive and negative forms is created. (Fig. 136)

Treatment of the Faces

Face treatment is very much the same as edge treatment.

In subtraction, holes are made on the faces. Any negative shape which does not lead to loose parts or weakening of the structure can be used. (Fig. 137)

Addition allows any shape with a flat base to be adhered to the flat faces. Additional shapes can always be fitted to negative shapes on the faces. (Fig. 138)

Half-cut shapes can always remain hinged or folded in and out on the faces of the prism. (Fig. 139)

Joining of Prisms

Two or more prisms can be used in one design by joining them in various ways.

Joining can be done easily by

face contact, whether the prisms are parallel or not parallel. The bond in this case is very strong as long as the glue is strong. (Fig. 140)

Edge contact is weaker because the area along the edges on which glue can be applied is very limited. In cardboard construction, it is possible that the face of one prism can be extended to form the face of another prism, in which case the strength of the face plane will be the strength of the bond. If the cardboard is thin, one prism is really hinged on the other one and the joint is a flexible one. (Fig. 141)

End contact doubles the height of the prism. In this case, there should be flat planes covering the ends, and the joining is actually done by adhesion of one plane to another, as in face contact. (Fig. 142)

The end of one prism can be joined to the face of another, making a T shape or L shape. If the ends of the prisms are mitred, an L shape can also be formed. (Fig. 143)

Two crossed prisms can be interlocked if the body of one prism is fitted into the body of another. (Fig. 144)

We can construct two crossed prisms which are integrally united to one another by constructing some of the double faces out of the same piece of cardboard. (Fig. 145)

Union of a number of prisms joined at the ends can lead to a framelike structure or a structure with linear continuity. (Fig. 146)

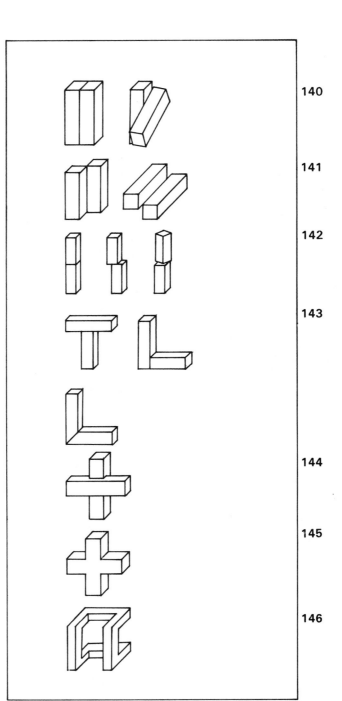

140

141

142

143

144

145

146

147

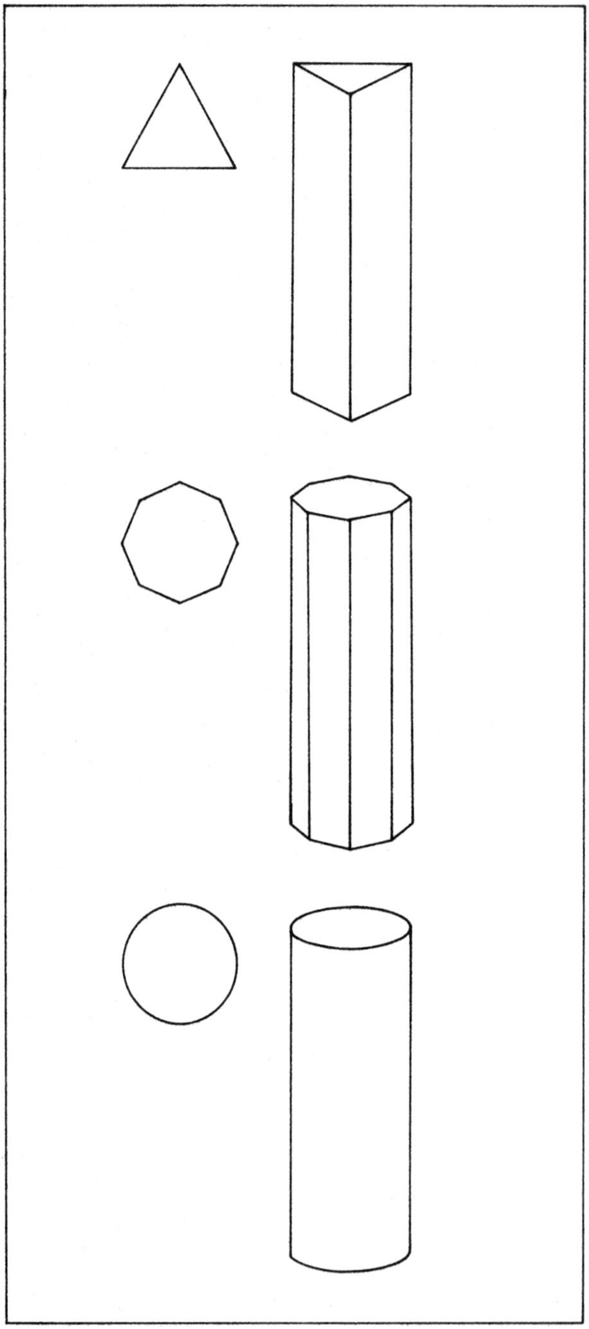

The Prism and the Cylinder

The minimum number of flat planes we can use for the sides of a prism is three, which results in a prism with a triangular top and bottom.

If we increase the number of sides in the prism, the top and bottom shapes will change from triangles to polygons. The more sides a polygon has, the less angular and closer to circular it becomes. For instance, an octagon is much less angular than a triangle, and thus an octagonal prism has a much rounder body than a triangular one.

By increasing the number of sides of a polygon infinitely, a circle may finally be reached. In the same way, by increasing the number of sides of a prism infinitely, a cylinder may finally be created. (Fig. 147)

The body of a cylinder is defined by one continuous plane, without beginning or end, and the top or bottom of a cylinder is in the shape of a circle.

Variations of a Cylinder

We may say that the standard cylinder consists of two parallel circular ends of the same size and a body perpendicular to the ends. From the standard, the following deviations are possible:

(a) the body can be slanting; (Fig. 148)

(b) the ends can be of any round-cornered shape; (Fig. 149)

(c) the ends can be nonparallel to each other; (Fig. 150)

(d) the ends can be of different sizes or shapes; (Fig. 151)

(e) the body can be bent; (Fig. 152)

(f) the body can expand or contract at intervals. (Fig. 153)

End and face treatments can be applied to the cylinder in the same way as they are applied to the prism.

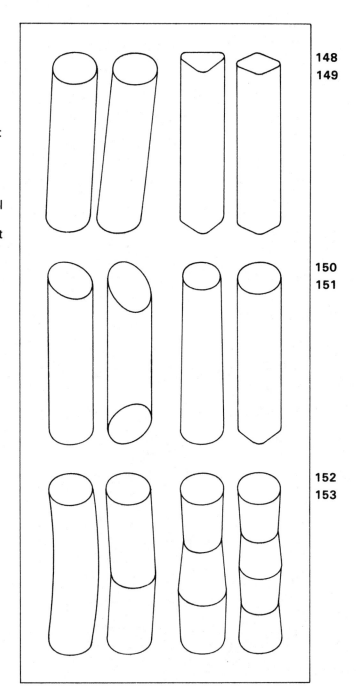

148
149

150
151

152
153

277

154

Figures 154 to 163 all illustrate different approaches in the use of prisms. Figure 157 is a single prism with surface treatment of the body and the faces, the other projects all explore possibilities of using prisms as unit forms in design.

Figure 154—numerous square prisms of varying heights have been used. Note that near the lower ends, the faces of many of the prisms have been trimmed into circular shapes.

Figure 155—this spiral design is made of a number of triangular prisms which rise gradually in height. The lower ends of the taller prisms have been shaped to produce an area of cavity for the accommodation of the shorter prisms which mark the beginning of the upward spiral.

155

Figure 156—this is another view of the same design illustrated in Figure 155.

Figure 157—the body shape of this prism has been much transformed. Face treatment also reveals some negative circular shapes in the inner layer of the construction.

156

157

158

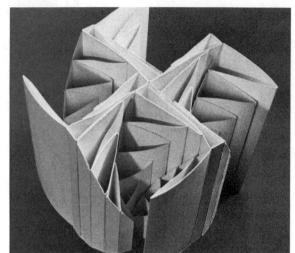

Figure 158—four sets of triangular prisms in gradation of size and shape have been used in this design.

Figure 159—this consists of three concentric layers. The innermost layer has the tallest but also narrowest prisms. The outermost layer has the shortest but biggest prisms.

159

Figure 160—this is constructed of seven prisms, all of which are bent sharply near the bottom, while also treated on the faces with zigzag patterns.

160

161

Figure 161—each prism is actually a wedge shape constructed of four elongated isosceles (equal-legged) triangles and has two flat-tipped ends. The spiral construction is the result of gluing a number of such prisms together by face contact.

Figure 162—triangular planes have also been used for the prisms in this design. Each prism consists of six triangular planes, and the ends are in triangular shapes which are open and not covered. The construction is made by edge and end contact.

162

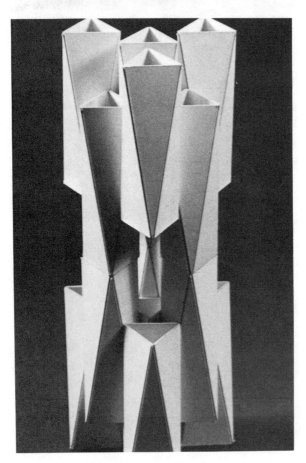

Figure 163—prisms used in this
design have been constructed
of three triangular planes and
one rectangular plane. The lower
end of each prism is in a triangular shape, but the top end is
only a slit opening between two
planes. The prisms are arranged
in a fanlike manner.

163

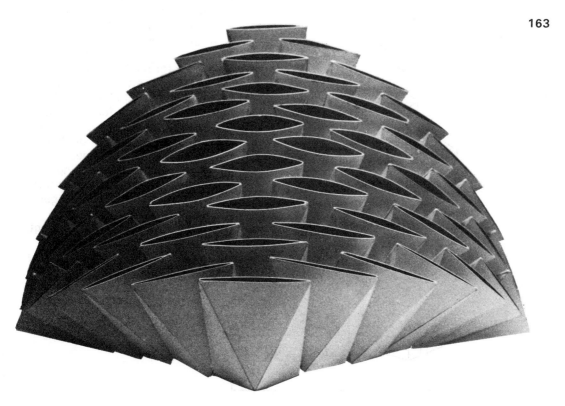

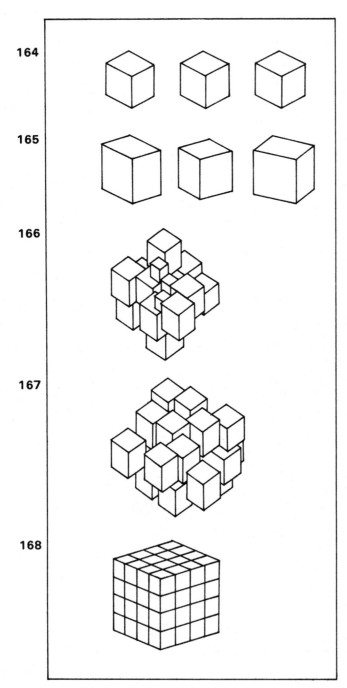

164

165

166

167

168

CHAPTER 5: REPETITION

Repetition of Unit Forms

Repetition of unit forms has been briefly mentioned in Chapter 1. We have also seen that many of the examples illustrated in Chapters 2, 3, and 4 contain unit forms in repetition.

In the narrowest sense, repetition of unit forms means that all the visual elements—shape, size, color, and texture—of the unit forms should be the same. (Fig. 164)

In a broad sense, identical color or texture among unit forms can constitute repetition. Of course, the unit forms have to relate to one another by similarity or gradation of shape as well, otherwise they cannot be grouped as unit forms. (Fig. 165)

Shape, in any case, is the most essential visual element when we speak of unit forms. Thus, when we speak of repetition of unit forms, repetition of shape must always be included. It provides an immediate feeling of unity even though the unit forms are rather informally arranged. (Fig. 166)

Visual unity is further strengthened when the unit forms are repeated both in shape and size. (Fig. 167)

If a high degree of regularity in organization is desired, such unit forms can be put together in a design guided by a repetition structure. (Fig. 168)

Repetition Structure

The wall structure described in Chapter 3 is already a kind of repetition structure, except that it is only two-dimensional in nature. (Fig. 169)

To obtain a truly three-dimensional structure, this wall structure can be extended forwards and backwards. In this way, it not only has a front view but can be seen properly from all sides. (Fig. 170)

We can define a repetition structure as one in which the unit forms, or the spatial cells containing them, are put together in regular sequence and pattern so that they all relate to one another in the same manner.

It is not easy to illustrate on paper the various types of repetition structure in three-dimensional design. The simplest way is to analyze these structures in terms of vertical layers or horizontal layers. Vertical or horizontal layers are actually the same thing in most symmetrical designs which can be turned sideways for a different viewing. (Fig. 171)

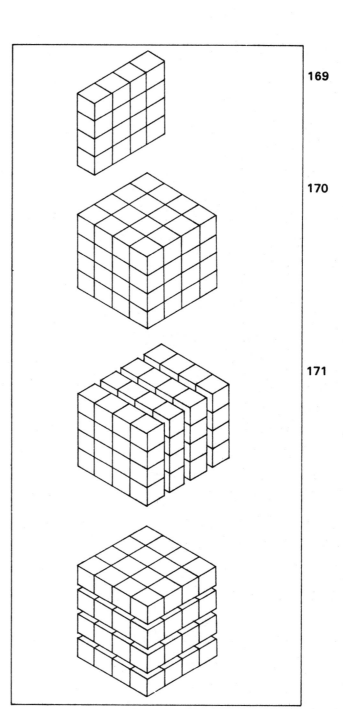

169

170

171

285

172

173

174

175

176

Arrangements of the Layers

To illustrate the organization of a repetition structure, let us start with arranging four layers of spatial cells or unit forms.

The simplest arrangement is to have each layer directly above the next. (Fig. 172)

Then we shift the positions of alternate layers. (Fig. 173)

Or we can arrange them in positional gradation. (Fig. 174)

Directional variation is also possible. Directions of alternate layers can be shifted. (Fig. 175)

Or we can arrange the layers in directional gradation. (Fig. 176)

Organization Within Each Layer

Within each layer, there are numerous ways of arranging the unit forms, and alternate layers can be arranged differently. We have illustrated nine spatial cells or unit forms in one layer to explore the various possibilities. First we arrange them in three rows and put them closely against one another. (Fig. 177)

The positions of the rows can be shifted. (Fig. 178)

There can be gaps between the spatial cells or unit forms. (Fig. 179)

If all the spatial cells or unit forms do not touch one another, the adjacent layer can be arranged differently to help hold the spatial cells or unit forms of the first layer in position. (Fig. 180)

Directional variation can be introduced among the spatial cells or unit forms. (Fig. 181)

Joining of Unit Forms

Spatial cells, which are usually of simple geometric shapes, can usually be joined to one another by face contact, but unit forms, when used without spatial cells, may be of shapes or in positions which demand various kinds of joining.

Face contact certainly gives the firmest bond. This can be full face contact or partial face contact. (Fig. 182)

Edge-to-face or edge-to-edge contacts tend to be weaker and may give flexible joints. (Fig. 183)

Vertex-to-face, vertex-to-edge or vertex-to-vertex contacts are generally difficult to control, and care must be exercised if such joints are necessary. (Fig. 184)

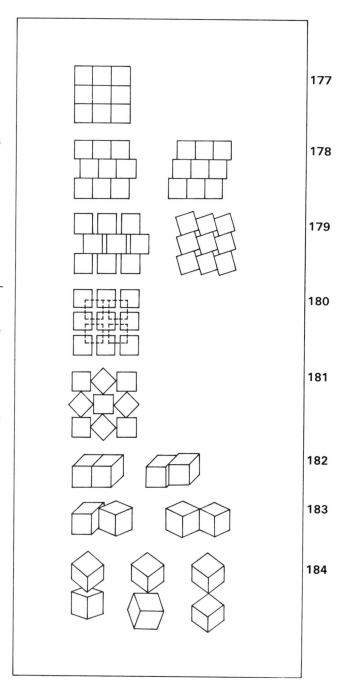

177

178

179

180

181

182

183

184

185
186

187

188

189

288

190

Square Prisms as Unit Forms or Spatial Cells

The structure becomes a bit more complex if the unit form or the containing spatial cell is not a cube with three equal dimensions. We have illustrated a square prism as an example, to see how many ways two or more of these units can be put together.

Certainly we can place one directly above another by face contact. (Fig. 185)

We can place one above another without aligning the edges. (Fig. 186)

The two prisms can be positioned in different directions. (Fig. 187)

They can be in edge-to-edge contact. (Fig. 188)

Three prisms can form more complicated shapes. (Fig. 189)

Four give wider possibilities of interesting combinations. (Fig. 190)

Once the relationship of the two or more prisms is established, the new shape can be repeated in a repetition structure.

L-Shape Unit Form or Spatial Cell

The basic square prism we have just seen can be composed of two cubes. Three cubes can make a basic L-shape which has a right-angle bend and two arms pointing towards different directions.

With an L-shape unit form or spatial cell, possibilities in construction can be quite challenging. (Fig. 191)

We can first study the L-shape as a flat shape to see how two or more L-shapes combine to form new shapes. (Fig. 192)

Then we can use two or more three-dimensional L-shapes to create new shapes which are truly three-dimensional in character. (Fig. 193)

Again, the new shape can be repeated in a repetition structure.

Unit Forms in a Repetition Structure

Most unit forms are far more complicated than the plain cube, the square prism, or even the L-shape. In organizing the unit forms into a repetition structure, the following points should be noted:

(a) unit forms cannot float in space and must be anchored properly. The influence of gravity cannot be ignored;

(b) strength of the structure must be taken into consideration.

(c) the front view should not be emphasized to the neglect of the other views;

(d) unit forms can interlock with or interpenetrate one another. Space between unit forms on one layer can be filled by unit forms of the next layer. Concavity and convexity can complement each other. (Fig. 194)

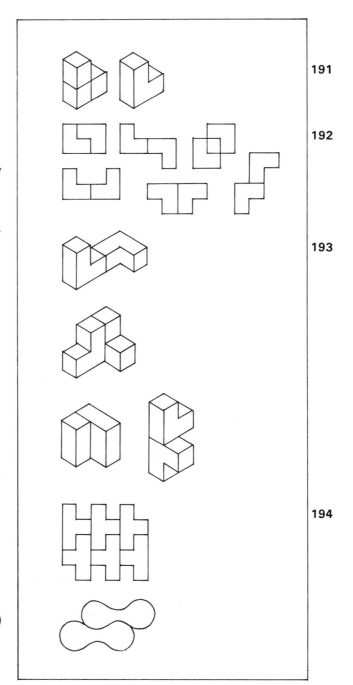

191

192

193

194

289

195

Figures 195 to 202 all illustrate the repetition of unit forms (including all visual elements) in a repetition structure.

Figure 195—there are six horizontal layers, each layer containing four unit forms. Each unit form is actually developed from a cube.

Figure 196—unit forms used in this design are also developed from a cube. Each unit form has square top and bottom, but a very narrow waist. There are three vertical layers, and it is interesting to notice how the central layer is fitted into the negative space between the left and right layers.

197

Figure 197—four horizontal layers comprise this design. Each unit form is made of a strip of thin cardboard split at both ends into two narrow bands. At each end, the narrow bands are curled and joined. The final shape is like the numeral 8 lying on its side.

Figure 198—The plane view of each unit form is a hexagon. The side view is a rhombus. The unit forms are joined to one another at the vertices, which are not pointed but flattened. There are three horizontal layers, with nine unit forms in each layer.

Figure 199—another view of Figure 198. The top view is now the side view.

198

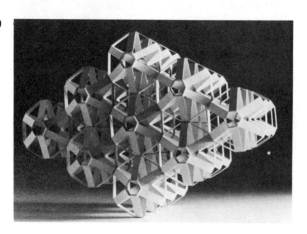

199

Figure 200—the unit form here looks like the letter X or Z, and is derived from a hollowed cube with side planes partially cut and removed. There are five horizontal layers altogether.

Figure 201—a Y-shaped flat plane is used for construction of the spherical unit form. To do this the three arms of the Y-shape are curled and joined together. The design is built of seven horizontal layers, but the number of unit forms for each layer is in gradation.

200

201

202

Figure 202—the unit form for this design is remarkably simple. It is a triangular piece that has been slightly curled. The joining is either by vertex-to-vertex or vertex-to-edge contact. The structure may be rather fragile, but it gives the design an attractively delicate effect.

Figure 203—this is a different view of Figure 202.

203

CHAPTER 6: POLYHEDRAL STRUCTURES

The Platonic Solids

Polyhedra are fascinating shapes, which can be adopted as basic structures in three-dimensional design. Among them are five fundamental regular geometric solids that are of prime importance. As a group they are called Platonic solids, and include the tetrahedron (four faces), the cube (six faces), the octahedron (eight faces), the dodecahedron (twelve faces), and the icosahedron (twenty faces). Each is constructed of regular faces, all congruent, and their vertices are regular polyhedral angles.

The tetrahedron contains four faces, four vertices, and six edges. Each face is an equilateral triangle. (Fig. 204)

If it rests on one of its faces, the plane view is an equilateral triangle. If it rests on one of its edges, in a rather unstable way, then its plane view is, unexpectedly, a square. (Fig. 205)

The tetrahedron is the simplest among the Platonic solids, but it is the strongest structure that can be made by man.

The cube is the best known shape among the Platonic solids. We have mentioned it frequently right from the beginning of this book. It contains the three primary directions and is indispensable for the establishment of the three basic views (see Chapter 1).

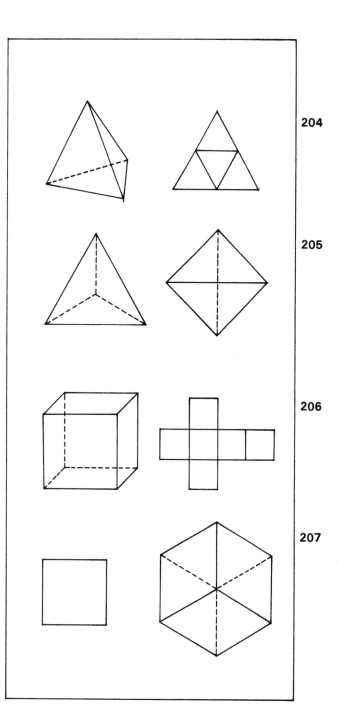

204

205

206

207

295

208

209
210

211

212
213

296 214

215

There are six faces, eight vertices, and twelve edges in a cube. Each face is a square. All angles are right angles. (Fig. 206)

If it rests on one of its faces, the plane view is a square. If it rests on one of its vertices, then its plane view is a regular hexagon (six sides). (Fig. 207)

The octahedron is the dual of the cube. This means that to form an octahedron, each vertex of the cube is replaced by a face of the octahedron, and each face of the cube by a vertex of the octahedron. (Fig. 208)

An octahedron has eight faces, six vertices, and twelve edges. Each face is an equilateral triangle. (Fig. 209)

If it rests on one of its vertices, the plane view is a square. If it rests on one of its faces, the plane view is a hexagon (six sides). (Fig. 210)

The dodecahedron is composed of regular pentagons (five sides). It has twelve faces, twenty vertices, and thirty edges. (Fig. 211)

If it rests on one of its faces, the plane view is a regular decagon (ten sides). (Fig. 212)

The icosahedron is the dual of the dodecahedron. It has twenty faces, twelve vertices, and thirty edges. (Fig. 213)

Each face is an equilateral triangle, just as in the tetrahedron and the octahedron. (Fig. 214)

If it rests on one of its vertices, the plane view is also a regular decagon (ten sides). (Fig. 215)

The Archimedean Solids

Besides the five Platonic solids, which are completely regular polyhedra, there are quite a number of semi-regular polyhedra called the Archimedean solids. These semi-regular polyhedra are also constructed of regular polygons. The difference between the Platonic and the Archimedean solids is that each Platonic solid is built of only one type of regular polygon, whereas each Archimedean solid is built of more than one type of regular polygon.

Altogether there are thirteen Archimedean solids, but only the simpler and more interesting ones are introduced here.

The cuboctahedron is one which contains fourteen faces, twelve vertices, and twenty-four edges. (Fig. 216)

Among the fourteen faces, eight are equilateral triangles and six are squares. (Fig. 217)

If it rests on one of the triangular faces, the plane view is a hexagon (six sides). (Fig. 218)

The truncated octahedron is one which contains fourteen faces, twenty-four vertices, and thirty-six edges. (Fig. 219)

It is obtained by chopping away the six vertices of an octahedron, and replacing them by six square faces.

Among the fourteen faces, eight are regular hexagons and six are squares. (Fig. 220)

If it rests on one of the hexagonal faces, the plane view is a dodecagon (twelve sides) with

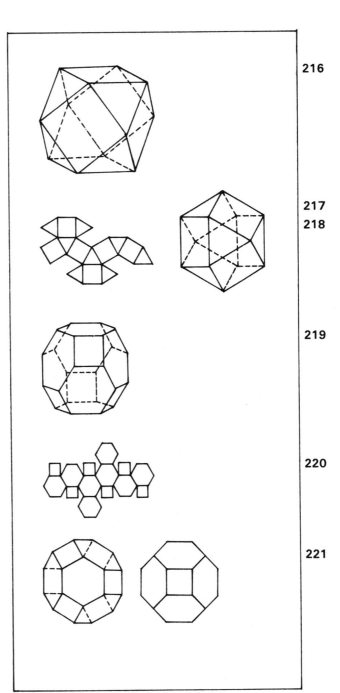

216

217
218

219

220

221

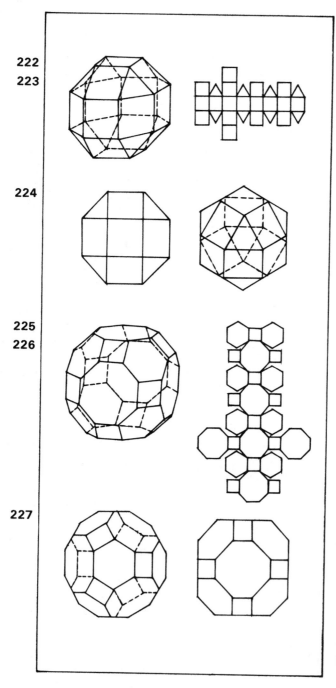

222
223

224

225
226

227

unequal adjacent sides. If it rests on one of the square faces, the plane view is an octagon (eight sides) with unequal adjacent sides. (Fig. 221)

The rhombicuboctahedron, or small rhombicuboctahedron, to distinguish it from the great one, which is described next, is a solid which contains twenty-six faces, twenty-four vertices, and forty-eight edges. (Fig. 222)

Among the twenty-six faces, eight are equilateral triangles and eighteen are squares. (Fig. 223)

If it rests on one of the square faces, the plane view is a regular octagon (eight sides). If it rests on one of the triangular faces, the plane view is a regular hexagon (six sides). (Fig. 224)

The great rhombicuboctahedron (or truncated cuboctahedron) contains twenty-six faces, forty-eight vertices, and seventy-two edges. (Fig. 225)

Among the twenty-six faces, twelve are squares, eight are regular hexagons (six sides), and six are regular octagons (eight sides). (Fig. 226)

If it rests on one of the hexagonal faces, the plane view is a regular dodecagon (twelve sides). If it rests on one of the octagonal faces, the plane view is an octagon (eight sides) with unequal adjacent sides. (Fig. 227)

Interesting designs can be developed from any of the polyhedra. All provide the fundamental structure for face treatment, edge treatment, and vertex treatment.

Face Treatment

If the polyhedron has been constructed so that it is hollow inside, the simplest face treatment is to make negative shapes on some or all of the faces, revealing the empty space inside. (Fig. 228)

Each entire flat face of the polyhedron can be replaced by an inverted or projected pyramidal shape, constructed of joined or interlocking planes. In this way the external appearance of the polyhedron may be transformed into a stellated polyhedral shape. (Fig. 229)

Separately constructed shapes can be attached to the faces of the polyhedron. (Fig. 230)

Edge Treatment

Along the edges of a polyhedron, shapes can be added or subtracted. When they are subtracted, faces are also affected because we cannot remove anything from an edge without removing a part of the adjoining faces. (Fig. 231)

Straight edges of the polyhedron can become curvilinear or bent. This will cause the flat faces to bulge or cave in, in accordance with the new edge shapes. (Fig. 232)

Each single-line edge can be replaced by double- or multi-line edge, and this will lead to the creation of new faces. (Fig. 233)

Interlocking of the face planes along the edges can take place in varied ways. (Fig. 234)

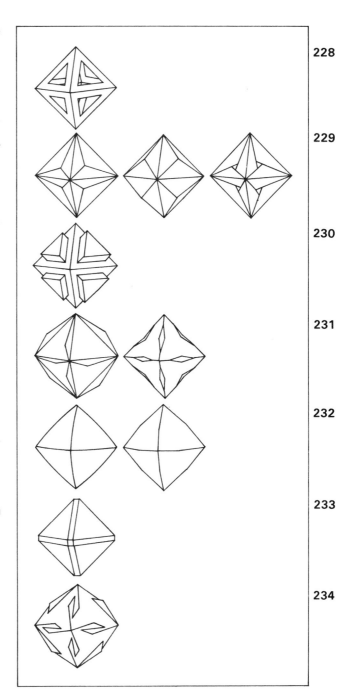

228

229

230

231

232

233

234

299

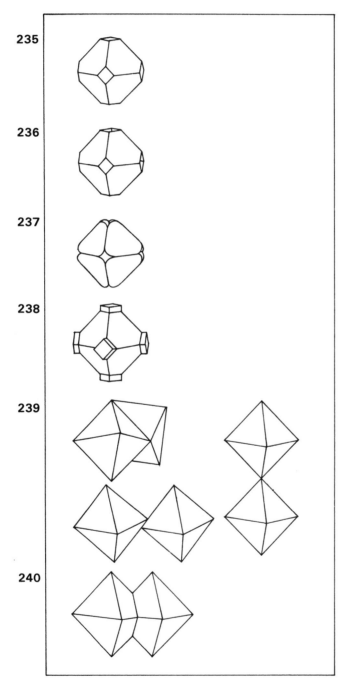

235

236

237

238

239

240

Vertex Treatment

Vertex treatment normally affects all the faces which join one another at the single point of the vertex. One way to treat vertices is by truncation, which means that the vertices are cut off and new faces are formed on the cut areas. Truncation usually leads to creation of a new polyhedral shape. We have already described the truncated octahedron among the Archimedean solids. The polyhedron illustrated here, however, is not an Archimedean solid because the triangular faces have not been transformed into regular hexagons after truncation. (Fig. 236)

If the polyhedron is hollowed, truncation reveals a hole at each vertex. Such holes may be specially treated so that the borders are not just simple straight lines. (Fig. 237)

Additional shapes can be formed on the vertices. (Fig. 238)

Joining of Polyhedral Shapes

For a more complicated structure, two or more polyhedral shapes of the same or different designs can be joined together by face contact, edge contact, or vertex contact. (Fig. 239)

For greater structural strength or for design reasons, vertices can be truncated during vertex contact, edges flattened during edge contact, or the volume of one polyhedral shape made to penetrate the volume of another. (Fig. 240)

Figures 241 to 255 illustrate poly-
hedrons with various surface
treatments. Some of the projects
show polyhedra used as unit
forms.

Figure 241—the structure is an
icosahedron. All its vertices have
been truncated, and in place of
the vertices are pentagonal holes.
Each of the triangular faces is
now a regular hexagon on which
a sunken-in circle and a projecting
pyramidal shape have been
constructed.

Figure 242—this is a dodecahedron with simple edge and face
treatments that do not transform
the original shape of the structure.

Figure 243—eight octahedra
have been used for this design.
Each octahedron is given both
face and vertex treatment. Face
treatment is simple: negative
circles are cut on all the faces.
Vertex treatment is complex: the
angles of the vertices are inverted
so that the octahedron appears
truncated.

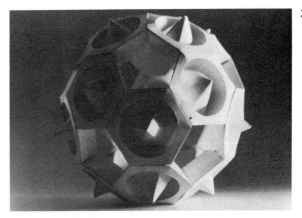

241

242

243

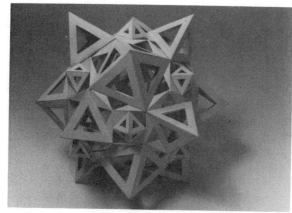

244

Figure 244—the structure for this complicated design is the great rhombicuboctahedron, which consists of octagonal, hexagonal, and square faces. Negative shapes are cut on all the faces and tetrahedral and semioctahedral shapes are added.

Figure 245—a negative hexagonal shape is made on each of the hexagonal faces of a truncated octahedron, through which one can see the interesting interior polyhedral shape. It is a linear octahedron set among inwardly pointing square and hexagonal pyramids built on the underside of the faces.

245

Figure 246—the structure of this design is also the truncated octahedron. All the faces have been stripped to the edges, revealing six layers of the same shape in size gradation contained inside.

246

Figure 247—face treatment has brought much transformation to this icosahedron. Each face is replaced by a projecting tetrahedron whose vertex is split open, with enclosing planes curled out and internal space revealed.

Figure 248—like Figures 245 and 246, this highly complex design has been developed from a truncated octahedron. Each hexagonal face is divided into six triangular sections, and each square face is divided into four triangular sections, all with cut and curled-out shapes. Additional shapes are also projected from sections of the hexagonal faces.

247

248

249

Figure 249—most parts of the faces of the truncated octahedron have been cut away. The main activity of the design takes place inside the polyhedral framework.

Figure 250—twelve truncated cubes have been used to compose this design. Each face of the cubes contains a negative circular shape which resonates visually with the triangular holes formed at the truncated vertices.

250

Figure 251—here the faces of the great rhombicuboctahedron have been treated with shapes projecting both inward and outward.

Figure 252—a dodecahedron has been used as the basic structure for this design. On each of the pentagonal faces, a pentagonal pyramid is built, but all the faces are stripped to the edges. The vertex of the pyramid, instead of projecting all the way out, is pushed inward. The result is a complicated design composed completely of linear elements.

Figure 253—this design is composed of two truncated octahedra, each of which shows a play of negative shapes and concave and convex forms.

251

252

253

254

Figure 254—there are eight truncated octahedra in this design altogether. Each contains inverted vertices and negative shapes.

Figure 255—this consists of ten cuboctahedra, each with curved edges and open faces. The effect is very much that of a linear structure with no straight lines at all.

255

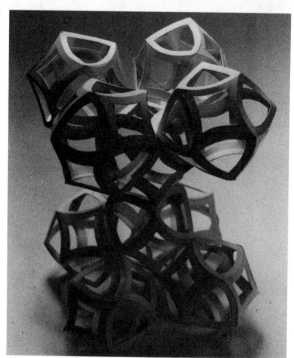

CHAPTER 7: TRIANGULAR PLANES

In the last chapter we saw that three out of five of the Platonic solids, the tetrahedron, the octahedron, and the icosahedron, are constructed of triangular planes. Triangular planes are also used for the construction of projecting or introjecting pyramidal shapes created from the faces of any polyhedron. Thus triangular planes are of considerable importance in three-dimensional design and cannot be ignored. (Fig. 256)

Equilateral Triangles

To explore the possibilities of construction with triangular planes, we can use a narrow strip of thin cardboard and divide it into a series of equilateral triangles. (Fig. 257)

Cutting one triangle from the strip, we have a flat plane with three equal sides and three angles of sixty degrees each. (Fig. 258)

Two linked triangles may be folded in any desirable angle. This can be a free-standing three-dimensional shape. (Fig. 259)

Three linked triangles can make a tetrahedron with one face missing. (Fig. 260)

Four linked triangles can make a complete tetrahedron. (Fig. 261)

Five linked triangles can make a double-tetrahedron with one face missing. (Fig. 262)

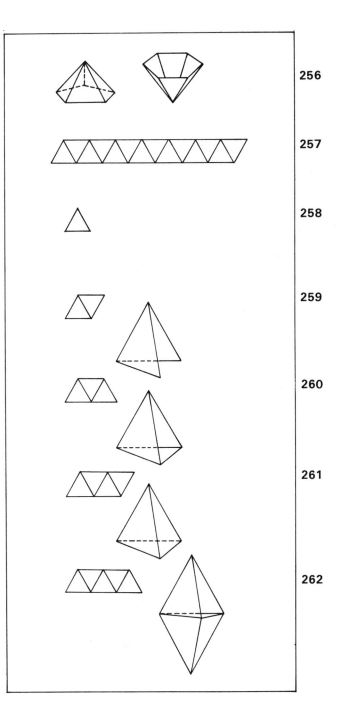

256

257

258

259

260

261

262

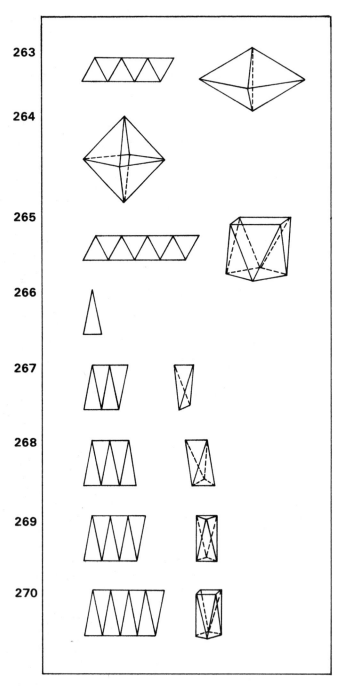

263

264

265

266

267

268

269

270

Six linked triangles can make a complete double-tetrahedron. (Fig. 263)

They can also form an octahedron with two faces missing. (Fig. 264)

Eight linked triangles can make a prismatic shape, with a hollowed square top and a hollowed square bottom. The two hollowed square shapes are of the same size but in different directions. (Fig. 265)

Isosceles Triangles

The equilateral triangles can be elongated to form narrow and tall isosceles triangles, with two equal sides. (Fig. 266)

Four linked triangles of this kind can make a much distorted tetrahedron which may also be described as a prism with two wedge-shape ends. (Fig. 267)

Five linked triangles can make a prism with an open triangular shape at one end and a wedge-shape at the other end. (Fig. 268)

Six linked triangles can make a prism with an open triangular shape at each end. (Fig. 269)

Eight linked triangles can make a prism with open square ends. (Fig. 270)

Examples using the prisms formed of isosceles triangles can be found in Chapter 4, in which Figure 161 contains prisms made of four linked triangles and Figure 162 contains prisms made of six linked triangles.

Unequal-sided Triangles

Just as a narrow strip of thin cardboard can be divided into a number of equilateral or isosceles triangles, it can also be divided into a number of triangles with unequal sides. (Fig. 271)

With six or eight linked unequal-sided triangles, we can construct prisms very similar to Figure 269 or 270 if all the angles of the triangles are acute angles.

Unequal-sided triangles of different shapes and sizes can be used to build irregular tetrahedra or octahedra which may become exciting elements in a design. (Fig. 272)

The Octet System

Just as squares can fill up two-dimensional space without gaps, cubes can fill up three-dimensional space without gaps. (Fig. 273)

Equilateral triangles can fill up two-dimensional space without gaps, but tetrahedra cannot fill up three-dimensional space without gaps. With three octahedra in edge-contact positions, we discover that the space left over exactly accommodates one tetrahedron. (Fig. 274)

Thus when octahedra and tetrahedra are used together, they can fill up three-dimensional space without gaps. This is called the octet system, and it can produce structures of amazing strength that use a minimum of materials. (Fig. 275)

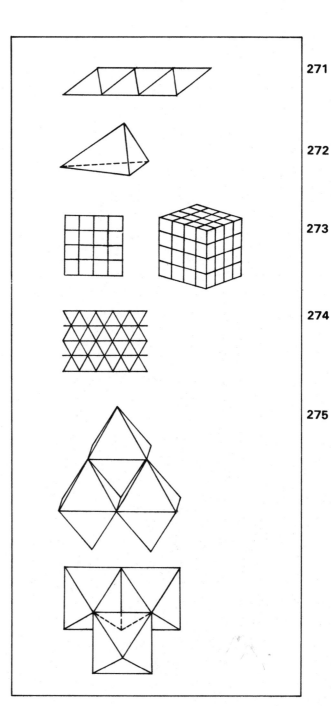

271

272

273

274

275

309

276

Triangular planes offer unlimited possibilities in design. Regular or irregular tetrahedra, octahedra, and pyramidal shapes can be joined together with unexpected effects. Figures 276 to 284 demonstrate some of the varied constructions that can be created from triangular planes.

Figure 276—eight linked triangles have been used to construct one unit form, which is similar to Figure 265. A number of such unit forms makes a ring, which is one layer of the design. Layers of the same construction but in diminishing sizes establish the structure for this design.

Figure 277—all faces of the tetrahedron used here are almost stripped to the edges. Six groups of these are arranged in a radiating manner.

Figure 278—a total of ten tetrahedra are used. Each has one of the vertices pushed in and then out in an interesting way.

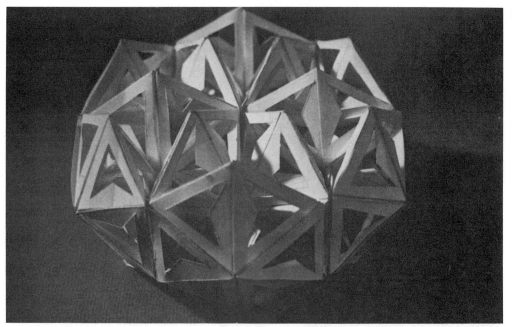

279

Figure 279—a number of tetra-hedra have been glued together by vertex contact. Structurally, this is not very strong, but the form has a feeling of openness, even though all the faces of the tetrahedra are solid.

Figure 280—each unit form is made of several triangular planes. The unit forms are glued to one another by face contact, forming a circular ring which is repeated several times in the final design.

280

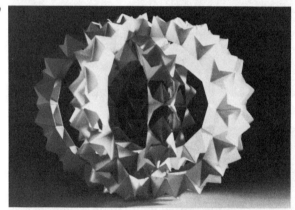

Figure 281—three folded tri-angular planes have been used to construct each unit form. Twenty unit forms in vertex contact make one large tetrahedral super-unit form, four of which are then put together in one design.

312

281

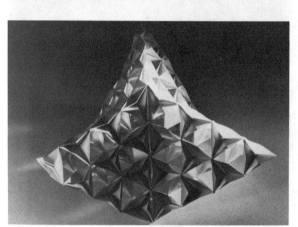

Figure 282—one element of the unit form is constructed of three linked and folded triangular planes. Four of such elements in vertex contact make one unit form, and these unit forms in vertex contact build the design.

Figure 283—each unit form consists of nine linked triangles, three of which are isosceles and six of which are right-angled. This results in a prismatic shape, with a triangular shape at one end and a hexagonal shape at the other end. An additional element built also of linked triangles is positioned inside the prismatic shape. The unit form is repeated fifty-five times in a triangular wall structure which is not flat but curved.

282

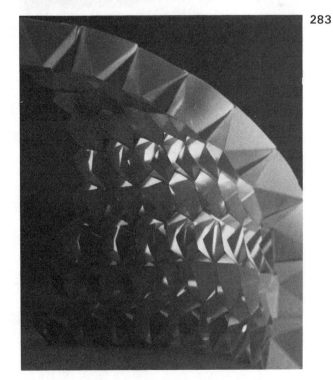

283

313

284

Figure 284—there are twenty-five unit forms in five layers, or five columns. Each unit form is an octahedron with one vertex pushed inward. The structure is built by means of face contact. An interesting aspect of this design is that each column is not perpendicular to the ground plane but slanting.

CHAPTER 8: LINEAR FRAMEWORK

Construction with Planes

So far we have been dealing with three-dimensional forms constructed of flat planes of even thickness. To construct any solid geometric form which consists of all flat faces and straight edges, we can cut the planes in the shapes of the faces and glue them together, with or without internal reinforcement.

For instance, a solid cube consists of six square faces. To build this, six square planes are required. The thickness of the planes is of little visual significance because it is normally concealed. (Fig. 285)

Construction with Lines

All geometric forms with straight edges can be reduced to a linear framework. In constructing this, each edge is transformed into linear materials which mark the borders of the faces and form the vertices where they join.

In any geometric form, there are always more edges than faces. Thus construction with lines is more complicated than construction with planes. Using the cube again as an example, there are only six faces, but there are twelve edges, and the twelve edges become twelve linear sticks which must be connected in order to construct the linear framework of a cube. (Fig. 286)

In our exploration of linear relationships, the sticklike elements

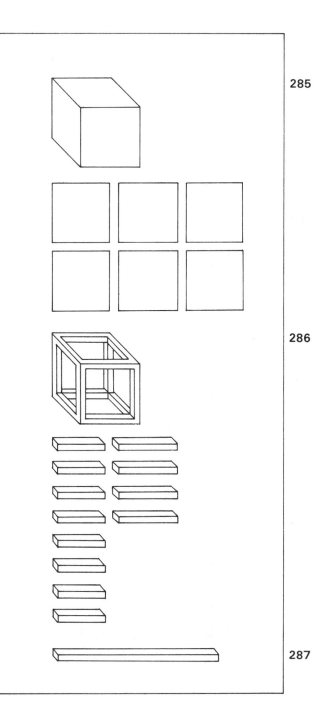

285

286

315

287

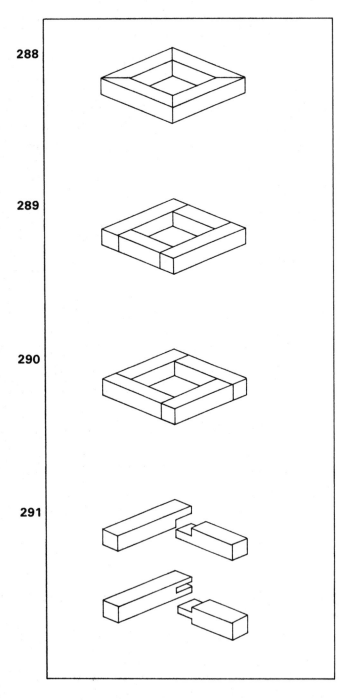

288

289

290

291

316

can be wooden sticks with square cross sections. The shapes are, in fact, elongated prisms with their own faces, edges, and ends. (Fig. 287)

Joints

In using wooden sticks for construction, we first need to know about joints. To build a flat square frame, four wooden sticks of the same length can be mitred and glued together. Such joints are neat and fairly strong. (Fig. 288)

A simpler way to make a flat square frame is to have two slightly longer and two slightly shorter wooden sticks with square-cut ends. The ends of the shorter pieces are glued to the side faces of the longer pieces. The length of the longer pieces equals the external measurement of the square frame, whereas the length of the shorter pieces equals the internal measurement of the square frame. (Fig. 289)

We can also use four wooden sticks, with square-cut ends, all of the same length. This is the simplest way of making a square frame. The external measurement of the final square frame is the sum of the length and thickness of a wooden stick, and the internal measurement of the final square frame is the difference between the length and the thickness of a wooden stick. (Fig. 290)

Joints made with square-cut ends are not as strong as those made with mitred ends. Stronger ends could be made if the end of one wooden stick overlaps another wooden stick, both having a portion cut away. This is called a half-lap joint. More complicated mortise-and-tenon joints can be made for still greater strength. Certainly though, for making small models, complicated joints are not necessary. (Fig. 291)

Components for Linear Framework

With a top and bottom square frame, we only need four supporting wooden sticks, cut to the length of the internal measurement of the square frame, to erect the cube. (Fig. 292)

Variations on the linear framework of the cube can be made in one or more of the following ways:

(a) the top or bottom frame, certainly, can be of a shape other than the square; (Fig. 293)

(b) the shape of the top frame can be of the same shape and size as the bottom frame, or of the same shape but not the same size; (Fig. 294)

(c) the direction of the top frame can be the same as or different from that of the bottom frame; (Fig. 295)

(d) the top frame can be tilted in space and nonparallel to the plane of the bottom frame; (Fig. 296)

(e) the supporting sticks can be all of the same length or of varying lengths; (Fig. 297)

(f) the supporting sticks can be all perpendicular or at an angle to the bottom frame; (Fig. 298)

(g) the supporting sticks can be parallel or nonparallel to one an-

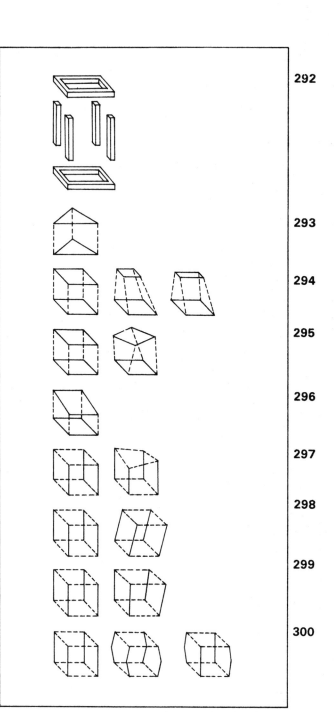

292

293

294

295

296

297

298

299

300

317

301

302

303

318

304

other; (Fig. 299)

(h) the supporting sticks can be straight or bent, or a mixture of both kinds. (Fig. 300)

Repetition of the Linear Framework

So far we have seen how a simple linear framework can be constructed. To take this further, we can repeat the section of linear framework as many times as desired by placing one unit above the next. Each section can be considered as one unit.

If each unit has parallel top and bottom frames of the same shape, size, and direction, and parallel supporting sticks of equal length, then by placing one unit on another in the same direction, we will have a vertical structure with straight edges. (Fig. 301)

Normally, the top frame of the unit below becomes the bottom frame of the unit above.

If each unit has parallel top and bottom frames of the same shape and direction, but not of the same size, this means that the supporting sticks, though of the same length, cannot remain parallel to one another, and the resulting structure will have zigzag edges. (Fig. 302)

If each unit has parallel top and bottom frames of the same shape and size, but not of the same direction, this means that the supporting sticks, again, cannot remain parallel to one another, and the resulting structure will have a twisted body. (Fig. 303)

If each unit has nonparallel top and bottom frames of the same shape and size, this means that the supporting sticks will have to be of unequal lengths, and the resulting structure will have a curved or bent body. (Fig. 304)

Stacking of Repeated Units

Repeated units can be stacked so that the bottom frame of the unit above does not coincide exactly with the top frame of the unit below. The units can be shifted gradually in position or direction. (Fig. 305)

The column thus created can be placed horizontally if it cannot remain stably in a vertical position or for aesthetic reasons. (Fig. 306)

In more complex structures, repeated columns can be used.

Addition and Subtraction

Within the top or bottom frame, or between supporting sticks, or inside the space defined by the linear framework, additional linear shapes can be positioned for strengthening the structure or just making it more interesting. (Fig. 307)

After this additional support, it is possible that some or all of the original supporting sticks, or part of the top or bottom frame, can be removed for aesthetic or other reasons. (Fig. 308)

Sticks which compose the top or bottom frame or are between the two frames can exceed the length of the cube. (Fig. 309)

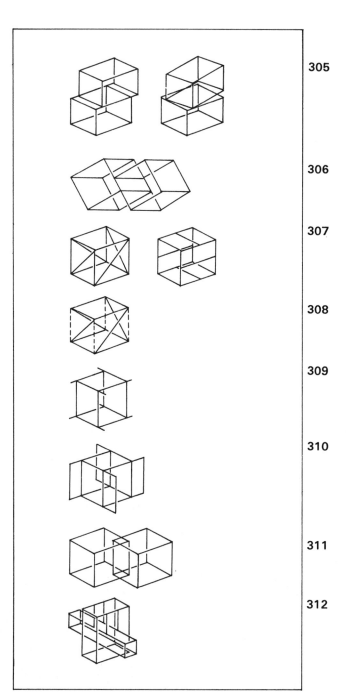

305

306

307

308

309

310

311

312

319

Additional frames can be formed outside the linear framework. (Fig. 310)

Interpenetration

Interpenetration occurs when part of one linear framework is inside the space defined by another linear framework. (Fig. 311)

A smaller linear framework can be suspended inside a larger one with additional supporting or hanging elements. (Fig. 312)

Figures 313 to 318 are all projects in construction of linear frameworks. Some of the examples in earlier chapters, made of cardboard but with all the faces stripped to the edges, could

be looked upon as projects of this kind too. They are figures 196, 198, 200, and possibly 277.

Figure 313—here nine units of linear framework have been used. Each unit is constructed of two square frames and four parallel supporting sticks of the same length. The units are glued to one another in directional rotation.

Figure 314—this structure consists of two units, each divided into four sections, with one section of the top unit overlapping one section of the bottom unit. Diagonal lines are erected inside the units, replacing all vertical supporting sticks.

313

314

315

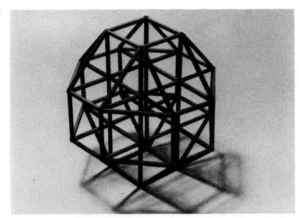

316

317

Figure 315—the structure is a rhombicuboctahedron, inside of which additional linear elements are developed that link the vertices.

Figure 316—here each unit is the framework of a cube and the units are in gradation of size and direction, one inside another.

Figure 317—there are four units in this design. Each unit was originally the framework of a cube but most of its vertical and horizontal elements have been removed after the addition of diagonal elements to the structure.

Figure 318—the structure contains five layers, with four units in each layer. Each unit is a slanting prismatic shape.

318

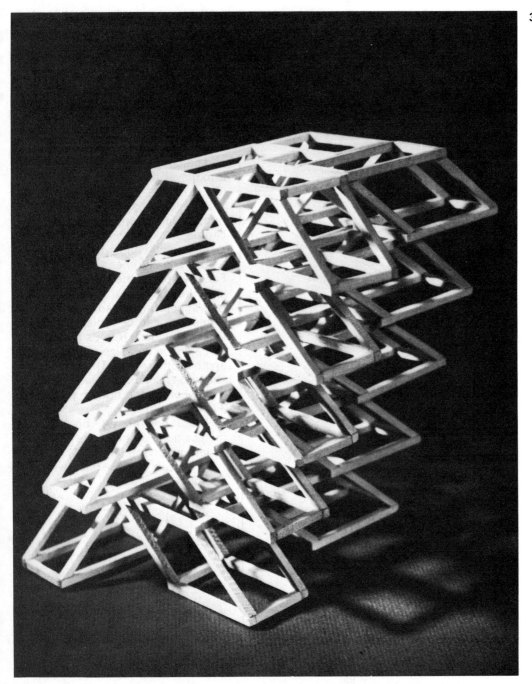

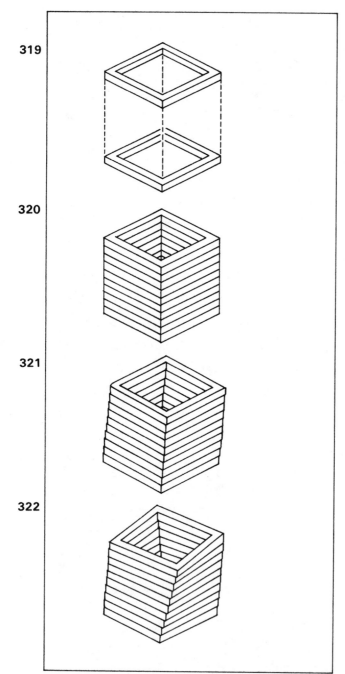

319

320

321

322

324

CHAPTER 9: LINEAR LAYERS

Building Up of Linear Layers

In the last chapter we saw how linear frameworks could be constructed. If we take away the supporting sticks from a linear framework, we are left with a top frame and a bottom frame, which can be considered two layers, a top layer and a bottom layer. (Fig. 319)

Between these two layers a number of intermediate layers can be stacked, and the shape thus erected will be the same as the original linear framework. For example, if the framework is in the shape of a cube, the four supporting sticks of the framework can be replaced by layers of square frames in the same shape and size as the top and bottom frames. The resulting shape has solid side planes, but hollowed top and bottom planes. (Fig. 320)

Now, if desired, we can shift the positions of the layers to make a slanting prism. (Fig. 321)

Or we can rotate each layer gradually. (Fig. 322)

Variations and Possibilities

To simplify our thinking process, we can use a single wooden stick for each layer and see what variations and possibilities we can have.

First of all, the two ends of the wooden stick can be shaped in whatever way is desirable. (Fig. 323)

In building up the layers, the sticks can be all of the same length or have varying lengths. (Fig. 324)

We can position one stick directly above the next, but we can also arrange them in positional or directional gradation. (Fig. 325)

The body of the stick can be specially treated. (Fig. 326)

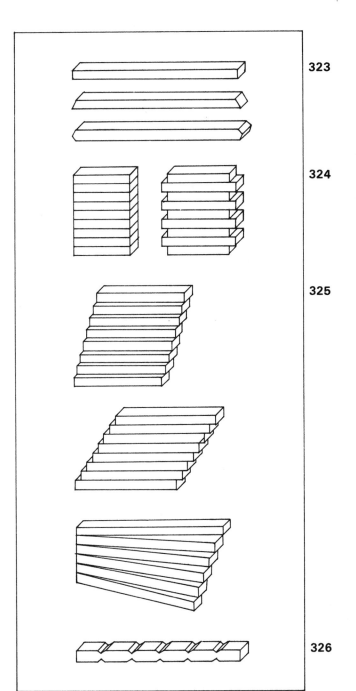

323

324

325

326

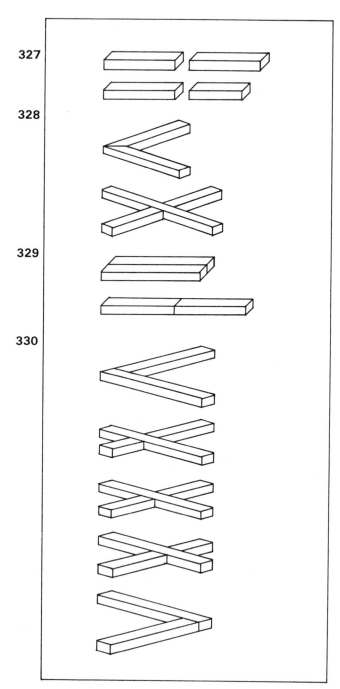

327

328

329

330

Gradation of Shape in Layer Construction

Possibilities in gradation of shape can be explored if we have more than one wooden stick in each layer. Suppose we have two sticks in each layer of our construction. The two sticks can be of the same or different lengths. (Fig. 327)

They can be joined at one end to form a V-shape, or they can cross each other to form an X-shape. The angle of joining or crossing can vary from one layer to the next. (Fig. 328)

They can also be glued together laterally or longitudinally. (Fig. 329)

Let us observe the following example in layer construction. The top layer is a V-shape with the joint pointing to the left. In the layers immediately below this, the two sticks begin to overlap each other gradually in a half-lap joint, forming an X-shape. The central layer is an X-shape with the intersection right at the middle. In the layers immediately underneath this, the intersection of the X-shape moves gradually to the right. Finally it becomes a V-shape with the joint pointing to the right and it marks the bottom layer. (Fig. 330)

With more sticks for each layer, and positional and directional variations, more complicated effects easily can be achieved.

Figures 331 to 338 all show the use of linear layers in three-dimensional structures.

Figure 331—each layer is a simple square frame in this seemingly complex construction. The square frame is in gradation of size as well as gradation of direction.

Figure 332—there are four groups of linear layers. In each group, a wooden stick rotates and becomes longer and longer. The four groups are joined together in an X-shaped structure.

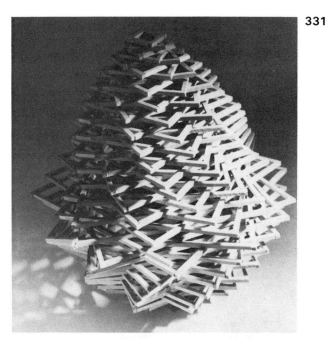

331

332

Figure 333—similar to Figure 332, here we also find rotating sticks forming curved planes, four of which are put together in one design.

Figure 334—this contains twenty groups altogether, each constructed of six rotating sticks in gradational lengths. The overall shape of this design is an irregular tetrahedron.

Figure 335—there are only two groups of rotating sticks in this design. All sticks are of the same length.

333

334

335

336

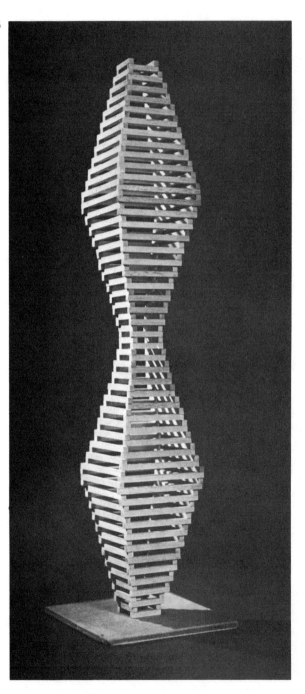

Figure 336—here each square frame is separated into two layers, one layer with two sticks pointing forward and backward, and the next layer with sticks pointing sideways. Gradation of the size of the square frames, created by gradation of the lengths of the sticks, has made this into an interesting towering shape.

Figure 337—similar to Figure 336, we have sticks pointing at different directions in alternate layers. The lengths of the sticks remain unchanged, but the distance between two parallel sticks in each layer narrows and widens gradually.

Figure 338—this is shown on page 100. It is constructed more or less on the same principle as Figure 337.

338

CHAPTER 10: INTERLINKING LINES

Interlinking Lines on a Flat Plane

On a flat plane let us draw two straight lines of the same length and on each of them mark seven equally spaced points. (Fig. 339)

Interlinking lines can be created by joining the points on one of the straight lines to those on the other. If the two straight lines are parallel and we join the points in the order of their positioning, a pattern of parallel interlinking lines are produced. If we join the points in the reverse order of their positioning, the interlinking lines will all intersect one another at one new point which is half-way between the two straight lines. (Fig. 340)

If the two straight lines are nonparallel, interlinking lines may all be parallel, or in directional gradation, or in intersection at many new points. In the last case, a curved edge is produced although the interlinking lines are all straight. (Fig. 341)

If the two straight lines are joined to each other at an angle, interlinking lines may all be parallel, or in intersection at many new points. In the latter case, a curved edge is also produced. (Fig. 342)

If we mark the equally spaced points not on straight lines but along an arc of a circle, interlinking lines created between those points may be all parallel, or in intersection at many new points, producing a curved edge, as in the examples above. (Fig. 343)

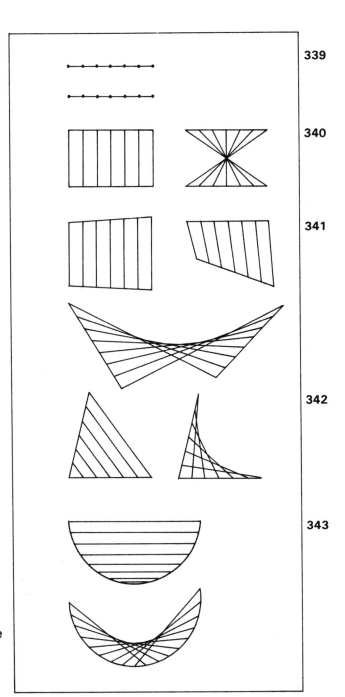

339

340

341

342

343

Interlinking Lines in Space

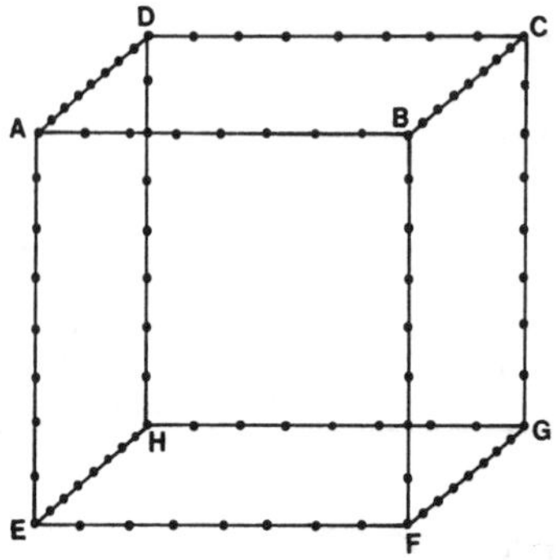

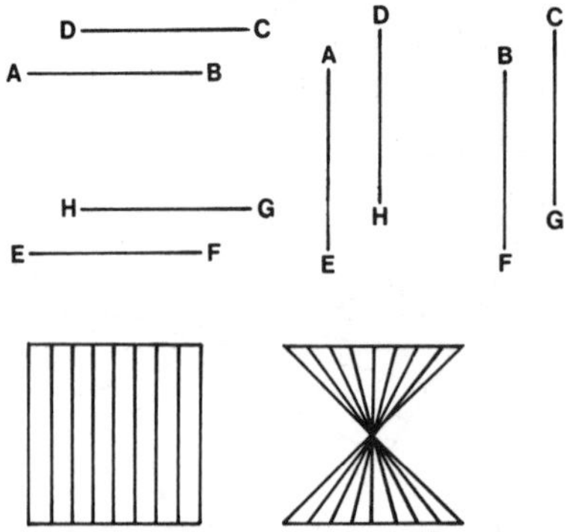

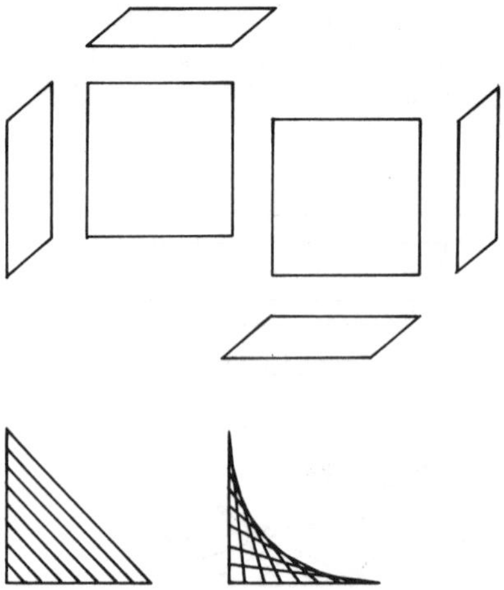

To explore possibilities of inter-linking lines in space, we can use a linear framework in the shape of a cube, with vertices A, B, C, D, E, F, G, and H. On each of the edges, represented by sticks, seven equally spaced points are marked between the vertices. (Fig. 344)

AB, CD, EF, and GH are parallel sticks. So are AE, BF, CG, and DH. Interlinking lines developed between parallel sticks have the same results as those on the flat planes illustrated in Figure 340. This means that they are either all parallel or in intersection at one new point. (Fig. 345)

AB, BC, CD and DA are sticks on the same plane. So are sticks DA, AE, HE and DH; or sticks AB, BF, EF and AE; or sticks CD, DH, GH and CG; or sticks EF, FG, GH and HE; or sticks BC, CG, FG and BF. Any two adjacent sticks from the above groups can produce interlinking lines similar to those illustrated in Figure 342. (Fig. 346)

344

345

346

As we have seen, sticks which are parallel to each other or on the same plane produce interlinking lines basically of two-dimensional nature. Three-dimensional effects can be achieved only if the sticks are nonparallel and on different planes.

For instance, sticks AB and FG in Figure 344 are nonparallel and on different planes. To develop interlinking lines, we can either connect A to F and B to G, or connect A to G and B to F. (Fig. 347)

If we connect A to F and B to G, the interlinking lines can form a surface which is slightly curved. (Fig. 348)

If we connect A to G and B to F, the curved surface formed by the interlinking lines is even more prominent. It is not only curved but twisted. (Fig. 349)

Other pairs of sticks which can produce similar effects are AB and HE, AB and DH, AB and CG; BC and EF, BC and GH, BC and AE, BC and DH; CD and HE, CD and FG, CD and AE, CD and BF; DA and BF, DA and CG, DA and EF, DA and GH.

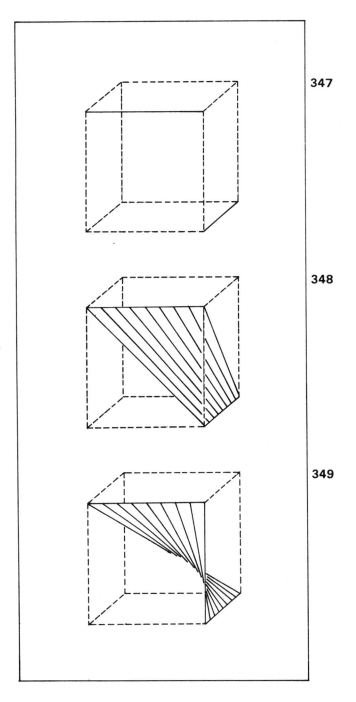

347

348

349

335

350

351

352

336

353

Materials and Construction

The linear framework always must be made of rigid material, such as the wooden sticks, in order to stand firmly and provide strong support for the interlinking lines. (Fig. 350)

With a rigid linear framework, the interlinking lines may be of rigid or soft material. Rigid interlinking lines can simply be glued to the faces of the members of the framework, and their ends are normally shaped to facilitate adhesion with maximum face contact. (Fig. 351)

If the interlinking lines are of soft material, such as thread made of cotton, nylon, or other substances, they can be tied or fixed by some means to members of the framework. (Fig. 352)

Soft interlinking lines must be stretched taut between two anchoring points and, in doing so, tension is created. The framework has to be strong enough to withstand such forces. (Fig. 353)

Planar Construction for Interlinking Lines

If a linear framework is not used, we can use simple planar shapes in a construction for the development of interlinking lines. Planar construction may be stronger than a linear framework if the material used is of adequate thickness and rigidity.

Clear acrylic sheets are ideal for this purpose, as the transparency of the material allows full display of the intricacies of interlinking lines. Opaque material may tend to become too prominent as a form and at least partially obstruct vision of the play of interlinking lines.

Interlinking Lines Within a Transparent Cube

To explore the effect of curved surfaces formed of interlinking lines with as little interference of the framework as possible, we can use six square acrylic sheets to build a cube. (Fig. 354) On the top plane, a number of evenly spaced tiny holes forming a circular shape can be drilled. The same can be done on the bottom plane. (Fig. 355)

Now we can construct interlinking lines with nylon or cotton thread between the top and bottom planes.

If the interlinking lines are all parallel to one another and perpendicular to the top and bottom planes, the result is a cylindrical shape. (Fig. 356)

If the interlinking lines are all slanting, and nonparallel to one another, the result is a hyperboloid with a continuous curved surface. (Fig. 357)

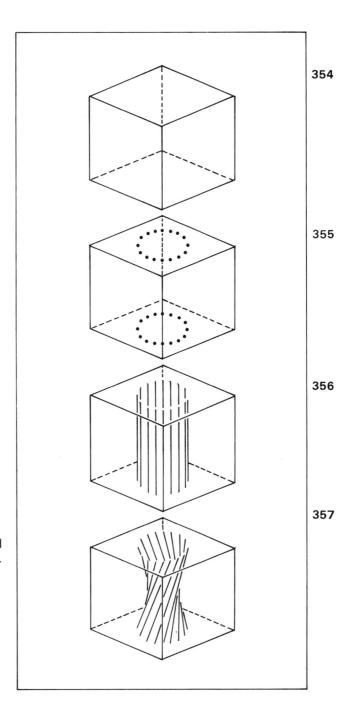

354

355

356

357

337

358

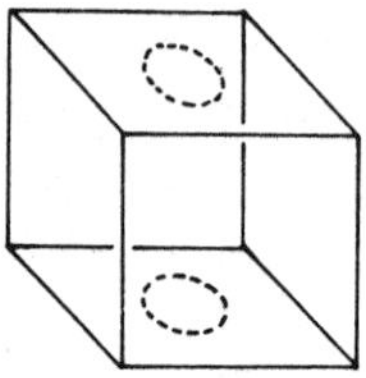

359

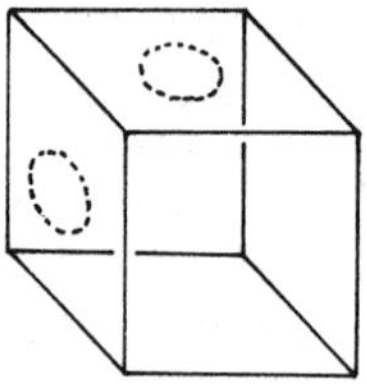

360

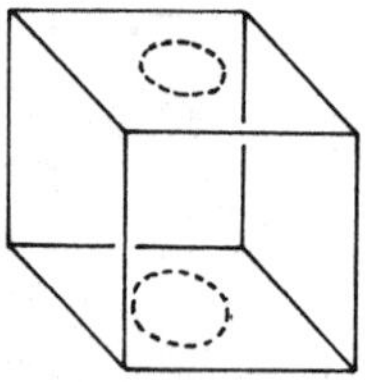

361

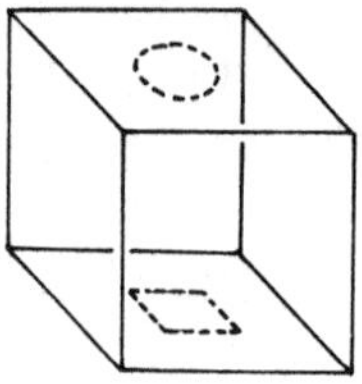

338

362

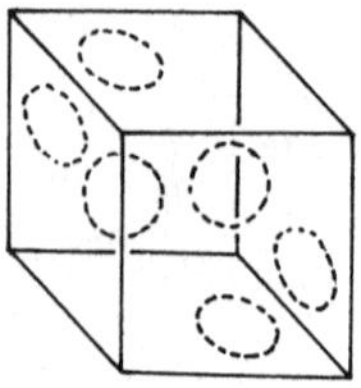

More complicated and interesting results can be achieved by varying the design just described in one or more of the following ways:

(a) the position of the circular shapes can be moved from the center towards the edges or corners of the top and bottom planes; (Fig. 358)

(b) one or both of the circular shapes can be moved to the side planes of the cube; (Fig. 359)

(c) the size of the two shapes can be different; (Fig. 360)

(d) one shape can be different from the other. Both can be non-circular if desired; (Fig. 361)

(e) several sets of interlinking lines can be constructed within the same transparent cube. (Fig. 362)

Figures 363 to 368 illustrate projects using rigid wooden sticks for the construction of interlinking lines. Figures 369 to 374 feature interlinking lines in soft materials.

Figure 363—rigid interlinking lines are constructed within the framework of a cube. The four vertical supporting sticks of the framework are removed afterwards.

Figure 364—here a spiral shape is cut from a flat plane. It is raised and lowered, supported by the interlinking lines.

363

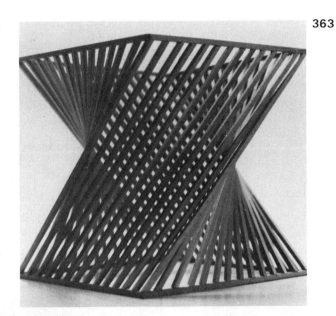

364

Figure 365—the framework is a strong one, composed of vertical, horizontal, and diagonal members. All interlinking lines are parallel to the ground plane, but they are in directional gradation, forming gentle curved surfaces.

365

340

Figure 366—the framework is an octahedron. Six sets of interlinking lines are developed near the six vertices.

Figure 367—six triangular frames rotating around a common axis form this framework. The whole structure is reinforced by interlinking lines which enclose the space inside with curved surfaces.

366

367

341

368

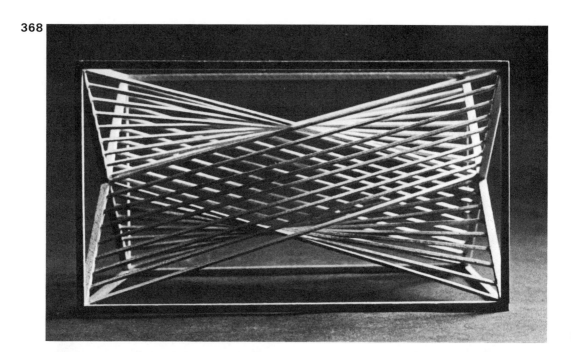

369

Figure 368—here the framework is built of two square frames and four parallel connecting sticks of the same length perpendicular to the square frames. Within each square frame, an X-shape is erected, and interlinking lines are developed between the two X-shapes.

Figure 369—eight isosceles triangular frames have been used for this octahedral framework. One stick is added inside between two opposite vertices to strengthen the structure, but two sticks of the outside framework are removed. Soft cotton thread is used for the interlinking lines.

Figure 370—the framework consists of three curvilinear plastic sticks. Nylon thread winds up and down and forms an interesting network among the curves.

Figure 371—four planar shapes of the same shape and size and five circular discs of varying sizes, all made from clear acrylic sheets, have been combined in this structure. Interlinking lines in nylon thread are developed between the circular discs as well as between the discs and the outside supporting shapes.

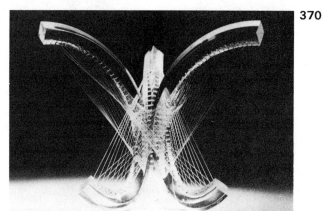

370

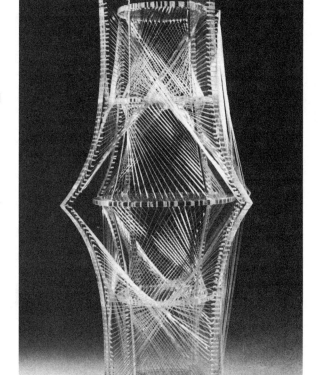

371

343

372

Figure 372—here a spiral plastic band has been used for the development of interlinking lines.

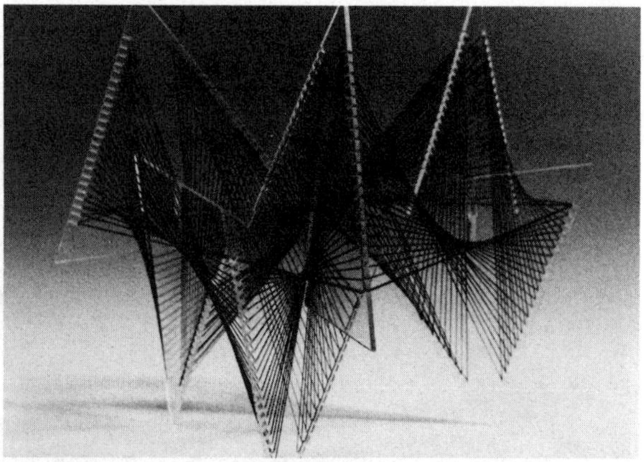

Figure 373—several triangular shapes made of clear acrylic sheets compose this structure. The main interest of the design is the interlinking lines, which stand out sharply among the transparent planes because of the dark color of the cotton thread.

Figure 374—in this design, the planar shapes, made of opaque acrylic sheets in dark color, are more prominent than the nylon interlinking lines, which are transparent and colorless. The effect is just opposite to that of Figure 373.

373

374

GLOSSARY

These are the key terms used in particular sections or throughout the text, arranged in alphabetical order. This arrangement may be different from that in the index, where the adjective component of a term is usually preceded by the noun component. Readers can use the glossary to obtain definitions and refer to the index to locate relevant parts of the text. Specific computer terms, which have been explained in the general introduction, are not included in this glossary.

Abstract form. A form that makes no reference to anything in our daily environment.

Active structure. A structure with structural lines that actively divide space into restrictive structural subdivisions, and can intercept and crop forms.

Addition. The union of two or more overlapping forms to make a larger form.

Anomaly. The presence of some irregularity or variation in a design where strict regularity generally prevails.

Attribute. Visual appearance of a line or an enclosed area. A line can have attributes of weight, color, and pattern; and an enclosed area can have a fill with attributes of color and pattern.

Background. The void space behind all positive forms in two-dimensional design. Shapes generally hidden behind other shapes sometimes also form part of the background.

Basic grid. Equidistant vertical and horizontal lines making identical square subdivisions in a repetition structure.

Body. The elongated plane within the two edges of a line or the narrow volume inside a prism or cylinder.

Calligraphic shape. A shape composed of freely made lines and marks revealing the effects of a particular tool.

Centrifugal structure. A kind of radiation structure with structural lines radiating from the center, or its vicinity, in all directions.

Centripetal structure. A kind of radiation structure constructed with groups of bent or curved structural lines pressing towards the center.

Closed path. A path that makes a complete enclosure, showing no end points.

Color. How light is reflected to and perceived by the eye from the surface of a shape or form. This may be related to its pigmentation with application of ink or paint. Color, in a broad sense, includes not only the spectral hues, such as red, orange, yellow, green, blue and purple, but also black, white, and all the intermediate gray shades.

Composition. The general visual result obtained with the arrangement of shapes or forms within a frame of reference, with or without the conscious use of a formal, semi-formal, or informal structure. See also *Formal composition*, *Informal composition*, and *Semi-formal composition*.

Compound form. A form established with different component forms that remain distinguishable.

Concentration. A way of distributing shapes or forms with increasing density in desired areas.

Concentration structure. Arrangement of shapes or forms with concentration occurring at predetermined points, lines or areas to achieve a semi-formal composition.

Concentric structure. A kind of radiation structure with layers of concentric circles or polygons as structural lines surrounding a common center.

Conceptual elements. Invisible elements that are the structural components of a form.

Constructional elements. Structural components in three-dimensional solids.

Continuance. Repetition of unit forms in one or more directions. Two-way continuance establishes a border. Four-way and six-way continuances establish an all-over pattern.

Contrast. Relating forms of the components of forms to emphasize their differences in one or more aspects, such as shape, size, color, texture, direction, and/or position.

Contrast structure. Arrangement of shapes or forms to achieve effects of contrast in direction, position, space, or gravity in order to establish an informal composition.

Cylinder. A three-dimensional form with circular or oval cross-sections.

Depth. An illusion of receding deep space behind the picture plane.

Dilation. Increasing the size of a shape.

Direction. The orientation of a shape with reference to other shapes or to the frame.

Division. Splitting of one shape into two or more shapes.

Dot. A tiny and compact shape visible to the eye.

Edge. The border of a line, shape, or plane.

Elements. Invisible structural components or visible constituents of a form, composition, or design. See also *Conceptual elements*, *Constructional elements*, *Visual elements*, *Relational elements*, and *Practical elements*.

End. The extremity of a line, or the top or bottom of a vertically placed prism or cylinder.

Face. A physical plane defined with edges and vertices in a three-dimensional solid.

Figure. The positive shape or form occupying space.

Fill. Color, pattern, or texture occupying the interior of a shape whose outline is bounded by a closed path.

Flat form. A form that is paper thin with no significant thickness.

Form. Any visual entity comprising all the visual elements of shape, size, color, and texture, suggesting or embodying plane and/or volume. See also *Abstract form*, *Compound form*, *Flat form*, *Man-made form*, *Natural form*, *Negative form*, *Plural form*, *Positive form*, *Representational form*, *Singular form*, *Superunit form*, *Unit form*, and *Verbal form*.

Formal composition. Composition displaying order of strict regularity, implying the existence of an underlying formal structure.

Formal structure. A structure effecting arrangement of unit forms to establish a formal composition showing a particular kind of regularity.

Frame of reference. The surrounding edge of a composition. This could be the edge of the paper that contains the design, or a specially drawn linear frame defining the design area.

Geometric shape. A shape composed of straight lines and/or circular arcs.

Gradation. Gradual change of a series of unit forms in an orderly sequence. Gradation of shape, size, color, texture, direction, and position may be affected separately or in combination.

Gradation structure. Arrangement of unit forms with gradually increasing or decreasing space between them in an orderly sequence.

Gravity. Heaviness or lightness of a form showing the effects of instability and movement or of stability and balance.

Grid. Regularly spaced vertical/horizontal lines or dots for positioning forms in a composition. See also *Basic grid*.

Ground. Negative space occupying the void in the background.

Illusory space. The seeming presence of volume and depth in two-dimensional design.

Inactive structure. A structure just to guide positioning of shapes or forms in a composition.

Informal composition. Composition with irregular arrangement of shapes or forms, obtained with or without the use of an informal structure.

Informal structure. Arrangement of shapes or forms to attain a particular effect of contrast or concentration, showing some kind of irregularity.

Interpenetration. A situation of overlapping forms where the overlapped area changes into a negative form or displays a different color.

Intersection. A situation of overlapping forms where only the overlapped area is visible.

Invisible structure. A structure displaying no visible structural lines.

Line. A path traced by a moving point or a series of points, with a beginning and an end, or two end points. A conceptual line has length but no breadth. Line as form has both length and breadth. Line also forms the border of a plane.

Man-made form. A representational form derived from an object or environment created by man.

Multiplication. Creating multiple copies of a form.

Natural form. A representational form derived from any living organism, plant, inanimate object, or anything existing in the natural world.

Negative form. A hollowed shape surrounded by solidly filled areas.

Negative space. Space that is not filled or occupied.

Organic shape. A shape composed of softly flowing curves.

Open path. A path with end points that are not joined.

Overlapping. A situation of forms with one partially hiding another.

Outline. A continuously surrounding line with bends and/ or curves defining a shape that may be hollowed or filled.

Path. Straight or curved linear linkage between points. A path becomes a visible line with attributes of weight and color. See also *Open path* and *Closed path.*

Path of gradation. The way a unit form gradually changes in shape, size, color, direction, and/or position.

Pattern. Unit forms covering a surface with strict regularity.

Pattern of gradation. The order of arranging or distributing unit forms in gradation.

Picture plane. An imaginary transparent plane within the frame of reference coinciding exactly with the physical surface of the paper or any other material on which shapes and forms are displayed. Some of the shapes or forms could be seen as above or behind the picture plane with advancing or receding effects in space.

Plane. The surface covering the space that is enclosed within the outline of a shape. Plane also defines the external limits of a volume.

Plural form. A form established with repeated unit forms.

Point. A mark locating position for any line or shape. It has no length or breadth and is not meant to be visible.

Polyhedral structure. A three-dimensional structure with regular arrangement of repetitive vertices, edges, and faces.

Polyhedron. A geometric solid composed of many faces.

Position. Placement of shapes or forms at specific locations within a frame of reference.

Positive form. A form that is filled with color, pattern, and/or texture and that occupies space.

Positive space. Space that is occupied by a filled shape or positive form.

Practical elements. Elements pertaining to the communicative and functional aspects of a design.

Prism. An elongated three-dimensional structure with angular cross-sections.

Radiation. Rotation of unit forms around a common center to achieve a radiating effect.

Radiation structure. Arrangement of unit forms in regular rotation or concentric dilation. See also *Centrifugal structure*, *Centripetal structure*, and *Concentric structure.*

Reflection. Flipping a shape to establish its mirrored image.

Relational elements. Elements governing the placement and interrelationship of forms in a composition.

Repetition. Repeated use of one form. Generally, repetition of a form includes repetition of its shape, size, color, and texture — as well as its direction, position, space, and gravity — but repetition can be restricted to shape or any specific element, with variations of the other elements.

Repetition structure. Arrangement of forms so that they are all equidistant from one another vertically as well as horizontally.

Representational form. A form representing something that exists in our daily environment.

Rotation. Changing the direction of a form.

Semi-formal composition. Composition featuring a formal structure incorporating some irregularity, or composition featuring an informal structure incorporating some regularity in the arrangement.

Serial planes. A series of planes orderly arranged in a row to suggest a volumetric form.

Singular form. A form with fully integrated components that cannot be individually distinguished.

Shape. The characteristics of a line or a plane, or the appearance of a form from a particular angle and distance. A planar shape is normally defined by an outline and this can be filled with color, pattern, and/or texture. Shape is the most important element among the visual elements. Shape and form are sometimes used almost synonymously; but shape excludes all references to size, color, and texture, while form encompasses all such elements. See also *Calligraphic shape*, *Geometric shape*, and *Organic shape*.

Similarity. A relation of forms resembling one another in shape. Similar forms can vary in size, color, texture, direction, and/or position.

Similarity structure. Arrangement of forms in similar but not identical structural subdivisions.

Size. The dimensions of a form, or its comparative largeness or smallness.

Space. Voids surrounding and between forms. The forms, however, can be referred to as occupied space, with the voids as unoccupied space. See also *Illusory space*, *Negative space*, and *Positive space*.

Spatial cell. In three-dimensional design, a spatial unit for the construction of a column, row, layer, or wall structure.

Structure. A way of arranging forms in a specific order. See also *Active structure*, *Centrifugal structure*, *Centripetal structure*, *Concentration structure*, *Concentric structure*, *Contrast structure*, *Formal structure*, *Gradation structure*, *Inactive structure*, *Informal structure*, *Invisible structure*, *Polyhedral structure*, *Radiation structure*, *Repetition structure*, *Semiformal structure*, *Similarity structure*, *Visible structure*, and *Wall structure*.

Structural lines. Lines, usually invisible, used to construct a structure and to make subdivisions for positioning forms in a composition.

Structural subdivision. A two-dimensional spatial cell made by structural lines in a structure.

Subject. Recognizable content in a representational form.

Subtraction. A situation of overlapping a negative form on top of a positive form, to the effect that a portion of the positive form is removed, revealing more of the background.

Subunit form. Repetitive component of a unit form.

Superunit form. A group of closely or loosely related unit forms used repeatedly in a composition.

Surface. The covering plane within the outline of a shape.

Symmetry. A shape or form with its mirrored image in a bilateral arrangement.

Tactile texture. Texture that can be felt with the hand.

Texture. Tiny marks or shapes in a rather even distribution covering the surface of a shape. These can be slightly irregular or strictly regular, forming a pattern. See also *Tactile texture* and *Visual texture*.

Touching. A situation with forms whose edges or corners are in contact with one another without overlapping.

Translation. Changing the position of a shape without changing its direction.

Union. Merging of overlapping forms into one larger form.

Unit form. A form used repeatedly in a composition. See also *Subunit form* and *Superunit form*.

Verbal form. A form based on written language, such as characters, letters, words, and numbers.

Vertex. Convergence of edges and faces in a three-dimensional structure, forming a protruding tip.

Visible structure. A structure with structural lines that have attributes of weight, color, and probably also pattern or texture.

Visual elements. Visible characteristics contributing to the appearance of a form.

Visual texture. Texture that can be seen by the eye but cannot be felt with the hand.

Volume. Three-dimensional space enclosed by planes.

Wall structure. Arrangement of three-dimensional unit forms to erect a vertically oriented plane.

Weight. Attribute given to a line that helps to establish its breadth.

INDEX